The Creative Art of Troublemaking in Education

T0384989

Drawing on a lifetime's experience and research in education, Frank Coffield brings together some of his previously published papers to assess the impact of a wide range of national educational policies and to examine the role of the state in public education.

He concludes that damage has been done to education by political parties of both right and left and that damage will not be reversed until: further, vocational and adult education receive the same levels of commitment and resource as other sectors; serious steps are taken to tackle Britain's unacceptable levels of poverty; and the powers of the state are reduced.

Among the unresolved challenges highlighted are the plight of young people from deprived estates; their tactics in dealing with unemployment; the task of improving learning, schools, inspection, and system governance; the failure to increase productivity being blamed solely on education; and the dysfunctional and undemocratic political framework on which education reform is forced to depend.

An essential read for anyone in education, this provocative criticism of our past and current educational 'system' provides an accessible as well as a humorous critique of educational policy and politics.

Frank Coffield has been a Professor of Education at the Universities of Durham, Newcastle, and UCL Institute of Education at the University of London.

The Creative Art
of Troublemaking
in Education

Frank Coffield

Routledge
Taylor & Francis Group

LONDON AND NEW YORK

Designed cover image: © Getty Images

First published 2025
by Routledge
4 Park Square, Milton Park, Abingdon, Oxon OX14 4RN

and by Routledge
605 Third Avenue, New York, NY 10158

*Routledge is an imprint of the Taylor & Francis Group, an informa
business*

© 2025 Frank Coffield

British Library Cataloguing-in-Publication Data
A catalogue record for this book is available from the British
Library

ISBN: 978-1-032-75914-2 (hbk)
ISBN: 978-1-032-75910-4 (pbk)
ISBN: 978-1-003-47614-6 (ebk)

DOI: 10.4324/9781003476146

Typeset in Optima
by KnowledgeWorks Global Ltd.

The great historian A.J.P. Taylor once said: 'Conformity may give you a quiet life; it may even bring you to a University Chair. But all change in history, all advance, comes from the nonconformists. If there had been no troublemakers, no Dissenters, we should still be living in caves'.

This country needs its troublemakers, nonconformists and dissenters as never before. (1993, *The Troublemakers*, London: Pimlico: 14)

Contents

Acknowledgements

I wish to acknowledge that permission was kindly granted by the following publishers to reproduce previous writings of mine, most of which have been shortened or re-edited to save space: Neil Wilson Publishing for extracts from *A Glasgow Gang Observed*; Sage for the article 'Entrée and Exit' from the *Sociological Review*; the *Journal of Educational Policy* for the two articles in Chapters 6 and 15; Wiley for the two articles from the *British Educational Research Journal* in Chapters 8 and 11; University College London Press for the extracts in Chapter 9, 12, 13, 16 and 17; and University College Union for the article in Chapter 14. The firms that published the articles in Chapters 4, 5, 10 and 18 no longer exist and so could not be contacted. Penguin/Random House were repeatedly contacted to give permission for the quote from A.J.P. Taylor but have to date not replied to requests. Tracking down suitable forms of the articles for this anthology proved difficult because PDFs had to be converted into Word files. Two people helped me way beyond the call of duty: Dr Antono Olmedo of Exeter University and Matt Coward-Gibbs of York St John's University.

I am grateful to the friends who took the time and trouble to comment on the Introduction and Final Comments: Maggie Gregson, John Lowe and Reiner Siebert. Nearly every one of the 17 chapters was improved by the selfless interventions of Tony Edwards who died recently, but not before he showed me by example how to be a professor of education. Two other people deserve my deepest thanks. Robin Alexander suggested this collection of writings and has supported me throughout the process of putting it together, not least by his insightful and constructive criticisms. My wife, Mary, has spent incalculable hours pulling these 19 chapters into a publishable form. She has been my unflagging support throughout. I could not have completed this task without her. Finally Lauren Redhead and Bruce Roberts of Routledge have proved to be considerate editors with whom it has been a pleasure to work.

Chapter 1

Introduction

The power of the state has grown enormously. It has inflicted extensive damage on education and it needs to be severely pruned. To prune a tree does not mean that it should be pollarded, but that dangerous branches and dead wood are lopped off to promote new, healthy growth; and the more severe the pruning, the stronger the shoots. Education can take no more from the blundering, interference, negligence and aggrandisement of the state.

There will, however, always be indispensable roles for the state: to pay teachers and fund crucial infrastructure; and beyond education, to intervene decisively in a crisis such as the COVID pandemic. But the conclusion reached above has become unavoidable as a result of my reflection on more than 50 years spent teaching and researching in education. This book is a collection of 17 articles written during that period, all of them about England, apart from the first one. Re-reading them has made it clear that the problems addressed are still with us, some in an even more virulent form. The chapters which follow provide the evidence for this harsh verdict on successive governments since 1988; I will do my best to let that evidence speak for itself before presenting in the final chapter possible ways forward.

Balance sheets can be found elsewhere which detail the strengths of English education, including the resilience of, and innovations created by, our institutions; successful measures such as Sure Start and the huge investment in new buildings during the 2000s.[1] There is simply no space here to do justice to this topic.

The English education 'system' is unrecognisable from the one I entered decades ago because there is no longer anything that could be called a coherent system. We need to free our schools, further education colleges and universities from the deadening hand of the Department for Education (DfE), no matter which political party is in power.

This book contains two innovations. First, most books on education concentrate on primary schools or on the academic streams in secondary schools which lead on to universities. Instead, I will draw most of my evidence from the neglected further, adult and vocational sector (henceforth FE) which caters for millions of students on a huge variety of courses.

DOI: 10.4324/9781003476146-1

Second, after a short introduction, each chapter will begin with an anecdote, printed in italics, the subjects of which include such luminaries as Boris Johnson, Saint Paul (not often found in the same sentence), Sir Karl Popper and Sir Peter Ustinov. The themes addressed in this book are so serious that they need to be balanced by humour, not to make the problems more bearable but to celebrate the indomitable spirit of humans, especially when they find themselves in trouble. Some of the anecdotes relate directly to the chapter they precede, others do not.

Before introducing the main themes of this book, let me explain two key terms: 'power' and 'the state'. David Hargreaves defines power as 'not so much a possession as a relationship between two or more persons or between some sort of body or institution and persons'.[2] The relationship between the DfE and the teaching profession has fallen apart as the former has accumulated power over not only *what* is taught in schools but also *how* and *when* it is taught and assessed, thus undermining the professional autonomy of teachers.

The rot began with the 1988 Education Act which gave ministers unprecedented control over education. That Act enabled primary and secondary schools to opt out of local government oversight, but the irony was that heads were given control of school budgets for which they had no training but lost control over the curriculum. The outcome has been a contradictory mix of centralisation and decentralisation. Since then, every Education Act, passed by Conservative and Labour administrations, has further increased the powers of ministers so that centralisation has been, not creeping, but galloping.

Nearly every aspect of state education is now decided by ministers, without meaningful consultation, from details such as the length of the school day, through academies being run as state schools, to specifying the precise approach to be taken in the training of teachers. The outcome, according to the Institute for Government, is that education is 'experiencing a full-blown workforce crisis',[3] with many of the most experienced staff, head teachers especially, leaving the profession in droves while 'the government is missing initial teacher training targets by a huge margin'.[4]

Such losses are unsustainable and the conclusion must be that the 30-year experiment in central control, which both main political parties have embraced, has failed and we must change course. Education is far too extensive and complex a social system ever to be micro-managed successfully from the centre and the attempts *to* do so have been hubristic.

The best evidence for this failure, which is presented in Chapter 13, comes from the FE sector, the treatment of which by both main parties has been shameful. As well as bearing the brunt of the cuts since 2010, it has suffered from a permanent revolution in ministers, qualifications, programmes and agencies which no government would have ever dared to inflict on schools or universities, though they too can point to their own catalogue of government-imposed blunders.

A further word about power, which is not a monolith, but is widely diffused, with many centres. Teachers, parents, governors and students all have power – to varying degrees – but given that the teaching profession is almost six times the size of the British army, it is surprising that it has so rarely exercised its power, probably because with so many unions, it struggles to speak with one voice.

The DfE also exercises power through its 18 agencies, the best known of which are the Office for Students, the Education and Skills Funding Agency and the Standards and Testing Agency. Two agencies are called 'non-ministerial' departments, but Ofqual (which regulates qualifications, examinations and assessments in England) and Ofsted (which inspects all services that provide education and skills) are appointed and overseen by ministers. Indeed, Ofsted acts as the sergeant major of the system, putting the stick about and ensuring that the prevailing emotion in education is fear rather than trust.

As demonstrated recently, even the powers of the Prime Minister, although disproportionate in this country, are subject to checks and balances from a network of institutions such as the law, the media and the devolved administrations. Boris Johnson's prorogation of parliament and Rishi Sunak's Rwanda plan for immigrants were both judged illegal by the Supreme Court.

This brings me to a brief discussion of 'the state', which according to James C. Scott is 'a vexed institution that is the ground of both our freedoms and our unfreedoms'.[5] Of all the contentious definitions that exist, the one used in this book is:

> A system of power and authority that claims the legitimate right to use force, composed of institutions (ie government, legal system, military, police) that regulates society within its territory.[6]

So the concept of the state is much broader than that of government. The state is also resilient and resistant to change, especially change that would weaken its power, but it too has become overmighty and must be reduced to its essential functions.

This does not mean agreement with the ideology of some right-wing groups in the United States and in the United Kingdom who believe in a small state, the smaller the better. Rather, a distinction is being drawn between, on the one hand, those roles that only the state can play, for example, in an emergency by finding over £100 billion to bail out the banks or over £350 billion during the COVID pandemic; and the more regular financing of teachers' pay and capital expenditure on buildings. On the other hand, to change the metaphor, there is the imperative to slim down the bloated state by cutting out the layers of excess fat laid down, for instance, in each of the 38 Acts of Parliament relating to education in the 35 years between 1988 and 2023, more than one every year.[7]

It is time to introduce the 17 chapters that follow. These comprise extracts from books, journal articles or conference papers, some of which are difficult to find or no longer available because publishing houses have closed down. I leave it to the reader to choose whether to follow the sequence of chapters or to select those of most interest. What holds them together? First, the three red threads of social justice; intensifying class and regional equalities; and the continuing predicament of young working-class people struggling to find a decent job with sufficient pay to support a family and a home.

The second unifying feature is the spirit in which they were written. The stance taken is one of healthy scepticism, of creating constructive friction, where the status quo is challenged and where key official documents receive the criticism and sometimes the ridicule they deserve. As one of my neighbours, Rob Hyland, observed: 'If you don't shake the tree, no olives will fall'.

I have, however, long since disabused myself of the notion that researchers are speaking truth to power. Stanley Cohen contended: 'It is a pointless waste of time to "speak truth" to the Kissingers of the world, who already know the truth very well'.[8] Whether they know and don't care, as Cohen argues, is more debateable. More likely, they hope to get away with ignoring, twisting or denying the truth. Some politicians let viewers know by smirking that they are aware their audience know they are lying, but they do it to show their contempt for the electorate. The phrase 'the blob', that Michael Gove used of those working in education, sums up that attitude.

My experience has been that in opposition, some politicians are eager to receive 'killer facts' to use in debates, but once given ministerial office, they no longer listen, especially not to research which contradicts their settled views. My practice, however, has been not just to criticise but to offer alternatives.

The chapters have been grouped into five sections, each devoted to one theme. The first grouping on juvenile delinquency contains extracts from my first book, *A Glasgow Gang Observed*. This is the first time I acknowledge authorship, as the book was originally published under the pseudonym, James Patrick, my two middle names. The two extracts describe how I became a participant observer of a teenage gang and my first night out on the town with them.

The second article in this section, *Entrée and Exit*, was written with Carol Borrill and details an abortive attempt to contact a group of adolescents from a multiply deprived estate in a north-eastern city. Much, if not more, can be learned, not from a successful attempt to contact 'difficult to reach youngsters', but from a study of a conspicuous failure.

The next section deals with youth unemployment. I obtained a research grant to continue studying delinquency, but in the early 1980s, there was one all-consuming concern among young people: unemployment. The first article in this group, *How young people try to survive being unemployed*, written with Carol Borrill and Sarah Marshall, recounts how our sample used survival tactics rather than coping strategies to deal with being moved from the 'dole', to 'govvie schemes' to 'shit jobs' and back to the 'dole' (their words). The spectre of widespread youth unemployment is predicted to return as a result of artificial intelligence, so these tactics are likely to prove useful again.

Chapter 5, *Is there work after the MSC?*, charts the spectacular rise of the Manpower Services Commission, which was set up to provide 'a permanent bridge between school and work', but it had more success creating jobs for its own staff than for young people.

Section 3 moves on to the related themes of further education and the world of work. Chapter 6, *Britain's continuing failure to train: the birth pangs of a new policy*, recounts the work of an academic panel of which I was a member. It was set up by the government to analyse the causes of employers' historic underinvestment in training their own workers and to propose policies to rectify their reluctance. At the eleventh hour, the Prime Minister, Tony Blair, intervened to change the definition of failure from being *structural* to *individual*.

Resistance is Fertile: the demands the FE sector must make of the next government was a conference presentation and it becomes the seventh chapter of the book. It lists demands that this neglected and impoverished sector must make, such as turning lifelong learning into a statutory right for all citizens. These demands were first made in 2015, none have been met, but they remain as necessary as when they were first articulated.

Section 4 on *Enhancing Learning, Teaching and Assessment* would appear to be a switch in interest, but it was a logical extension of my research with FE colleges. At the time, government policy was extolling lifelong learning as if it were a wonder drug, which would solve a range of educational, social and political ills. Chapter 8, *Breaking the Consensus: Lifelong Learning as Social Control*, subjected this claim to critical analysis and found it wanting.

In one FE college after another, it was impossible to miss the posters in classrooms advocating 'learning styles'. Chapter 9 reports on a systematic and critical review of the main types of learning styles which found them to be theoretically incoherent and conceptually confused. I mocked this approach by inventing my own *Learning and Teaching Styles Questionnaire*, presented in Chapter 10, which sought to discourage the use of such crude instruments by ridiculing them.

There remains the vexed question of how to improve the quality of education. The government's strategy became *Rolling out 'good', 'best' and 'excellent' practice. What next? Perfect practice?* Chapter 11 shows how these terms were used interchangeably. This prompted the *question If there's no such thing as 'best' practice, how can we improve teaching?*, which forms Chapter 12. An alternative is proposed which avoids the problems inherent in the government approach.

By now, an intense model of reform was being applied to all the public services, but it was so flawed that, despite significant investments, it was doing more harm than good. This was the argument of a lecture called *Running ever faster down the wrong road: An alternative future for Education and Skills*, the subject of Chapter 13.

The fifth and final section deals with plans to improve educational systems. It begins with the claim, in Chapter 14, that *Government policy is no longer the solution*, a claim reluctantly reached by reflecting on the hyperactivity of ministers in every phase of education without any concomitant accountability.

Chapter 15 subjects to examination two highly influential reports and explains *Why the McKinsey reports will not improve school systems*. They were being used by governments to justify radical change, but the examination found them to be deficient in ten respects and other commentators, such as Robin Alexander,[9] have since added more.

Over these years, my views on the state's role in education slowly hardened, leading me to conclude that power within education needs to be redistributed. This is the theme of *'From Exam Factories to Communities of Discovery: the democratic route'*, written with Bill Williamson, extracts from which form Chapter 16.

Recently, the very existence of the inspectorate, Ofsted, has been questioned after the suicide of a primary school head whose school had been downgraded from 'outstanding' to 'inadequate'. Such one-word judgements make no sense when applied to any school, but when used to summarise the work of an FE college with 20,000 students and 30 departments, they are absurd. They remain, however, an integral part of Ofsted's methods. I reviewed the evidence for these and found them to be invalid, unreliable and unjust. Chapter 17, an extract from *Will the Leopard Change its Spots? A new model of inspection for Ofsted*, is, however, devoted to outlining the main components of this model. The leopard never had any intention of changing its spots, but an incoming government is here being offered ideas for a more humane and effective system.

This anthology ends, in Chapter 18 – *The music in the word 'education'* – with the most personal statement I have written. It takes me back to my origins in Glasgow, where I learned from my father, as he learned from his, to hear the music, the excitement and the hope in the word 'education'.

The final chapter 'Chapter 19', *Final Comments*, outlines ways to curtail the power of the state, while revivifying education. We live in dangerous times when a senior cabinet minister, Rory Stewart, reflecting on his years in office, felt compelled to conclude:

> Many of the political decisions which I had witnessed were rushed, flaky and poorly considered, the lack of mature judgement was palpable, the consequences frequently catastrophic.[10]

He found while working for Liz Truss in the Foreign Office 'a culture that prized campaigning over careful governing, opinion polls over detailed policy debate, announcements over implementation.'[11] All this before Boris Johnson became Prime Minister.

One of the main reasons for such incompetence is that our political system is an *'elective dictatorship'*, which Lord Hailsham, no left-wing extremist, described as: 'the absolute legislative power confided in Parliament, concentrated in the hands of a government armed with a Parliamentary majority.'[12]

For decades, our Prime Ministers have been acting as if they were Presidents. Their judgement therefore becomes all-important, but when the Prime Minister is an inveterate liar or an economic illiterate, then the case for root and branch change becomes unanswerable. Reversing the damage done to education will have to begin at the top.

Notes

1 Coffield and Williamson (2011: 34–45); Coffield (2007: 4–8).
2 David Hargreaves (2019: 150).
3 Institute for Government (2003: 2).
4 Institute for Government (2003: 3).
5 James C. Scott (1998: 7).
6 Open Education Sociology Dictionary (2023: 1).
7 Personal communication from Department for Education (2023).
8 Stanley Cohen (2001: 286).
9 Robin Alexander (2022: 329).
10 Rory Stewart (2023: 357).
11 Rory Stewart (2023: 356).
12 Lord Hailsham (1978: 127).

References

Alexander, R.J. (2022) *Education in Spite of Policy*. Abingdon, Oxon: Routledge.
Coffield, F. (2007) *Running Ever Faster Down the Wrong Road*. London: Institute of Education Press.
Coffield, F and Williamson, B. (2011) *From Exam Factories to Communities of Discovery: The Democratic Route*. London: Institute of Education Press.
Cohen, S. (2001) *States of Denial: Knowing about Atrocities and Suffering*. Cambridge: Policy Press.
Hailsham, L. (1978) *The Dilemma of Democracy: Diagnosis and Prescription*. London: Collins.
Hargreaves, D.H. (2019) *Beyond Schooling: An Anarchist Challenge*. London: Routledge.
Institute for Government. (2023) *Performance Tracker*. London: Institute for Government.
Open Education Sociology Dictionary. (2023) Definition of State. Accessed 22 November 2023.
Scott, J.C. (1998) *Seeing Like a State*. New Haven, CT: Yale University: Agrarian Studies Series.
Stewart, R. (2023) *Politics on the Edge: A Memoir from Within*. London: Jonathan Cape.

Part 1

Juvenile delinquency

Chapter 2

A Glasgow gang observed

The two extracts below come from the first book I published in 1973, *A Glasgow Gang Observed*, by Eyre Methuen, which began life as a thesis for Glasgow University. Pages 1–4 and 14–16 are from the third edition, issued in 2013 by Neil Wilson Publishing. Two brief reflections. I now wish to strengthen my argument about the role of the police in exacerbating the cycle of violence. They responded to the violence of the gang by themselves acting like a gang whose masculinity had been publicly challenged. Second, my conclusions in the book now seem to me to be overly individualistic and failed to give sufficient recognition of the structural position of all working-class adolescents in the United Kingdom. The central message of the book remains as relevant as ever: those who have no stake in this society will continue to rob, riot and fight with each other until we give them what we want for our own children: a high-quality education and vocational training, leading to a job and a home, worthy of a human being.

When I was a graduate student at Glasgow University in the late 1960s, B. F. Skinner, who at the time was the most influential and controversial figure in the Social Sciences, gave a public lecture on his life's work. He was dressed in a beautiful light grey suit, shirt and tie, and was accompanied by a young, long-legged blonde beauty. When he finished, I expected the serried ranks of Social Science professors to challenge him, but they remained mute. Skinner pleaded with the audience to ask him something, anything. Eventually a Glasgow working man in working clothes got to his feet and asked: 'Professor, what's the weakness in your theory?' Skinner replied: 'There is no weakness'. The Glasgow man interjected: 'That's the weakness'.

Entrée

I was dressed in a midnight-blue suit, with a 12-inch middle vent, three-inch flaps over the side pockets and a light blue handkerchief with a white polka dot (to match my tie) in the top pocket. My hair, which I had allowed to grow long, was newly washed and combed into a parting just to the left of the centre. My nails I had cut down as far as possible, leaving them ragged and dirty.

DOI: 10.4324/9781003476146-3

I approached the gang of boys standing outside the pub and Tim, my contact, came forward to meet me, his cheeks red with embarrassment.

'Hello, sur, Ah never thoat ye wid come'.

Fortunately, the others had not heard that slip which almost ruined all my preparations. I had not planned to join a juvenile gang; I had been invited. For two years, I had been working in one of Scotland's approved schools during my vacations from Glasgow University and Jordanhill College of Education. As a result, I applied for a full-time post as a teacher, was accepted and started work in August 1966. During the Easter and Summer holidays of that year, I had met Tim, who had been committed to the school some months previously. Thanks to some common interests, we quickly became friends; a friendship which was resumed when I returned to the school. In discussion with the boys, the topic of gangs and gang warfare constantly cropped up. One particular conversation in the middle of July I remember well. A group of boys were lying sun-bathing in the yard during their lunch hour. I was sitting on a bench among them, criticising boys who got into trouble while on leave. Tim, who had been on the edge of the group and lying face downwards on the ground, suddenly jumped up and asked me what I knew about boys on leave and how they spent their time. The honest answer was very little, nothing at all in fact. At this point, the signal for the end of lunch break was given and, as the boys put on their vests and shirts and walked over to their 'line', Tim sidled up to me and asked me to come out with him and see for myself.

This combination of invitation and challenge worried me during the holiday I had before taking up my permanent employment. While I knew from records that Tim was a gang member, with an older brother serving a sentence for murder, the realisation of what an opportunity was being offered me, coupled with a general feeling of well-being after three weeks in Italy, made me resolve to accept Tim's suggestion. The very fact that Tim wanted someone in authority to see 'whit the score wis' intrigued me. On my return, I made use of every possible occasion to discuss privately with Tim the most suitable time for me to meet him while he was on leave, the type of clothes I should wear, the bond of silence and loyalty which would have to exist between us, etc. At first, Tim thought that I should be introduced to his mates as an approved school teacher but I soon pointed out the dangers and difficulties of that arrangement. For a start, I would then have been unlikely to see typical behaviour. It was slowly dawning on me that the best solution to the problem would be for me to become a participant observer.

I realised, however, that this method of approach presented its own problems, the chief of which was to what extent I should participate. My greatest worry was that incidents might be staged for my benefit, that Tim's behaviour might be radically altered, for better or worse, by my presence. Tim's willingness to introduce me to the gang solved the problem of obtaining entrée. But from then on, I would have to play it by ear. I spent the month of September thinking and planning, as the tan on my face slowly disappeared to leave me as pale as Tim and the others. I consulted no one during this period as to what my role should be, my main reasons being a need for total secrecy and a fear of being stopped. Privately, I came to the conclusion that I must be a passive participant – a conclusion that became increasingly difficult to abide by, as I shall explain later. I had read, but not fully appreciated, Michael Young's thoughts on the 'Interpenetration of observer and observed' in his book *Innovation and Research in Education*. A sentence of his was to remain in my mind: 'The main problem, and excitement, of the social sciences is how to cope with the involvement of observer in observed …'. Not only had I to recognise the fact that I was bound to change what I was observing just by observing it, but I also had to contend with the problems of role confusion. The situation of my being a middle-class teacher during the week and a member of a juvenile gang at the weekend produced a very real conflict for me. In fact, it was the internal struggle between identification with the boys and abhorrence of their violence that finally forced me to quit.

To overcome the problem of background, I decided to present myself as Tim's 'haufer' (i.e., the best friend in the approved school), who was out on leave at the same time, and 'havin' nae people' (i.e., relatives) had been befriended by Tim. This proved to be a simple but effective answer to questions about where I lived.

A third problem was that of language. Born and bred in Glasgow, I thought myself *au fait* with the local dialect and after two years of part-time work with these boys, I considered myself reasonably familiar with their slang – another serious mistake as it turned out. So confused was I on the first night that I had to 'play daft' to avoid too many questions and also to enable me to concentrate on what was being said.

The plan was to meet Tim on the Saturday evening of his next weekend leave. Boys from Glasgow and the surrounding area were allowed home for a weekend once a month and for Sunday leave in the middle of the month. I began to concentrate on making my physical appearance acceptable to the group. I was prepared to give my age as 17, although this point was never questioned. In fact, I was able to pass myself off as the mate of a 15-year-old boy; my exact age remained indeterminate but apparently acceptable. Clothes were another major difficulty. I was already aware of the importance attached to them by gang members in the school, and so, after discussion with Tim, I bought the suit I have described in the first paragraph. Even here, I made two mistakes. First, I bought the suit outright with cash instead of paying it up, thus attracting both attention to myself in the shop and disbelief in the gang when I innocently mentioned the fact. Second, during my first night out with the gang, I fastened the middle button of my jacket as I am accustomed to do. Tim was quick to spot the mistake. The boys in the gang fastened only the top button; with this arrangement, they can stand with their hands in their trouser pockets and their jackets buttoned 'ra gallous wae'.

One point of cardinal importance remains to be explained: namely, how an approved school teacher could develop such a close relationship with a pupil. I was the youngest member of the staff and looked it, and this as much as anything else made my relations with the boys easier and more informal. A common set of interests – football, swimming and pop music – helped to further my connection with Tim. He for his part showed an intense curiosity about my home, family and middle-class background and I was especially curious about him. Our conversations during the evenings and weekends when I was on duty, plus the camaraderie engendered by a week's camping with a group of boys, including Tim, seemed to ensure a closer relationship than usual between teacher and pupil in a normal day school. But the bond of loyalty thus forged was soon to be tempered in far more testing circumstances.

Allowing the characters to speak for themselves presents two final problems – those of obscenity and unintelligibility. I must warn the reader that some of the phrases used, apart from predictable swearing and blaspheming, are extremely crude and are only included to convey a total picture of the conversations I heard. The second difficulty is more intractable. Whole pages may at first glance appear to be extracts from *Oor Wullie* or *The Broons* (characters in strip cartoons of Glasgow life), but such is the dialect. A glossary is included as an appendix to the book to enable the reader to translate the main text into English.

On the Friday night as I left school, I reminded Tim for the last time that I was coming purely as an observer. At first he had been amused and delighted at my acceptance of his offer; later, as I made detailed preparations with him, his attitude became one more of incredulity. I now understand why.

The first night

Tim had told me that on Saturday nights, the boys normally met between six and eight at a pub close to the centre of the city. I had heard its name before and knew it to be on one of the main approach roads from the north-west side of the city. The arrangement with Tim was that I would see him around seven o'clock; an arrangement which I kept, to Tim's obvious astonishment. Despite all my planning, despite all our detailed discussions and last-minute reminders, he had remained unconvinced of my intentions.

The boys had just decided to move into the pub as I approached them, this being one of the reasons why they did not hear Tim's opening remark. As we in turn entered the pub, I saw that Tim was wearing the weekend clothes he kept at the approved school: a casual shirt with large brown and yellow diamonds as the pattern, grey checked trousers and black shoes. In addition, he now had on a black leather shortie coat which he realised would have been stolen if left at the approved school. Tim had been released on leave from school at about 10 o'clock that morning, had travelled home and gone straight to bed, only getting up in time to go out for the evening.

Inside the pub, the gang broke into little groups of three or four and drinks were ordered. 'Baggy', a large fat boy who was dressed, I was happy to see, in the same style as myself (apart from his pink and black striped socks), ordered pints of beer for himself, Tim and me. Even on the following day, I found difficulty in recording the first few minutes of this meeting – a failure of memory due, I think, to my nervousness. However, within a short time, it was established that I was an approved school boy, a fellow inmate of Tim's and a housebreaker. I saw from Baggy's face that this last claim had been a mistake. On our return to school, Tim told me that the gang, although con-victed numerous times for shop-breaking, had never broken into a home. 'It's yir ain people – people just like yersel'. Tim's own conviction for attempted housebreaking with intent seemed to belie this protestation, or so I thought until I learned that under the law of Scotland, 'housebreaking' covers the forced entry of 'any roofed building', i.e., shops, factories, garages, as well as private houses. I gave my own first name, thinking that this was the saf-est approach; Tim never quite became accustomed to addressing me in this way, though lately he seemed to derive much enjoyment from the exercise. I confessed to be 'dain' ma Hoosey' (serving my time at an approved school) 'fur screwin' hooses' (housebreaking). Baggy 'wis in the mulk', working for Scottish Farmers; his round lasted from 5.30 to 10.30 every morning, leaving him free for the rest of the day. For this, he earned 'eleven poun' – no bad for a seventeen-year-auld'.

Tim spent his time answering shouts of welcome from boys already en-sconced around the bar and from those who were still arriving. He was add-ing little to our conversation, perhaps out of embarrassment. I, for my part, wanted to say as little as possible and avoid answering questions, as both the answer and the accent it was delivered in were liable to be wrong. Happily, Baggy liked talking and I asked questions or nodded approval when appropri-ate. I learned that he had spent one year in the Merchant Navy but had not been permitted to go ashore when off the coast of South Africa because he had 'nae papirs'. Baggy was bitterly resentful about this, though I didn't fully understand the point. No chance was given me to enquire further, as Baggy turned with relish to a description of the sword which he kept down the side panels of a scooter he had bought for £20 from a boy in the Maryhill Fleet. Here we went off at a tangent again. This time I missed the point of the story about the boy, whose name I have forgotten, but whose father was a book-maker, able to make the gift of an Austin Mini to his son. Baggy was obviously envious; suddenly he dropped this subject and instead told me how he had been able to afford the scooter. He had stolen 'trannies' (transistor radios) and hub caps from cars outside the main hotels in Glasgow, turning the collection into money through dealing with a 'punter' at Charing Cross.

This word I remembered to ask Tim about. Although in the context the meaning of 'punter' was clear enough, on that first night I was often com-pletely at a loss as to what was being talked about. The fact that I was able to

clarify difficulties or obtain more information from Tim in school proved in-
valuable. Otherwise I doubt if I could have continued. Tim, I was well aware,
had given me minimal information about the gang prior to my first outing,
but after that he could not have been more helpful. For instance, Tim told me
later that the word 'punter' was 'a normal man where you live who never gets
caught', to whom you took stolen goods and traded them in for guns, 'blades'
or money. 'Ye can even take a packet of Persil tae them and get somethin' oan
it'. Tim then told me that one of his older brothers, Pete, had 'done a joab', a
wages snatch for a bookmaker in return for a gun, an Italian biretta. Another
brother, Mick, had been so jealous that he had 'gone doon to the coffee stall
at Charing Cross and asked for a punter'. A man had then left and later re-
appeared with someone who told him what kind of a gun he had and what
price it was. In this manner, Mick had acquired a sawn-off double-barrelled
shotgun. One other item of knowledge I was to pick up myself about punters:
they were the people who sold bottles of wine at extortionate prices on Sundays when all other sources of supply were closed. The word was also generalised to mean a member of a 'team' or gang, as in the much used phrase 'Ya
Cumbie punter'.

Meanwhile, I was listening to Baggy's description of the battle with the
Milton Tongs at the Bishopbriggs Bowling Centre. Running out of the building, he had taken his sword from the scooter, cut one boy and the rest had
scattered. 'A bunch o' crap-bags, thae Milton Tongs'. At this point, Pat Nolan
entered the pub, saw Tim and came to join us, insisting on buying drinks
all around. Pints of lager, heavy beer and bottles of Newcastle Brown were
ordered. Pat was about five feet four, slightly built, with protruding teeth.
What he lacked in height, he made up for in noise. Within minutes, we heard
that during the week he had been 'up fur R and D' (charged with riot and
disorderly behaviour). The fine had been £50. With the actions of a cashier
slapping money down, he reconstructed the scene: 'Wallop! Wallop! Pied'.
During the laughter, he saw two men entering the bar who looked to me
like Indian students. Tim whispered to me, 'Watch Pat. He hates thae Pakies.
Watch him stare at them'. Pat shouted something which I didn't catch to the
other boys in the room, who all turned and began to stare at the new entrants.
Sensing the atmosphere, the two young men withdrew as Pat and the other
boys exploded with laughter. This incident led Pat to reminisce about 'the big
darkie in the Calton Tongs, a big Pakie he wis – thoat he wis a gemmie – came
doon Maryhill hissel' and wis ripped' – by Tim's elder brother Mick.

Now Tim began pointing out boys in the pub to me: '"Big Hauf" the boy wi'
glassies and his front teeth missin', had taken on the two McCormick brothers
and 'chibbed' them. 'Peam' used to live in Maryhill before his family flitted to
Drumchapel, but he still travelled into town to meet the boys every Saturday
night. Frank Murphy, a boy with a crewcut and a large ugly scar stretching
from the tip of his chin to his ear, was the centre of attraction. He had, I was
told, 59 stitches on the side of his face; he had been 'ripped' only a few

weeks ago: 'It wis in the papirs'. Then my attention was directed to Tommie McConnell whose claim to fame was that he had punched a boy through the window of a large department store in town. During this identification parade, I was becoming increasingly aware that I would have to excuse myself for a trip to the toilet, and so, using the approved school jargon (which I had already noticed was acceptable), I claimed to be 'burstin' for the can'.

Chapter 3

Entrée and exit

We decided to work in an area where, in one week in 1982, more than 4,000 young, unemployed 16–18 year olds were chasing 12 jobs. The article was published in *The Sociological Review* (31, (3), August 1983, 520–545) and was written with Carol Borrill. Having received a research grant, we attempted (and failed) to carry out a participant observation study of groups of older adolescents. The local authority was providing seriously inadequate facilities for seriously deprived young people. A Liverpool policeman commented on the Toxteth riots as follows: 'Society throws these kids into a dustbin and expects us to keep the lid on'. To this day, the Youth Service remains in the front line – for cuts, estimated at over 70% since 2010.

At Durham, I used to take postgraduate students of education to visit different types of school. Once I organised a trip to a City Technology College. We arrived in time for morning assembly in the hall where the pupils were sitting in their houses named Romans and Hebrews etc. The students and I were arranged in a semicircle on the stage behind the headteacher who wore a black academic gown. He began by quoting the famous lines from St Paul's letter to the Corinthians, 1:14: 'Though I speak with the tongues of men and of angels and have not love, I am become as sounding brass or a tinkling cymbal'.

He then asked: 'Who'd like to ask a question about this morning's reading?' All eyes went down in an effort to evade his gaze. He began pacing up and down the aisles, encouraging someone to speak. Finally in exasperation he called on a small girl: 'Elizabeth, you've always got something to say for yourself. What do you want to ask?' Poor Elizabeth, her neck bright red with embarrassment, asked in a piping voice: 'Please Sir, did the Corinthians ever write back?'

Introduction to study and area

This chapter describes an abortive attempt to make contact with a group of older adolescents from a multiply deprived estate in the centre of a main city in the north-east of England. One of the central aims of the chapter will be to help other researchers avoid the mistakes and pitfalls awaiting those who,

DOI: 10.4324/9781003476146-4

flush with the success of receiving a research grant, are perhaps over-anxious to establish relationships of mutual trust and respect with their target populations. The natural history of this episode will be described in as dispassionate a manner as possible, one major incident will then be analysed, and finally some general conclusions will be drawn from the experience. The literature is replete with examples of successful attempts (e.g. Spencer, 1964; Farrant and Marchant, 1970; Holman, 1981, etc.) to establish contact with 'difficult to reach' youngsters; it is just possible that as much, if not more, could be learned from a detailed study of a conspicuous failure.

We were attempting a participant observation study of groups of older adolescents and had obtained grants from both the SSRC's research initiative into 'Young People in Society' and from Durham University. (The views expressed are, of course, our own.) Our aim was to present with empathy a rounded picture of the ordinary, day-to-day activities of groups of older adolescents who would appear as recognisable human beings rather than walking concepts from either the psychological or sociological literature.

It is also necessary to introduce the social, economic and physical context within which the action took place. In economic terms, the Northern Region is a depressed area which continues to decline. For more than 20 years, it has suffered huge job losses, particularly in coal mining (60,000 jobs lost since the mid-1960s), iron and steel and shipbuilding. A recently published report on the economic prospects for the Northern Region (Robinson, 1982) made it clear that in terms of unemployment and Gross Domestic Product, the North was in 1980 close to the bottom of the EEC regional league table. In fact, the North was sandwiched eleventh from the bottom of the table between Calabria and Lazio in Southern Italy. The report's forecast was for further decline with a 20% unemployment rate in five years' time, which, they argued, 'more realistically reflects the implications of continued regional disadvantage within a national low growth context' (p. 27).

The Down Dale[1] estate was built in the inter-war years close to the Centre of Shipton, a sprawling city of over 200,000 people in the north-east. The local labour market has a very restricted range of professional, managerial and other white-collar jobs, with less than half (8.5%) of the average figure for England and Wales (17.6%) of Social Class I in the 1971 Census; and more recent factory closures, particularly in the textile industry, have severely reduced the number of semi-skilled and unskilled jobs. As a result, the Manpower Services Commission reported in 1980 that the young unemployed of Shipton had the most limited job opportunities in the Northern Region. (The ratio of young unemployed to job vacancies was eight times higher than the national average in both 1978 and 1979.) The first returns from the 1981 Census show that since 1971, unemployment has increased by 127% and that male unemployment was over 25% in five wards and as high as 37.4% in one. The unemployment figures have, of course, risen even more steeply since April 1981, and the local Careers Office was able to place only

50% of the school leavers in real jobs after two years. To put the point more graphically, in one week in September 1982, more than 4,000 young people aged 16 to 18 who were either unemployed or on government schemes were chasing 12 jobs.

These statistics are therefore not just an irrelevant or standard introduction to the area: they are a grim reflection of the social structure within which young people live from day to day. A special government programme was established in Shipton in 1977 and a stream of reports over the next three years highlighted a multitude of deficiencies, including the following: nearly half the unemployed were unskilled male labourers; mortality rates were well above the regional and national average, particularly the perinatal mortality rate (24 per 1,000 in Shipton, 21 in the Northern Region and 19 in England and Wales); Shipton had more children in care (8.5 per 1,000) than either the regional average (7.9) or the national average (7.4); 50% of these children were admitted to care because of family breakdown, compared with 29% regionally and 35% nationally; the percentage of households without a car was much higher (75.3%) for the inner area of Shipton than for Shipton itself (63. l%) or the national average (42.2%): in 1978, Shipton was one of the ten local authorities in the country with the highest proportions of pupils receiving free school meals; only 14.4% of Shipton's fifth-form pupils remained at school compared to 27.5% nationally (in some of the inner area schools, the percentage fell as low as 4.7%): only 4.6% entered full-time further education, compared with 14.0% nationally (in the inner area, the percentage dropped to 0.5%): it is difficult to imagine a percentage lower than 0.5% and such low staying-on rates are still (1982) the lowest anywhere in England and Wales.

Two general remarks summarise this and other statistical information. First, the young people of Shipton, when compared with their contemporaries in either the Northern Region or in the rest of England, are growing up in an area of acute urban deprivation and with the most limited educational opportunities in the country. Second, the indicators of deprivation by ward in Shipton make it clear that the problems are concentrated in the inner urban areas: we chose to work in the Down Dale estate, which is situated in one of the most deprived of all the wards. In response to the publication of the statistical reports mentioned above, the local authority set up a number of programmes to combat urban deprivation in general and the low achievement of school children and the poor employment prospects for school-leavers in particular.

The Down Dale estate was built in the 1920s and 1930s and is now caught between two trunk roads which service a series of large, industrial estates. Most people, therefore, tend to drive at speed past the estate along the dual carriageway. Entrance to the estate is far from obvious as many of the side roads are closed off by cement bollards to prevent young children from wandering into the traffic, which consists mainly of heavy lorries. The houses, which are all owned by the local authority, are built from dull red bricks and the front doors of many are painted over with nicknames. Some residents have attempted to protect the roses in their front lawns by erecting wooden fences, but others, who are increasingly in the majority, have abandoned their gardens to roaming dogs and to the litter dropped by passers-by. Because of the very high level of unemployment, men of all ages can be seen shopping, collecting children from primary schools or just sitting on their doorsteps. The shops in the centre of the estate have their front windows boarded up and the boards are daubed with slogans and nicknames. The pubs and garages are situated on the periphery of the estate and on the main roads leading into the centre of the city. Despite the general atmosphere of private poverty and public neglect, it is not being suggested that the estate is socially disorgan-ised or comparable to some of the most stigmatised estates in Glasgow or Liverpool. There was evidence of considerable community spirit, which had organised trips to the seaside for the Mothers and Toddlers Club, street par-ties to celebrate a royal wedding and political meetings to protest about local conditions. Similarly, life in Shipton itself has a positive aspect to it; there are excellent sporting facilities, extensive public gardens, a network of supportive and extended families and intense local loyalty to the area.

Local histories of the area, however, reveal that the problems of poverty, unemployment, slum housing, ill-health and poor education did not sud-denly come to the fore in the 1960s or 1970s but have been endemic in Shipton since it became an early boom town in Victorian times. To take one example from the sphere of education, provision for technical and commer-cial education was seriously inadequate, especially when one considers that Shipton was above all else an industrial town. An inspector's report for 1909 showed that less than one-fifth of the money levied for higher education was devoted to technical education and that only 1.6% of the population attended evening schools, compared with a national average of 2.3%. Shipton had to wait until the Second World War for a technical institute to be established. It is therefore no surprise that the proportion of professional people is, and always has been, very low: in 1865, for example, out of a total population of 39,000, there were 6 lawyers, 12 doctors, 27 teachers, 9 chemists, 1 land surveyor and 158 publicans.

Working in two clubs

One of the local authority programmes to combat deprivation was based in the Down Dale estate and, in part, consisted of a club for unemployed young people, which met in the afternoon, and an evening club for them and their younger siblings. The two authors joined a team consisting of a youth and community worker, his assistant, and two part-time helpers; at planning meet-ings, it was decided to run the clubs in a very informal, relaxed style, which was, however, to be supported by some basic rules to ensure a minimum of good order. The rules which were agreed upon were as follows: that no drink-ing of alcohol and no glue sniffing would be allowed within the club; that the age range admitted would be 14–21, with younger boys and girls being kept out; that staff would actively support each other, particularly if there was any trouble, and that difficult decisions would be discussed at meetings after the club had closed; that a subscription of 10p per visit would be paid by each young person; that a representative of each age group would be selected to join the staff in running the club; and that more activities (e.g. trips in a mini-bus, five-a-side football for boys, and gymnastics for girls) should be organised to avoid the problems encountered in the past. At a number of points during these preliminary meetings, hints were dropped by the local workers that the young people could be 'disruptive', 'anti-social' and 'difficult to control' at times. With hindsight, it seems possible that, in our eagerness to launch our own project with a suitable group of young adults, we discounted or played down these hints. On the other hand, hints were all that we were offered: we were not given any account of the incidents in the recent past which had involved another outside worker. At any rate, the mutual agreement allowed us to begin our research while the members of the team were able to recruit two unpaid helpers, one of whom (C.B.) wanted to work specifically with adolescent girls for whom little, if any, provision had been made in the past.

Our first impressions of the building where both clubs were to be held were of a tatty, modern structure covered externally and internally with slogans and nicknames which had been either painted or chalked up. The outside walls had two sizeable holes, which, we were told, had been created by the younger children wriggling into the building. Inside, there was a distinctive smell which we soon discovered came from the ladies' toilet which was blocked and out of use, both sexes using the gents' toilet. In addition to the toilets opposite the main entrance, the building consisted of nothing more than an internal door leading to one large room, the walls of which were lined with cupboards of various sizes, all of which had been broken open. In one corner of the room, there was a kitchen area with running water, but the surfaces were so dirty and the bins were so full of rubbish that serving young people tea or coffee could have become a health hazard. Underneath some discarded curtains in the kitchen lay a broken fire extinguisher; and week after week we noticed that the litter bins were not emptied with the result that the floor in the main room became littered with torn newspapers, dirty cloths, cigarette stubs and sweet papers. The centre did have a caretaker, but he had become disheartened over the seven years it had been in operation, because it had been so regularly knocked about and abused. Each time the clubs met, tables for pool, ping-pong and football were brought out into the centre of the room and the colour video TV set (together with cues, etc.) were collected from the caretaker's home. These latter items were also returned there after use for safekeeping.

The first meeting of the reconstituted club for older, unemployed young people took place on a sunny afternoon in mid-September 1981. Inside the hall, about half-a-dozen boys aged between 18 and 22 were watching (or sleeping through) a video film of *Dirty Harry*. After the film, a few desultory games of table tennis and pool were played, but as the afternoon wore on, the boys slowly drifted away to find out how their bets had fared.

About a dozen young men attended this afternoon club and they themselves thought that very few, if any, girls would turn up because they weren't likely to be interested in pool or table tennis, and anyway, they added that the girls would be put off by the swearing. One girl had attended the club in the past, but she had been 'more like a lad than a lass'.

The young men did not accept the person they called the 'boss-woman', a senior youth worker who dropped in one afternoon to see how the young assistant of 21 was coping on his own. She felt that the young men had such dismissive attitudes to women in general that they found it particularly hard to relate to a woman in a position of authority.

The young assistant tried to encourage some of the club members to play dominoes or cards, but those who were not playing table tennis or table football preferred to sleep with their heads slumped on the tables. One or two slept all afternoon and only woke up to go home to watch television. The older boys, who all seemed to come from very large families ('I've seven brothers and a few sisters'), were married and had very young children. They were keen to find sufficient money to buy football strips for a full team and so join a local league. They needed money to hire a pitch for a season; the local authorities charged £25 for a poor playing surface and £88 for a first-class one, and there were no reductions for the unemployed.

The afternoons were generally filled with a staple diet of ping-pong, pool and TV video films. Once a fishing trip was organised, rods were hired from a youth centre, and four members went off for the afternoon. Their visits to the pub were of necessity restricted to the day they collected their unemployment benefit.

The older boys appeared to have drifted into long-term unemployment and had become apathetic and listless as a result. There was no discussion of potential jobs (there were none to discuss), no job searching and no talk of moving house in search of work. They talked about devising means of filling in time in the most pleasant way possible. They displayed no bitterness and no political anger; there was only the occasional flash of temper from a 17-year-old who would throw his bat across the room if he lost a game of table tennis.

Two of their number, Billy and Cliff, were looked upon by the others as leaders of the group and they also seemed to play a central role on the estate; they acted, for example, as bouncers if the teenagers held a disco and wanted it controlled. Billy was six feet tall, well-built and good-looking; his arms were heavily tattooed. He was 21, married with a young son, and had been unemployed for three years. He was captain of their football team, a natural leader with an engaging sense of humour and an infectious laugh who often diffused arguments with a timely joke. He was able to tease others without provoking trouble, he seemed to take more care over his appearance, and he tended to win at games such as dominoes. He was so respected by all and sundry that the senior youth workers had strongly encouraged him to take a course in youth and community work. As this would mean leaving the area, Billy had consistently refused. He did, however, voluntarily help the workers with the younger adolescents. Cliff was smaller, quieter and was said by one part-time worker (on little or no evidence) to be more ready to solve problems by force. He too was married with one child and was also being coaxed by the youth workers to become a full-time paid STEP[2] worker, a post he finally accepted. Relationships with these and other young men were beginning to develop when an incident at the evening club brought us up sharply.

Against our expectations, a younger set (14–17 years old) of boys turned up for the evening club and a still younger group (12–16 years old) of girls. Almost all of the boys who had left school were unemployed and they spoke of spending their time lying in bed until early evening when they came out onto the streets looking for something to relieve the boredom. They were receiving (in September 1981) £15 unemployment benefit, of which they were giving their parents £10 for bed and board, thus leaving them with £5 a week for all entertainment, transport, clothes, records, beer, etc. The membership of one local recreation centre cost £11 to join, although there were cheaper alternatives. None of these facilities were used by the young people.

The clothes of the younger boys and girls varied considerably. Some of them were dressed in 'punk gear' with haircuts to match, others were dressed in well-cut jeans and polo-neck jerseys, while others still appeared to have little or no money to spend on clothes. Boys and girls in the latter group wore dirty, shabby clothes which looked like hand-downs. As a group, they looked like the typical deprived children of the inner city: most were small and underweight for their age.

Both of us experienced great difficulty at the beginning in understanding the local dialect. Phrases such as 'The crack was canny' (The conversation was lively) or 'a canny few' (a good many) were quickly understood, but whole sentences were passing over our heads. At times we would ask youngsters to repeat their question, but often we would fail for a second time to follow them, we then had to decide whether to risk asking for a further repetition or to pretend to have understood and make a response which it was hoped would be appropriate. The young people were all very tolerant of our difficulties in engaging them in ordinary conversation, although on one occasion one of us was playfully addressed as though the boy was trying to get through to a large, slow-witted, deaf child.

We started to get to know some of the young people who attended the club regularly. We suffered some 'sample attrition' as one or two boys appeared in court for stealing cars, etc., and were 'sent down'. Most of the boys aged 16 and 17 regularly displayed a heavy macho image of themselves. Typically, Stew, the only strong, well-built boy who was also one of the few in full-time employment, indulged in some light-hearted sword-play with a billiard cue, poking it into the stomachs or chests of boys and girls alike. He would burst out laughing and break off his 'fencing' just at the point when his opponent began to get riled.

The ability to deliver clever ripostes was much prized, particularly in the constant banter which went on between boys and girls. The banter often and quickly became a slanging match where all sorts of sexual accusations were hurled backwards and forwards. Witness the dialogue between Stew and Sharon who had been locked all evening in a running verbal and physical contest:

Stew: Do you want me to come down and kick your fucking mask off?
Sharon: If you've got a horse, jump on and fuck off.

Both of these remarks were greeted with laughter by a large audience, as though they were original witticisms and yet they were used habitually by each individual as parting shots. It may, however, be better to see these interactions as a positive feature of their relationships, which appeared to be strengthened as a result.

In the evenings, the audience for such exchanges always included a group of much younger children aged between 5 and 12. They constantly ran into the main room (sometimes by pushing aside the tables which blocked the holes they had made in the outside walls) and had to be thrown out or they disrupted all the activities by running around shouting, bumping into players and preventing any conversations from getting underway. They were still on the streets after the club closed at 9.30 p.m., they all smoked, cadged cigarettes where they could and ran to the local pubs for the older boys to buy them large bottles of cider at 90p (and so earning the 10p change). At the end of the evening, they also collected the empties for which they received a further 8p a bottle. If not admitted to the club, they hammered on the outside door, on one occasion breaking one of the windows. Those we spoke to on the steps of the club were, at the ages of 7, 8 and 9, unable to tell the time or read the most elementary reading books which could be found in the cupboards. Despite their behaviour, the children were held in very obvious affection by the young people and by the workers; it was very difficult to refuse a cold and wet 7-year-old, dressed in thin clothes and rubber sandshoes, who wanted to sit in your lap while you talked to his older brothers, sisters or cousins.

The children, at serious risk to themselves, jumped on and off the bumpers of the mini-bus and chased it along the street, as it set out or returned from trips. These excursions were in part arranged to relieve the crush in the main room on evenings when more than 20 youngsters turned up. About 12 adolescents and two members of staff set off in the mini-bus to visit, on one occasion, a local farm and, on another, the local airport. To try to avoid the children clambering over the vehicle, the new, part-time member of staff who was driving the mini-bus picked up the young people, who in the meantime had bought beer and cider, at a pre-arranged spot some distance from the centre. The children, however, always found the mini-bus and managed to leap on to it before it sped off. That was not the only danger: on one occasion, the back door of the local authority mini-bus could not be locked or even closed. The handles were tied together with a piece of string and when one youngster bumped against them, the doors burst open in transit. Both of the trips which we joined seemed to us rather pointless; it was dark when the farm was reached, and at the airport, there were no planes taking off or landing and no observation tower or balcony. The physical appearance of the young people, and their shouting and milling about, quickly brought on the scene security officers who shepherded us all out of the building. The mini-bus did not return directly to the centre but aimlessly toured the darkened streets until the time came to close the club. The youngsters responded to what they called 'the boredom' of the trips by running around screaming as soon as they got out, by pinching what they could when they arrived, or by carving their initials into the wooden seats when they were back in the vehicle.

It was on one of these trips that we first noticed Gloria. She was a stockily built girl with long blonde hair who was still at school, where she boasted of shouting 'fucking bastard' at teachers. Both boys and girls used the words 'crazy' and 'mad' to describe her behaviour; they were at one and the same time wary of her and easily influenced by her. The workers thought she was 'really moody' and 'a really weird kid'. (Later, we learned that she came from a 'disturbed' family, some of whom were in trouble with the police.) One evening Gloria picked a fight with another girl, a fight which ended with them rolling on the ground, tearing each other's hair; she was only quiet when 'necking' in a corner with her boyfriend, Malc. He seemed able to control her aggression and her swearing by taking her aside and talking gently to her. It was one of the part-time workers who brought the fight between the two girls to an end and he was bitten for his pains. Gloria's boyfriend, Malc, then put his hand over her mouth to prevent her from swearing, and insisted that she stay outside in the rain until she cooled off. She accepted Malc's discipline.

Gloria was not the only girl in the club who became involved in physical fights. Sharon fought with both boys and girls. In the course of one evening, she was three times thrown over the same hedge (to the great annoyance of the owners) by Stew, whom she insisted on calling a 'poof', a term she backed up with a stream of explicit sexual obscenities. At one point, she was chased so hard that she ran for protection to her grandmother's house, which was just within sight of the centre. Stew and his mates tried to drag her out of the doorway, while her grandmother struggled to pull her in. The few older girls we met on the steps of the club refused to enter; in the words of one of them, everybody in the club was 'either a bitch or a poofter'. Behind the aggressive ribaldry and the tough posturing displayed by both sexes, we suspected that the relationships between boys and girls were based on long association and deep knowledge of each other which resulted in mutual support, sympathy and even tenderness at times. The bravado may be nothing more than a facade for the youth leaders, ourselves and the rest of the outside world.

The boys were all concerned about portraying strong masculine images of themselves. At the earliest meetings with Tom, a 17-year-old 'half-caste' who was small and thin for his age, he presented himself as a boy who hated lying in bed all day, who got up regularly at 8 a.m. and who helped his unemployed father (who himself was only in his early forties) to create vegetable patches in neighbours' gardens for an extra £2 a day. Tom claimed to have been on a Youth Opportunity Programme but, as it had led to no job, he had become very cynical about the whole scheme. The fieldnotes of our first encounter with Tom described him as 'a sensible, level-headed boy'.

Within two weeks, Tom had dropped the socially acceptable response and was admitting that he lay in bed all day and that in general he 'pissed about'. He was also not above 'taking the piss' out of researchers. He was keen on clothes and he was dressed in a new outfit every time we met him. One evening, besides dyed grey hair, he sported tartan trousers and a tartan jacket, a white tee-shirt and an anarchist badge, all of which he claimed to have stolen. Tom was bright, articulate and seemed to be alone in being politically aware. He boasted to us that he could steal all he wanted in life, namely, clothes, drink, cigarettes, etc. He had no interest in possessing larger items such as a car or a house. 'Work', he explained, 'just gives you scraps of paper for slavery. I just *take* what I want'. He admitted to having three or four convictions and seemed not to care whether it was three or four: by such means, he sought to convey his contempt for the proceedings. His last appearance in court, apart from having no effect on him, had cost him a £10 fine. How had he been able to pay it out of the £5 he was left with every week? 'My Nana paid it for me', he replied with much laughter.

Tom introduced Bob one evening. Bob, although the same age, was even slighter than Tom, had closely cropped blonde hair and was wearing a new pair of Doc Martin boots. Bob described how he had 'blasted out' (was on the run from a remand centre) and how 'the busies' (the police) were combing the estate looking for him. Bob cadged fags and money from most of the older boys in the centre and, at the same time, tried to sell them a new pair of trousers, which he claimed to have stolen earlier that day.

Two or three sets of brothers also attended the club, including 'Evo' (so called because of his habit of glue sniffing) and 'Stew'. They came from a family of six, four boys and two girls. Evo was the older of the two, being 19 years old; his hair was dyed blonde and his clothes and general style were punk. He spent his evenings quietly playing pool, but we were told by the workers that they had had difficulties in restraining him physically when he had been sniffing. His younger brother, Stew, brought glue into the club one evening, but the youth worker who spotted him turned a blind eye. There was a lot of talk about glue sniffing sessions on different parts of the estate, but, in the opinion of the older boys who attended the afternoon club, the practice was virtually confined to the 14- to 17-year-old boys and girls. The older boys looked with contempt on glue sniffing which they saw as a relatively harmless practice of young adolescents; it was something they would soon grow out of and something only excitable middle-class adults took seriously.

We concentrated on making contact with the oldest teenagers who turned up in the evenings, but the majority were under 16, and this was especially true of the girls. Among the older group was Andy, a small, slightly built boy, with blonde-dyed hair who had to be told by the 16-year-old Smithey the words for 'cockpit', 'wing', etc., when we were at the airport. Smithey had a pinched, gamin face, a shock of black hair and apparently only one set of clothes: dirty black drainpipe trousers, a black tee-shirt, red socks and black shoes with thick soles.

The incident

Out of a total of some 20 to 30 people, these were the youngsters whom we were just beginning to get to know, when, during the fourth week of our involvement, one of us (F.C.) had the aggression of the whole group directed towards him.

As I approached the club, the younger children were hammering on the outside door and had already smashed one of the glass panels, which had recently been replaced. Two boys under 10 years of age were standing on the roof and were urinating onto the front door. The trainee youth worker came out at this point and told them to 'piss off'. As the adults and teenagers laughed, the young boys and girls (including the two on the roof) slipped into the club, where they ran in circles around the main room avoiding capture.

Inside, the boys were attracted to the new darts set which had been left by the afternoon club. As soon as they began quarrelling about the score, the darts were used as weapons, although interestingly none landed on target. When the part-time workers tried to calm them down, the boys pretended to throw the darts at them. When the young trainee intervened, they began throwing the darts between his legs, inching towards his feet with every throw but still without hitting the target.

There were more than 30 young people in the club that evening, all crammed into one room. The noise made by the screams of the children, as they were caught and thrown out, mingled with the quarrels of the adolescents. Before the young trainee's face, Sharon stripped a table tennis bat of its rubber cover and, when this produced no reaction, she asked him directly what he was going to do about it. He replied that he would replace the bat next week; this was not, however, the practice in the club. When asked why she had torn the rubber from the bat, Sharon answered: 'You didn't see nothing, you've got no fucking eyes to see'; and with that she walked away. Tom and Andy were openly drinking large bottles of cider and cans of beer in the club and both had spent the afternoon sniffing glue. They turned to writing on the walls with purple chalk. Tom chalked up in large letters, 'YOU CAN'T VOTE ANARCHIST, YOU CAN ONLY BE ONE!' Andy wrote 'THE SYSTEM MIGHT OF [sic] GOT YOU, BUT IT HASN'T GOT ME!' When no one made any move to stop them, other boys began drawing pictures of male and female genitalia on the walls of the main room.

Some of the girls, watching from the internal doorway, started chalking up their own names; others began to pick at a large pre-existing hole in the plaster of one of the inside walls. Shortly, they were tearing out handfuls and were joined by some of the younger boys. As the plaster board fell on the floor, the trainee worker and one of the part-time workers used a brush and shovel to clear the debris away, having earlier succeeded in getting the girls to clear away most of their own mess. The trainee at one point turned to settle an argument between two boys who were throwing darts at each other in a less controlled manner. Two other boys began undoing the zip of his trousers and the dart players announced that they had found a new target.

Across the room, a new girl in dirty and ill-fitting school clothes, carpet slippers and bare legs, which were red from scratching, was having a slanging match with Sharon. The two of them began fighting, rolling over on the ground, pulling each other's hair and scratching. When I saw blood on Sharon's cheek, I separated her from the new girl who was straddling her. I was immediately surrounded by the older boys who claimed that I had been 'hitting lassies'. The new girl added that I had pulled her hair and touched her breasts while separating her from Sharon.

Two boys had now forced open a cupboard which had been repaired and for which new locks had been fitted by the Mothers and Toddlers Club. They found squares of thick cardboard which they began flicking across the room and into the faces of the children. One girl of eight received a slight cut just below her eye and so I decided to point out the dangers to the boy responsible. He immediately challenged me to a fight outside and began pushing me in the chest. I explained to him that the cardboard was thick enough to give someone a serious eye injury and turned away. Ricky, a 12-year-old, straightaway flicked a card into my face. The immediate group became quiet as they waited for my response. I told him quietly but firmly that, if he did that again, he would have to leave. He smiled, picked up another card and flicked it into my face. I told him he would have to leave, took him by the arm and began moving him towards the door. After only a few steps, he broke from my grasp and began flaying around in all directions with his arms and feet; he then started throwing chairs and knocking over tables. His face was red, his lips were flecked with spittle and his words became incoherent. He was now in the centre of the room and for a few minutes he could not be approached, as he was hurling whatever was near him at anyone and everyone. His elder brother finally grabbed him from behind, pinned his arms to his side and held him on the ground to stop his legs from thrashing around. All the while he whispered in Ricky's ear, calmed him down and then carried him outside.

Because of the confrontation, I was now accused by one boy after another of 'picking on Ricky', and challenged to fight outside. The older boys then left the club, but not before a number of them warned me that I would be beaten up on my way out. One of them chalked up the message 'FRANKIES [sic] GOING TO GET FUCKED', as he left. Another, dancing about in front of the group, pushed a heavy, bone-handled gents' hairbrush into my hand and ordered me to clean the floor with it. The boys were now openly competing with each other to see who could go furthest; as they continued to raise the stakes, appeals from me for calmness and reasoned argument were brushed aside. The floor now had a new layer of cardboard cards, chalk and plaster from the wall which was still being picked to pieces by the girls. We learned later that at this point, Andy told the part-time workers that the quarrel had nothing to do with them and so they should stay out of it.

When the club closed, I went outside and was immediately surrounded by the older boys who began pushing and jostling me and telling me that I was about to be beaten up. The other workers, who were returning the equipment to the caretaker's house, ran across and formed an escort around me. We began walking smartly towards the main road but as we moved under a bridge, the boys broke into two groups to prevent either an advance or a retreat. The girls were grouped together, some 20 yards behind, watching and shouting. Twice as we had walked towards the bridge, the hairbrush had been thrown at us but each time it had missed. Now under the bridge, we were threatened with stones, half-bricks and the odd bottle; some of these objects were thrown but none landed on target. As the boys closed in on us from each direction, we began to be punched and kicked.

I decided, as the verbal threats were being directed solely at me, to break through the boys ahead and to run up to the main road to prevent us all from being trapped underneath the bridge. I plunged through the boys who had blocked off the pavement by positioning themselves between the railings and the wall of the bridge, and, pursued by the whole group and a shower of missiles, I reached the main road where I saw a local bus stopping some two hundred yards away. I ran towards it and got on, but the driver refused to close the doors or to move off. Although he could hear the noise of the stones and bottles hitting his bus and could see the boys who were now running alongside, he insisted on receiving the exact fare. All I could find was a £1 note, so he told me to get off. Some female passengers began shouting hysterically, as the front runners, Tom and Andy, now tried to board the bus. They both shouted obscenities and spat in my face, as I pushed them off the bus; at the same time, I avoided the half brick with which Tom kept trying to hit me on the head. Eventually, the driver drew away from the kerb, as the whole group of boys arrived and began kicking and hammering on the sides of the bus.

The bus now sped along the road but was shortly overtaken by a police car which had been passing. The police stopped the bus and I went out to speak to the two officers. They decided to wait for ten minutes to allow the boys to clear off the main road and to avoid a confrontation; they then drove me back to my car and I joined the other workers in a pub to discuss what had happened.

Other meetings were later held to inform the youth workers who had not been present and to develop a strategy for coping with the situation. With the exception of one part-time worker, we all agreed that we should attempt to discuss the incident with the young people at the next meeting of the club. Some senior youth workers turned up to that meeting, at the start of which there were almost as many adults as youngsters and none of those who had been centrally involved. As the evening wore on, some of the older boys and girls began to drift in; eventually, Tom and Andy sloped in, both looking very sheepish and guilty. All the young people were acting self-consciously, saying 'thank you' and 'please' in exaggeratedly polite voices. However, no discussion was held that night – or any night – as many of the young people who were central to the incident did not turn up. One young girl was overheard explaining to her friend who had been absent on the night in question that Frank had been attacked by the boys because he had 'picked on Ricky'.

At meetings with the other workers, however, the following information emerged for the first time, although it proved impossible to establish the 'facts', as we received not only different accounts from different people but also differing accounts when the same people were asked about the same events on different occasions. Two senior workers were of the opinion that in the recent past there had been other violent outbursts at the club and, more frequently, at other similar clubs in the area. They told us, for example, that one young man had been 'victimised' by the boys and girls, had become a 'scape-goat' and had been 'drummed out of the club', having suffered some damage to his leg by falling off the mini-bus when demonstrating the dangers of clambering over the vehicle. To others who had seen the incident, such words as 'victimised' and 'drummed out' were too emotive and exaggerated. What is agreed is that the young man had to take four to five days off work. Other incidents we were told about concerned the full-time youth worker who had tried to impose some order one evening and, in response, a 10-year-old had 'walked all over' his new car. On another occasion, Stew had gone berserk and had thrown chairs through the windows; Evo had also become physically uncontrollable one evening after a session of glue sniffing. The part-time workers had also witnessed Ricky's explosive behaviour and knew that the young people were generally more tolerant and understanding of his outbursts. None of this information was passed on to us before we began attending in the evenings.

The club in the Down Dale estate was not the only one in Shipton to run into trouble. During the very same period, there were violent incidents in two other youth clubs in Shipton, and there was a long history of similar problems in the deprived districts. Indeed, the only qualified youth worker had been withdrawn after the first week to sort out financial troubles in another club; this left an untrained 21-year-old in charge every evening from then on. In the opinion of the most senior youth workers, the Down Dale estate and the social problems presented by its young people were typical of the borough. If the level of deprivation was so well known by senior workers, then we should expect explanations for the inadequate response to come from them and their superiors rather than from those struggling at the coal face.

Discussion

Many factors need to be taken into account to explain why one of us was singled out for such aggression. The past history of the club itself is obviously relevant as is the occurrence of similar behaviour in other youth clubs serving similarly disadvantaged areas. The limitations of the physical setting also played their part in that all the young people were regularly crowded into one large room; there were no facilities for breaking the group into more manageable numbers and there was nowhere for quiet conversations to take place or relationships to develop. The excursions in the mini-bus, which helped to ease the crush in the centre, created further problems which at the time appeared to be neither acknowledged, discussed nor acted upon. We later learned that the trips in the summer months had been much more of a success, but those young people who had been out on a trip tended to return 'rather high', hence the practice of returning only when the club was about to close.

In our opinion, there was also a serious failure right from the start in keeping to the set of rules which had been agreed upon; these rules were in fact never made explicit to the young people nor their agreement to them sought. An attempt, for example, was once made to collect subscriptions, but only the more amenable youngsters handed over their money. When they saw that others refused to pay up, they demanded to be refunded. The failure to impose even some minimal amount of order led to a series of confrontations, each one more serious than the one before. It was as though the boys and girls were constantly prodding the adults into laying down some guidelines and, when the adults refused, their behaviour became steadily more outrageous. The youngsters appeared to us to be testing the limits of acceptable behaviour, just as they would have done with a new teacher, and they seemed upset that there were no limits. They even invaded the bodily privacy of one worker without repudiation. Some of the leaders seemed to be prepared to accept almost any behaviour in case a confrontation led to a violent outburst. We witnessed a series of retreats and submissions, which finally helped to produce the very behaviour they were supposed to render less likely. The youth workers had no united policy (one of them thinking that violence should be met with violence and that the disciplining of the young people should be carried out by the strong arm of Cliff, one of the natural leaders on the estate); there were no formal, regular meetings before and after each session to discuss approaches, we were not party to any internal criticism of the very limited activities on offer, and only one of the three regular workers was attempting to get to know the young people individually and their family backgrounds. We found ourselves working in a setting which appeared to us to have no visible structure, no agreed policy, no regular self-evaluation and no support from senior staff.

There had in fact been a fundamental difference in approach and aims among the workers. Two of them appeared to us to want strict rules, tight control and adult decisions to be imposed on the members of the club. The other two were in favour of breaking away from the regimented practice of the past, of 'riding the storm' which they anticipated would blow up as a consequence and so giving the young people the opportunity to learn from their own mistakes and to take responsibility for their own club and for themselves. (Although it took over a year for the behaviour of the young people to change significantly, the latter view finally prevailed.)

Even if the workers had been much more experienced, skilful and united, they would still have had an uphill task, because the young people as a group presented a formidable array of problems. Their very number created difficulties, as did their drinking and glue sniffing. The latter was making the management of clubs far more exacting because the boys regarded it as a legitimate reason for 'acting crazy' and because there was so little knowledge about its effects. On the night of the incident, only two boys (Tom and Andy) were known by some of their friends to have been drinking and sniffing beforehand: but two in such a condition were sufficient to excite the others. Once the trouble had started, both of those boys became more affected than the others with the group spirit and seized the opportunity to increase their reputations in front of a large audience. Apart from the girls, that audience included Ricky's elder brother, who was one of the few not to be affected by the group spirit; for example, he did not participate in the 'aggro' in any way.

All of them talked of being bored, both those at school and those who were unemployed. The latter particularly came out in the evenings after a day in bed, looking for excitement and stimulation. After the incident, some of the boys talked vaingloriously of 'having run other workers out of town' and for them violence was clearly pleasurable. As Fox has argued (1977: 137): 'We have to face up to the fact that violence generates tremendous excitement, either in participation or in observation, and this seems to be a universal and deep-seated facet of our behaviour ...'. The boys and the girls also struck us as being rather immature: some of the boys were chronologically 17 but could have passed physically for 14. They were also very obviously deprived in a wide range of senses: of money, clothes, leisure facilities and job opportunities, and some always looked underfed and hungry. The general deprivations of the area were just as marked in the faces and the bodies of their younger brothers and sisters; there was every likelihood that they would grow up to be similarly bereft of education, of marketable skills and of any understanding of their relative poverty. Some were just as noticeably deprived of affection.

A few personal factors need to be added. Neither of us had time to establish relationships with these young people and, in fact, we were still learning the names of some. We were hampered by a lack of knowledge concerning the behaviour of individuals (e.g. Ricky's outbursts) and of the group as a whole (e.g. previous attacks on other workers). We were also outsiders who had much to learn about the language of these young people and their inherent rules. One of the part-time youth workers, for example, later claimed that the young people operated with only two rules. The first was that they themselves (and not adults) would intervene in fights before anyone was seriously hurt. I (F.C.) broke this rule unwittingly when separating the two girls. It is worth pointing out that this part-time worker also broke their rule in parting two girls but the relationship which he had established with them prevented any accusations or escalation.

Second, they were prepared to take turns at pool or table tennis. We would add a third rule: they were more tolerant and more protective of any of their number who was seen to have a special problem. I again blundered unknowingly when dealing with Ricky and committed a tactical error of telling him in front of a large group that, if he flicked another card in my face, he would have to leave. This was tantamount to challenging him to go on, as the only alternative for him was to back down and lose face in front of all his mates. In retrospect, it was also a mistake to take him by the arm. Pik (1981: 140), when analysing confrontations, wrote: 'Physical handling, even something so slight as catching at the sleeve of a child's, jacket, may trigger a violent response'. With hindsight, it was perhaps naive to make 'appeals for reasoned argument' in such an emotionally charged atmosphere; as McGuiness (1982) phrased it, the incident illustrated 'the inadequacy of a merely cognitive approach'. It might also have been preferable to focus attention on the injured girl, thus encouraging the group to care for her and perhaps even control the card-flicker. Instead, by laying down the law, I pushed the group into siding with one of its members who was being disciplined by an outsider. The loyalty and mutual caring which the group displayed towards each other could have been used in a positive way. One final stress factor should also be taken into consideration. I arrived at the club a few minutes late because of protracted meetings over reductions in the staff of the department in which I work and was consequently anxious and tired. As the 'aggro' developed, my own masculinity and that of the other workers became involved. As is so painfully obvious with hindsight, the action I took was in no way planned: I reacted immediately and thoughtlessly.

A large number of interacting factors have been introduced to help explain the aggression: a past history of difficulties in running the club, inadequate premises, workers who lacked a united policy, outsiders who mishandled situations through lack of knowledge and the youngsters themselves who, flushed with alcohol and glue, responded aggressively to the slightest frustration and who actively sought trouble as a means of increasing their status and decreasing their boredom. In our view, the behaviour of the young people had been steadily deteriorating since we first put in an appearance and the weakness of some of the workers only hastened the crisis. The precipitating factor in most people's eyes (and ours) was the fact that I happened to choose (from all those who were acting up) the one boy who was granted a greater licence by the others. Even then, if those workers who knew of the special treatment accorded to Ricky had intervened or had shown a united front, then the subsequent events might have been avoided. It is also interesting to speculate whether C.B., if she had been present, or any other female worker would have been able to head off the aggression.

Conclusions

Shipton was and is providing seriously inadequate facilities for seriously deprived young people. The centre was admitted to be 'seriously inadequate' by local officials and, more recently, in response to protests by residents, local politicians have promised that it will be upgraded and extended. At the time of writing, however, there continues to be no youth and community provision for the ward; indeed, there is still no full-time worker in the Down Dale estate. Even more serious, there is still no coordinated policy among local authority departments (e.g. Education, Social Work, Housing and Youth Service) for the Down Dale estate. In accordance with government plans, the local Education Committee was forced to make cuts in spending in both 1980–81 and 1981–82: the Youth and Community Service was one of the main areas singled out for cuts.

It is difficult to avoid asking why such conditions have been tolerated for so long in an area which has been controlled politically by the Labour Party for generations. The purpose here is not to use the language of blame, which is so easy to employ, but rather to tease out the complex interactions between amateur, conservative and democratically elected councillors and professional, bureaucratic and hierarchical local officials. To take a specific example, local youth workers and local teachers are left to cope with (and are unable to change) the problems created by the concentration of multi-problem families in certain streets on the estate. The reasons for such concentrations are many and interacting and are rarely the result of any simple policy of 'dumping'; on the other hand, there is little evidence as yet of a dispersal programme or of decentralised services. The picture is still one of uniform provision of all services, irrespective of special local needs.

The Youth and Community Service appeared to us to be under considerable strain; trained personnel were being removed to deal with crises, leaving the untrained exposed and vulnerable. There also needed to be a concerted policy, with agreed aims and approaches, which was adhered to by all the workers acting as a team. Work with such deprived youngsters needed to be supported by experienced, senior workers who encouraged self-evaluation. The *ad hoc* way in which decisions were made at all levels was inadequate to the task.

A more general comment about youth and community workers in such areas seems appropriate. Youth workers, policemen and prison officers are, to use Everett Hughes's term (1967), 'good people doing the dirty work of society'. Lee Rainwater (1974) extended this point when he wrote: 'The dirty workers are increasingly caught between the silent middle class which wants them to do the work and keep quiet about it and the objects of that work who refuse to continue to take it lying down'. Those in charge of youth clubs in deprived areas are the agents of society, they work long, unsociable hours in poor conditions for very modest returns and are expected to absorb many of the frustrations and aggressions of young people. In the words of a Liverpool policeman who was commenting on the Toxteth riots of 1981: 'Society throws these kids into a dustbin and expects us to keep the lid on'.

The staple diet of 1950s boys' clubs, namely, films, ping-pong and pool for unemployed young people, remained part of the routine. Yet what appears as merely playing ping-pong with a young boy can be the vital early steps in the build-up of a relationship. The workers were finding difficulty in moving the group on to other activities. It was certainly easier to criticise the provision being made than to suggest feasible alternatives, and the psychological literature (Jahoda, 1979, 1981; Hartley, 1980, etc.) has only recently reawakened its interest in the topic. The suggestions for helping people to cope with unemployment which are contained in that literature (e.g. Winfield, 1981: 353–4) all appear to us to be rather functional. Older boys, however, would have been better employed teaching their young brothers, sisters and cousins how to read.[3]

We noticed that what the younger children *were* learning was how to drink, smoke, sniff glue and become delinquent by imitating those adolescents in their community whom they admired. We remarked on the immaturity of the social behaviour of these adolescents, particularly in relationships between boys and girls. We would hypothesise that the flamboyant 'aggro' they displayed towards each other was often more a front than a reality; we did observe, however, examples of boys treating girls in dismissive, chauvinist ways.

It is important to record that, despite all the 'aggro' and all the shouting, running, punching, kicking and throwing of missiles during the incident, *no one was hurt*. This finding would support the work of Marsh (1978) and many others, who have argued that such fights are not unstructured, anarchic free-for-alls, but 'choreographed, seemingly rehearsed, stereotyped' (Fox, 1977: 144). It is not being suggested that the boys were following a set of explicit rules as though they were participating in a ritualised game; rather, the existence of implicit rules is being deduced from the way the fighting broke off at the very point when someone could have been seriously hurt, and from the fact that the target of their aggression was *allowed* to escape and so the incident could be brought to an end.

Sufficient rewards had been gained from their controlled 'aggro' without pushing the violence too far. They had regained control of their club (perhaps no bad thing in itself), they had manufactured enough excitement to fill the following days and weeks with discussions of exploits and possible repercussions, and they had, in Albert Cohen's (1955: 28) phrase, derived much pleasure from 'making themselves obnoxious to the virtuous'.

With regard to the running of the club, it was clear that a set of formal rules which, for instance, banned swearing or smoking, would simply have driven these young people away. And yet we feel that they wanted a minimum of good order to be established by themselves which would have allowed activities to take place. Every capitulation by the staff raised the temperature and the result was a series of crises which had ended in the past with the club being closed.

The imposition of activities, outings and rules prevented the club from starting where the young people were. The ban on alcohol and glue sniffing simply excluded two of the most important topics for discussion and reflection. The inner resources and motivation of the young people remained untapped by the failure to involve them in the construction and negotiation of a curriculum.

This experience has also re-emphasised the need for new workers to learn the immediate past history of the groups they are joining and to be sensitive to their informal rules. To have been informed before we met these young people that they preferred to control their own fights and that certain youngsters had particular problems which were treated leniently by their contemporaries would have eased our entrée. The passing on of such information is simply good professional practice. A concentration, however, on the microrules of social interaction, important as these undoubtedly are, will not explain all the behaviour of these young people and may lead us to underplay the far greater significance of social deprivations in their lives. Billy, for example, had all the personal qualities and the social skills to break out of his background; no one was more in tune with the implicit rules of his culture and yet when the chance presented itself for him to be trained elsewhere, he chose to remain within the community he knew. A deep knowledge of the inherent rules of aggression will not explain that decision.[4]

Within the same social conditions, however, there were marked individual differences among the group. There were quiet, polite, self-effacing girls, as well as Sharon and Gloria, who swore and fought like boys. There were boys like Smithey and Ricky's elder brother who refused to join in the 'aggro' and who made their disapproval clear later. Some were more politically aware, more intellectually able and slightly more affluent through parental support, and yet they were all confronting the prospect of long-term unemployment. Their individual differences appeared slight compared with the social deprivations they had in common. Overall, a more useful comparison may be between the young people of the Down Dale estate and students of the same age attending the local universities of Durham and Newcastle, not only in terms of money expended on education and on grants but also on the quality of living accommodation, on sporting and recreational facilities and on career guidance. Certainly, there is a small but growing problem of graduate unemployment, but the prospect facing the young people in the Down Dale estate is that 'many of them will never work at all' (Robinson, 1982: 123). Most of the young people we met will only be 34 years old in the year 2000, by which time they are likely to have been unemployed for eighteen years and will be facing a further twenty-six years of unemployment before 'retiring' at 60.

Even before the incident, we had begun to wonder whether involvement with this club was even in the short-term interests of our project. The age of the group (and particularly of the girls) was too young for our stated purposes. Moreover, the physical set-up prevented us from having the kinds of relaxed discussions which we wanted to have with young people and was unlikely to change in the foreseeable future. We regretfully decided to find other groups with which to work.

We hope that those workers who knew the group before we arrived and stayed with them afterwards will place this 'snap-shot' in a much wider context in a later article. We also wish to thank them for their comments which have improved this article: all of us hope to take it back to the young people themselves for *their* comments and an article from them would present perhaps the most interesting account of all. Negotiating the foregoing account has emphasised for us the point made by both Ginsburg (1980) and Rommetveit (1980) that 'genuine ambiguity and multiple meanings' are part and parcel of any social interaction.

Notes

1 The names of all places and people are pseudonyms.
2 Special Temporary Employment Programme, designed specifically by the Manpower Services Commission for the long-term unemployed.
3 We have since learned that such a scheme has recently begun.
4 A year later, Billy joined a part-time Youth and Community Work course; so much for the pretensions of social scientists.

References

Cohen, A.K. (1955) *Delinquent Boys: The Culture of the Gang*. New York: Free Press.
Farrant, M.R. and Marchant, H.J. (1970) *Making Contact with Unreached Youth*. Manchester: Youth Development Trust.
Fox, R. (1977) The inherent rules of violence. In Collett, P. (ed) *Social Rules and Social Behaviour*. Oxford: Basil Blackwell, 132–49.

Ginsburg, G.P. (1980) A conception of situated action. In Brenner, M. (ed) *The Structure of Action*. Oxford: Basil Blackwell.

Hartley, J. (1980) Psychological approaches to unemployment. *Bulletin of the British Psychological Society*, 33, 412–14.

Holman, B. (1981) *Kids At the Door*. Oxford: Basil Blackwell.

Hughes, E. (1967) Good people and dirty work. In Becker, H. (ed) *The Other Side*. New York: Free Press, 23–36.

Jahoda, M. (1979) The impact of unemployment in the 1930s and the 1970s. *Bulletin of the British Psychological Society*, 32, 309–14.

Jahoda, M. (1981) Work, employment, and unemployment: Values, theories and approaches in social research. *American Psychologist*, 36, 184–91.

Marsh, P. (1978) *Aggro: The Illusion of Violence*. London: Dent.

McGuiness, J.B. (1982) *Planned Pastoral Care*. London: McGraw Hill.

Pik, R. (1981) Confrontation situations and teacher-support systems. In Gillham, B. (ed) *Problem Behaviour in the Secondary School*. London: Croom Helm, 127–47.

Rainwater, L. (1974) *Social Problems and Public Policy*. Chicago: Aldine.

Robinson, F. (1982) *Economic Prospects for the North. Centre for Urban and Regional Development Studies*. University of Newcastle upon Tyne.

Rommetveit, K. (1980) On 'meanings' of acts … In Brenner, M. (ed) *The Structure of Action*. Oxford: Basil Blackwell.

Spencer, J. (1964) *Stress and Release in an Urban Estate*. London: Tavistock.

Winfield, I. (1981) Psychology and centres for the unemployed: Challenge or chimera? *Bulletin of the British Psychological Society*, 34, 353–355.

Part 2

Youth unemployment

Chapter 4

How young people try to survive being unemployed

The job interview consisted of two questions: 'Are you disabled?' and 'What size boots do you take?' The North East of England suffered huge job losses from the 1960s onwards in coal mining, iron and steel and shipbuilding and nothing was done to replace such highly skilled work. The impact on young people was particularly severe, so Carol Borrill, Sarah Marshall and I set out to find out how they were faring. We wrote this article which was published by the magazine *New Society* (since defunct) on 2 June 1983 (332–4) where we described how young people were using not 'coping strategies', but 'survival tactics'. The one 'coping strategy' that outsiders might have expected the young unemployed to adopt – political action – was conspicuous by its absence.

In 1984, a group of primary school headteachers contacted me to say that they were delighted with the quality of our students who did teaching practice in their schools. So many of them, however, came from the south east of England that they tended to return there after graduation rather than joining the staff of a local school. In response, Durham University set up a programme whereby local married women with the required A levels could take a part-time course to qualify as primary school teachers. Many of these new recruits to the profession gained first-class honours degrees because they were motivated, experienced in dealing with young children and keen to improve the lot of their families.

One such student told me how, after being accepted onto the course, she received a written invitation to join one of the colleges. The invitation came with a questionnaire, the last question of which was: 'Do you row?' She wrote: 'I don't think my husband and I quarrel any more than other couples'. No sooner had she done so than she realised what the question was really about.

Billy is 20 years old, has been on one government scheme since leaving school at 17 and has been unemployed continuously now for 14 months. He has never had a real job. When he goes to sign on, he presents himself with a challenge: he never takes a biro with him, preferring always to ask pointedly for a pen, which he carries off with him openly and then breaks outside the office, discarding it on the pavement, where it can be seen.

DOI: 10.4324/9781003476146-6

Len is 19, and works part-time on a Community Enterprise scheme, clearing rubbish from a beach with a squad of manual labourers. He knows the job could be done in a fraction of the time by a machine. When he was interviewed for the job, he was asked only two questions: 'Are you disabled?' and 'What size boots do you take?' He had repeatedly 'grafted and grafted' for hours at jobs demanding hard labour, only to be told to undo his own work in the afternoon. He has reacted to the pointlessness of the tasks by throwing his spade every so often into the sea.

Such means of hitting back at authority are not typical of our sample of 47 young men and women from the north-east, aged between 17 and 21. At any one time, half of them are unemployed, while the other half are best described as having moved in and out of 'shit' jobs and 'govvie' schemes. (Their words.)

Only two of our sample are involved in any form of political action (one is a member of the Militant Tendency, while the other supported an animal welfare rights candidate at the local elections). The majority are politically uneducated, not to say apathetic.

How well do those who are unemployed cope with their predicament? The strategies they devised to cope with secondary school would probably have eased their transition to the world of work (in much the same way as Paul Willis described it for lads in the West Midlands in his book, *Learning to Labour*). But now there is no shopfloor culture for many of them to join. There is no easily identifiable group like teachers or bosses to oppose or resist. The 'counter-culture' they developed at school is left without anyone to counter.

None of the young people in our sample were prepared in any way by their schools for unemployment, never mind long periods of it. In such circumstances, it is no surprise that they have fallen back on the 'local scripts' or tactics developed over many years by working-class communities in the north-east, a region which has had to live with unemployment for over 50 years. Our young people are – in the absence of any other form of help – dependent on the resources of their local communities.

These techniques are sometimes described – by psychologists and others – as 'coping strategies'. But they are more like *survival tactics*. In everyday language, 'coping' suggests a competition on equal terms; to a psychologist like Gordon Allport, 'coping' is purposive, conscious and non-spontaneous. Both meanings of the word are inappropriate to our sample. And 'strategies' imply a long-term view and a command of resources which they do not have.

We set out here the different survival tactics the young unemployed use. Each of the tactics is best thought of as being on a continuum. The eight tactics are not mutually exclusive; they often overlap. What they have in common is that they all contribute to the young person's well-being, physical and psychological. The main theme which links them is the struggle to maintain two necessities of life: self-respect and income.

Family support

Besides much-needed moral encouragement, families provide our sample with substantial financial subsidies. On average, our young people give their parents £10 a week for their keep. If they are 18 or older, this leaves them with £13.65 a week to pay for improving skills, travel to Job Centres, saving for the future, clothes, 'snake bites' (cider and lager), 'tabs' (cigarettes), discos, concerts, newspapers and cups of coffee to help them pass the time. Those under 18 will now only be left with £5.80 a week after giving their parents their keep. Since April, they have lost £3.10 'housing requirement' if they live at home.

Young people borrow from their mothers before the arrival of their Giro cheques on Saturday mornings, so that they can go out on Friday nights. This applies to Terry, who is 17, and Hughie, who is 18. For such young people, who are seeking adult status, unemployment prolongs the period of child-like dependence on parents. The network of contacts provided by the extended family remains the best source of information about jobs.

Contact with peer group

Considering the amount of time created by enforced idleness, few of the young people we talked to spend long periods in the company of friends who are also unemployed. We expected that they would throw themselves more fully into social activities and into meetings with their partners.

But because of unemployment, their isolation has increased: some of them – and especially young women – have retreated into their own homes and stayed there for days on end. Pat, for example, is 18, and has been unemployed for eight months since leaving a Training Workshop; she spends seven days a week watching television in her own home, only leaving to watch it at her boyfriend's. Some have been able to build up their relationships with their regular partner. But others have found themselves quarrelling more. For example, two of our sample, Dave (19) and Herbie (21) will not go out if it means being paid for by their working lasses.

The pattern of meeting with their friends seems not to have changed as a result of unemployment. They are still geared to the occasional big night out. This is further reflected in their spending patterns.

Spending patterns

Most of our young people spend their money on one or two big nights out every fortnight, rather than spinning out their money by spending a little each day. Their spending makes sense in human, if not economic, terms. The Friday or Saturday night out drinking with friends – whether in single or mixed-sex groups – is part of the traditional culture of the area. Our young people want to be a part of the ordinary life around them, even if it means staying in the house for all the other days of the week.

The young unemployed feel a need to be a continuing part of their immediate culture alongside those of their friends who are working. Like workers, many of them maintain their self-respect by refusing to let us buy them drinks, even coffee, despite their lack of money.

Skills

Acquiring new skills is almost exclusively limited to learning to drive. But two of our sample, Jane (18) and Les (18) have had to give up even this, because of the prohibitive price of lessons. These currently cost between £6 and £8.

Skills which have already been learned can help pass the time. These include fishing, playing the guitar, motorbike and car maintenance, modelmaking and talking on CB radio. Ron, for instance, who is 20, spends long hours practicing with his own band, plays for free at local gigs and hopes to go professional.

Any extra money earned is minimal. These young people feel the pinch of poverty acutely: three of the young men were recently discussing their inability to afford new pairs of much-needed shoes.

In his study, *Poverty in the United Kingdom*, Peter Townsend included in his definition of poverty those groups in the population who lack the resources to participate in the customary activities of their communities. If the young people in our sample were to depend solely on their social security money, they would be excluded from the run-of-the-mill activities of their age group and of their neighbours. This is why they turn to other sources of income.

Fiddle jobs

For generations, in regions of high unemployment, work 'on the side' has been a vital means of defending self-respect, maintaining basic income and preserving existing skills. At least half of our sample have had such jobs at one time or another. Only one of them – a young woman – claims that it would bother her to have one. The jobs vary from tasks undertaken for family or neighbours (painting, putting in fireplaces, babysitting) to more organised work (window cleaning, tiling, delivering newspapers).

But on council estates where a large percentage of the residents are receiving state benefits, there may not be enough income around to finance such jobs. If your neighbours are all on social security, few of them can afford to have their windows cleaned.

There can be other problems, too. Terry and his brother were seriously threatened and 'scared off' by regular window cleaners who accused them of being 'on the fiddle' and on their patch. Les worked long hours for a newsagent who then began lowering the handout from £15 to £6, and finally to £1.70 – at which price only much younger lads would deliver his papers.

Lads from one estate told us how their local community is being split by someone 'shopping' those with fiddle jobs to the Department of Health and Social Security (DHSS). There are also periodic purges by the 'super-snoopers' as the special DHSS inspectors are called. The result is that whole communities and not just individuals feel under attack in their struggle to survive.

Sub-employment

This phrase describes the constant movement by working-class youngsters in and out of depressing jobs which would not attract anyone permanently. The wages, conditions and prospects are all poor. So few demands are made on the competence and creativity of young people in a 'sub-job' that they need time out to recover their self-esteem.

At one time, in the early days of our study, we found that our young people were worried not just by the prospect of unemployment but by the *quality* of the jobs they were offered. But now we find that after leaving a job and 'taking a breather', our young people can no longer find even a 'shit' job. They have exhausted the opportunities in relation to government schemes, and, of course, no one in their age group is eligible for the new Youth Training Scheme.

Routines

We have noted some routines which they have evolved in order to fill in 'awkward' times and places. Some of our lads deliberately stay up late, watching television or listening to records, or they stay out late wandering around the streets, so that the next day they can lie in bed to avoid the dead time of the morning. They don't leave the house until the afternoon. In the early evening, they are more relaxed about being seen on the streets because they feel less distinguishable from the employed.

The desire to be an ordinary member of society is evident. Even in communities in which the same lads say there is no stigma in being unemployed – because that is the status of so many local people – they seem to feel some disapproval.

Routines vary. Billy gets up early, keeps himself busy by running regularly and building model aircraft. Kate (18) organises her days around housework; cooking tea for her working parents; 'going over the town' shopping; and seeing her working boyfriend regularly in the evenings.

On the whole, these young men and women adopt similar tactics to survive unemployment. But their *routines* reflect traditional sex roles, as the examples of Billy and Kate suggest. Young women make more use of the resources of the family (developing relationships, for example), but they also take on many more domestic responsibilities.

Nancy (18) and Diane (18) helped out in family crises. Nancy cared for first her mother, and then her grandmother, during illnesses. Diane's mother died. She then spent most of her time running the home and looking after her younger brothers and sisters. Other young unemployed women are expected to help their mothers with the general day-to-day chores.

Defence mechanisms

A common tactic is simply not to talk about unemployment. Avoiding the subject altogether helps young people to deal with it (although it creates problems for researchers like us). Some avoid the topic deliberately. Terry is typical in this. He cannot bear to watch television programmes on unemployment because he knows 'all the bad points about it already'.

But most of them simply do not expound on their feelings. As Al puts it, 'Too much time to think on the dole – it makes you depressed'. Hughie, ten months unemployed, comments, 'I'd have taken to drink if only I'd had the money'.

Most of them report that there are no serious discussions of unemployment with friends who are similarly placed. Going out and drinking with friends is used as a way of forgetting about unemployment. The peer group is not a forum for political argument.

So the one 'coping strategy' which outsiders might expect the young unemployed to adopt – namely, political action – is conspicuous by its absence, at least among our sample in the north-east. The economic prospects for the region suggest that large sections of the young unemployed are likely to remain state pensioners for the rest of their lives. If that prediction were to become part of their consciousness – say, as a result of electioneering – then that may be the spark which sets alight a dry forest.

The names in the article are pseudonyms.

Chapter 5

Is there work after the MSC?

Did the initials MSC really stand for More Social Control? 1984 saw the tenth anniversary of the Manpower Services Commission which was set up by Edward Heath's government to deal with employment and training. Within a decade, it had become the biggest quango in Great Britain with a budget for England almost twice the size of that for all universities in the United Kingdom. This article appeared in *New Society* on 26 January 1984 (128–30) in an attempt to start a public debate about the values and ideology of this new giant in our midst. It records how the MSC moved from the creation of jobs to the provision of training. How are employers to be weaned off government schemes that have young people working for them for nothing? That question still needs to be asked of those many employers who fail to invest in their own workers.

When Peter Morrison was Minister of State in the Department of Employment, I invited him to give a talk on the Manpower Services Commission to our students. I introduced him to the audience by recounting the story of the billionaire who asked his three young sons what they wanted for Christmas. The eldest asked for a train set so he bought him British Rail. The middle son asked for a toy plane so he bought him British Airways. When the youngest asked for a cowboy outfit, he bought him ... the MSC.

Morrison's talk did nothing to appease the audience of experts from the world of Further Education and Youth Training. After his speech, the University hosted a lunch for him when I asked him about the impact of mass unemployment on communities in the North East. He replied, 'The market will sort these problems out. Anyway, people up here will never vote Conservative so let them rot'. He was wrong on both counts. The market, some 40+ years later, has still not sorted the problems out; and people in the red wall seats in the North East did vote Conservative in 2019.

On 1 January 1984, the MSC was ten years old. Happy Birthday, MSC, and all who sail in her! An anniversary of this kind, however, calls for an assessment of progress as well as for celebration. Within the space of ten years, the MSC has grown to be the biggest quango in Great Britain, and its growth

DOI: 10.4324/9781003476146-7

continues apace. Within the first decades of its existence, for example, the commission's annual expenditure has increased more than tenfold.

The questions I would like to ask are as follows: why has there been so little informed public debate about the central values and ideology of this new giant in our midst? At a time when 'cost effectiveness' and 'accountability' are the key words used in political debate, should not some questions also be asked about the effectiveness of the MSC, even if it is only ten years old?

Let us start at the beginning. As a consequence of the Heath government's Employment and Training Act, 1973, the MSC was set up on 1 January 1974 with a board of nine members under a chairman: three members from the Confederation of British Industry, three from the TUC, two from local government and one from education. As the song has it, it takes two to tango; but apparently it takes ten to quango. In its ten-year history, the commission has had only three chairmen: Sir Denis Barnes (1974–76), Sir Robert O'Brien (1972–82) and, since 1982, David Young.

The MSC in England is accountable to the Secretary of State for Employment and there have been five such secretaries to report to: Michael Foot (1974–75), Albert Booth (1976–79), James Prior (1979–81), Norman Tebbit (1981–83) and, since 1983, Tom King. In 1977, the commission decentralised to some extent and permanent Manpower Services Committees were appointed in Scotland and Wales under their own chairmen.

The MSC began with a secretariat of 40 and operated through two agencies: the Employment Service Agency (Job Centres and so on) and the Training Services Agency (TOPS courses and so on), which together employed some 19,000 staff in over a thousand separate establishments. The most recent annual report (for 1982–83) gives the head office staff as 908, with a further 1,268 in support services. In all the MSC currently employs a staff of 24,184, which is a cutback from a peak of 26,162 in 1979. The first conclusion, therefore, is that the MSC has had a considerable success in creating jobs … for its own staff.

The commission has also undergone a succession of internal structural changes, the main lines of which are given in the yearly organisational charts. The two agencies, for example, have now become three operating divisions, the Employment Division, the Training Division and the Skillcentre Training Agency, backed up by two support divisions – Corporate Services and Manpower Intelligence and Planning Divisions. In addition, there is a new unit to run the Technical and Vocational Education Initiative.

A second conclusion, then, is that the MSC exhibits many of the features of an 'adhocracy', as described by Henry Mintzberg (1979) in his book, *The Structuring of Organisations*. He argues that an organisation capable of sophisticated innovation is likely to have frequent structural change, to deploy teams of experts in ad-hoc projects, to abound in managers and to be youthful. Again, such an organisation tends to produce ever-shifting responses to an external crisis; in this case, the unrelenting rise in unemployment, especially youth unemployment.

The chief reaction of the MSC has been to throw money at the problem. The special programmes which were originally devised to cope with unemployment have undergone a series of changes: YOP became YTS, JCP became STEP, which became CEP and now CP. Together, these programmes now amount to roughly 66% of the commission's total budget.

The dramatic growth in annual expenditure can be seen in these figures: in 1974–75, the MSC's total expenditure was £125.4 million and in 1984–85, it was £2,072 million. Corresponding figures for the income of universities were £444.6 million and £1,304 million. The comparison with the university sector can be pursued further. It is not just that some universities (like my own, Durham) have had 150 years to plan for and cope with growth (to 5,500 students). It is also true that there is an official watchdog – the University Grants Commission – which closely monitors staff-student ratios, size of departments and so on. In addition, the Education Secretary, Sir Keith Joseph, has recently suggested an independent inquiry into the efficiency of British universities. I, for one, would welcome such an inquiry with open arms. All I wish to ask is: where is the permanent, official watchdog for the MSC? Where is the democratic scrutiny of *its* operations and *its* effectiveness? Appearing before House of Commons committees is not enough.

The MSC has, of course, been subjected to all manner of political pressures. Sir Richard O'Brien was sacked as chairman in 1982, despite being a skilled negotiator and well-respected in the worlds of both industry and training. This seems to have been direct political interference.

Besides this, there was a proposal in the government white paper, *A New Training Initiative* (December 1981), to lower the 'training allowance' to £15 per week. More recently, we saw the clumsy attempt by Peter Morrison, the Minister of State for Employment, to exclude from Youth Training Schemes 'matters related to the organisation and functioning of society in general … unless they are relevant to trainees' work experience'.

Such moves prompt the following questions: how autonomous is the MSC? How extensive is the interference by the Department of Employment and the Treasury? Considering the amounts of public money and executive power invested in the commission, should there not be greater public accountability and debate?

You do not have to be an industrial psychologist to guess that an organisation which has grown so fast, and in so many directions, is not likely to have well-established internal lines of communication. It may also tend to make a series of short-term tactical reactions to long-term structural problems. Because it feels unsure of itself, it is likely to respond defensively to external criticism.

In the year 1982–83, when the total expenditure was £1,343.2 million, the MSC devoted just under £2 million (or 0.148%) to external research. Only two million pounds to evaluate how effectively that massive total was being spent may seem like a very small sum. But at the very time social scientists are finding research money increasingly difficult to obtain, the MSC has become an important new source of funding. Is there not a danger that those academics whose research is financed by the commission may temper their criticisms of MSC programmes? And how many principals of further education colleges can afford to criticise the MSC publicly, when MSC gold has become the lifeblood of so many institutions? The MSC payments to colleges of further education totalled more than £100 million by 1980–81.

This brings me to the heart of the matter. How has this new body been able to amass so much power in such a short time? Has the MSC a clearly defined ideology? Or does it just muddle through, reacting to one crisis after another?

The MSC is certainly in need of an ideology to legitimate its daily operations and its very existence. The publications which pour out of its Sheffield headquarters in a technicolour torrent have little to say about the MSC's view of society, its image of the worker or its vision of the future. The major reports – especially those published in the last few years – are strangely similar in tone. They are brash and brief to the point of oversimplifying complex issues. For instance, *The Youth Task Group Report* begins by claiming that it 'is about providing a permanent bridge between school and work'. Such a claim is either naïve overconfidence or misleading propaganda.

A study of the earliest documents suggests two general remarks. It is clear, first of all, that the need for such a body as the MSC was widely recognised at the start of the 1970s in order to improve on the fragmented and inflexible arrangements of the 1950s and 1960s. The need for the MSC to develop and implement 'a comprehensive manpower policy' is just as urgent now as it was then.

Second, the liberal, open-minded tone of the first reports is in marked contrast to the more recent publications. Right from the beginning, for example, contingency plans were drawn up to deal with unemployment: 'We decided at our first meeting that special measures were needed to minimise the harmful and wasteful consequences of a significant rise in unemployment' (*Annual Report*, 1974–75).

One of the key aspects of those contingency plans was 'a work creation programme'. The Job Creation Programme blossomed for a few years, was then heavily pruned and finally eliminated. Why? The official documents record that between October 1975 and April 1977, as many as 76,734 temporary jobs of benefit to the community were created for people in the age groups 16–24 and 50-plus. Why has the MSC moved, in the main, over the years from the creation of *jobs* to the provision of *training*?

Within the limits of this article, it is not possible to do justice to all the multifarious activities of the MSC. In focusing on its schemes for young people, it is only proper for an educationist like myself to admit that the commission has brought considerable resources and attention to a group of young people whom the educational world (and especially the Department of Education) had hitherto largely ignored.

Having given praise where it is due, I would still contend that the principles underlying the New Training Initiative, of which the Youth Training Scheme is part, need much more public discussion than they have had. Most of the media criticism of these has been of detail, rather than of principle. Attention has been drawn to the shortfall in the numbers of young people entering YTS, to the quality of some of the training and to the financing of the whole programme. I would instead like to ask: why concentrate all the resources on training which does not lead to a real job? What is the likely impact on the motivation of those 'trainees' (note the new MSC terminology for young people) currently in YTS who cannot realistically expect employment at the end of their 'course'? What is the likely impact on the recruitment to YTS in 1984 and 1985?

Is it not the British and American experience that vocational training has failed and failed miserably, no matter what it is called (YOP, YTS or whatever) and no matter who provides it (schools, further education colleges, employers or MSC)? W. N. Grubb and M. Lazerson (1981) in the United States have shown how vocational training tends in practice to become highly specific and narrow. That criticism is already being levelled at certain Youth Training Schemes.

There are alternatives to YTS which are not being discussed. Why not turn our young people into employees (rather than 'trainees'), pay them a wage (rather than a 'training allowance') and give them legal rights to further education or training as happens in France? The wage may have to be increased in stages, as currently happens to apprentices in West Germany.

Such a proposal would run directly counter to one of the central values which is visible in MSC publications – namely, the paramount importance given to the needs and wishes of employers. For all the well-meaning rhetoric about the 'expectations and aspirations' of individual young people, it is quite clear from the MSC's *Youth Task Group Report* who the main beneficiaries of YTS are. I quote from page 7: 'Our aim is to provide for what the economy needs, and what employers want – a better equipped, better qualified, better educated and better motivated workforce'.

If anyone still has any doubts, perhaps David Young's exhortation to British directors will settle them: 'In short, the YTS … is attractive financially to employers. You now have the opportunity to take on young men and women, train them and let them work for you almost entirely at our expense, and then decide whether or not to employ them' (*The Director*, October 1982). But what is to stop employers from taking on a new group of 'trainees' each year and offering real jobs to a small percentage, or perhaps to none at all?

This is not such a flight of fancy. As has been pointed out by the pressure group, Youthaid, YOP and YTS have provided employers not with cheap labour but with free labour. YTS could be seen as a direct subsidy to industry and commerce by the taxpayer. Indeed, the MSC's intervention, far from promoting a recovery in the labour market for young people, could be said to be permanently damaging it.

How, for instance, are we ever to wean employers from MSC schemes now that they have become used to young people working for nothing? With some honourable exceptions, the training record of most employers in this country has been poor, to say the least. The admitted neglect of this age group by the education system has been matched historically by a failure on the part of the employers to invest in their own young workers. What is the evidence that employers have had a change of heart? Although both sectors have been equally negligent, failure to produce an educated, skilled and flexible workforce has been blamed solely on schools.

Another major issue, which lies behind this debate and which confronts us all, is: how are we to 'gentle the masses' in the late 20th century when the discipline of work is no longer available for all? The solutions of the 19th century – formal schooling and police forces – will be tried even harder (hence the new powers to be given to the police). And some technological inventions will help: porno and horror videos (and beer) help to lessen the frustrations and political anger of young men. It is hard not to interpret the insistence of the MSC on changing the 'motivation' and 'attitudes' of young people as a concern about social unrest among the disaffected.

References

Grubb, W.N. and Lazerson, M. (1981) Vocational solutions to youth problems: the persistent frustrations of the American experience. *Educational Analysis*, 3(2), 49–68.
Mintzberg, H. (1979) *The Structuring of Organisations*. New Jersey: Prentice Hall.

Part 3

The world of work and Further Education

Chapter 6

Britain's continuing failure to train

The birth pangs of a new policy

The politicians' obsession with increasing the supply, but not the demand, for skills helps to explain our continuing low levels of productivity. This article published in the *Journal of Education Policy* in 2002 (17, (4), 483–97) provides an account of an official attempt in the United Kingdom to generate both a new analysis of the underlying causes of under-investment in workforce development and a new policy to rectify the weaknesses. The account is based on the participation of the present author who was a member of the Performance and Innovation Unit's (PIU) Academic Panel on workforce development during 2001. Some limited success was had in changing policy-makers' understanding of the complexity of the problem, but changing policy to match the new understanding proved far more difficult.

All jobs have their exciting moments and their boring half hours, some far more than others. I took to repeating to myself the following four quotes.

Studs Terkel, the American writer best remembered for his oral histories of working-class employees, argued: 'The surprise is not that work makes huge demands of us. The real surprise is that we work far harder for the institution than the institution itself deserves'.

Maimonides was a Jewish philosopher, who in the 12th century AD, wrote **The Guide for the Perplexed**. *His advice on lifelong learning reads: 'Live as if you will die tomorrow, but learn as if you will live for ever'.*

I am also fond of Karl Marx's favourite motto: De Omnibus Dubitandum, translated as 'everything should be doubted'. Researchers must be the merchants of doubt or we are nothing.

Then there's the principle enunciated by Florence Nightingale: 'the very first requirement in a hospital is that it should do the sick no harm'. I'd willingly pay for a poster to be hung opposite the desk of the Secretary of State for Education which would read: 'It is the first requirement of this Department to do students, staff and educational institutions only the minimum harm'.

DOI: 10.4324/9781003476146-9

Introduction

The PIU was created by the Prime Minister in July 1998:

> to improve the capacity of government to address strategic, cross-cutting issues and promote innovation in the development of policy and in the delivery of the government's objectives. The PIU is part of the drive for better, more joined-up government. It acts as a resource for the whole of government, tackling issues that cross public sector institutional boundaries on a project basis
>
> (PIU 2001b: 115)

The unit, directed by Geoff Mulgan, reports to the Prime Minister, who thereby receives another stream of policy recommendations, independent from the Departments of State. Geoff Mulgan was previously the director of DEMOS, an independent think tank, 'committed to radical solutions to long-term problems'. As director of the PIU, he reports directly to the Prime Minister through the Cabinet Secretary, Sir Richard Wilson; he has also recently been appointed to lead the Forward Strategy Unit, which 'will do blue skies policy thinking for the Prime Minister' (PIU 2001: 115). More than 15 projects have already been carried out by the PIU on such themes as improving analysis and modelling in central government, on privacy and data sharing, and developing a strategy for the electronic delivery of government services. In late 2000, the PIU began to commission officials from several government departments, as well as specialists on secondment from the private sector to examine workforce development (PIU 2000).[1] The team was completely formed by April 2001 and its remit was – within a period of six months – to make a strong case for the benefits of workforce development; to analyse the roles of government, employers and individuals; and to recommend both a holistic set of practical policies and a strategy agreed by all the key stakeholders. This was no mean task in such a short period.

It is equally important to recognise what areas were omitted from the remit. Some of the main issues which were not part of the policy review were:

- the policy of raising the participation rate in higher education to 50% by 2010;
- the new structures of the Learning and Skills Council (which was established in 2000 to create a coherent system for post-16 learning, apart from higher education);
- the LSC's relations with the Regional Development Agencies, the Small Business Service and the Department of Trade and Industry; and
- the reform of qualifications, especially vocational qualifications.

One intriguing question which remains unanswered is why it was thought necessary (and by whom) to initiate the PIU enquiry into workforce development when the Department for Education and Employment has set up a National Skills Task Force (NSTF), which had just produced detailed proposals for a national skills agenda based on a very comprehensive set of reports. David Blunkett, the then Secretary of State for Education and Skills, asked the NSTF to advise him on 'developing a National Skills Agenda which will ensure that Britain has the skills needed to sustain high levels of employment, compete in the global market place and provide opportunity for all' (DfEE 2000: 11). Either the Prime Minister's office was dissatisfied with the proposals of the Task Force or it wished to wrest control of the issue from the DfEE and other interested departments; or a report from the PIU is now the way to speed up the development of new policies by avoiding the in-fighting between departments; but this is conjecture.

Reviewing the evidence

An overview of the literature on workforce development was commissioned by the Unit from Sandy Coleman and Ewart Keep (2001), the latter of whom is widely regarded as a if not *the* leading authority in the United Kingdom on policy in this area. More specific reviews were produced on 'Lessons Learnt from Overseas Experience' by David Ashton and Johnny Sung (2001); 'The Economic Benefits of Training to the Individual, the Firm and the Economy' by Stephen Machin and Anna Vignoles (2001); and 'Motivation for Workforce Development: the Role of National Culture' by David Guest (2001). These reviews collectively provide a well-balanced summary of the research literature, of the main gaps in our knowledge and of the general implications for policy. Some brief comments will be made on each paper to give a flavour of the evidence presented to the PIU team, who did not receive firm, final conclusions from the researchers, as will be seen.

Ashton and Sung conclude from their study of the ways in which other governments have approached the development of their workforce that 'The Americans use the market, the Singaporeans "shape" the market, but the British do not appear to have made up their minds' (Ashton and Sung, 2001: 17). Meanwhile, all employees in Denmark and Sweden are entitled to a year's paid educational leave. The international comparisons strongly suggest a lack of vision and consistency in the British approach, which has resulted in a 'plethora of provision, with overlapping jurisdictions' (Ashton and Sung, 2001: 17), and which is not linked together in one coherent policy. Ashton and Sung conclude as follows:

> Training is essentially a derived demand. It has its origins in the ways we organize work. If we organize work along Taylorist lines, then we make few demands on the abilities of the majority of the labour force. If we organize it in terms of high performance working practices, then we make much heavier demands on the labour force. For this we need a more substantial

training input and we learn to make more effective use of the workplace as
the arena through which we deliver the appropriate skills

(2001: 18)

The burden of their argument is that too many British firms are stuck in Tay-
lorist forms of production, while countries like Singapore and Denmark are
successfully helping employers to re-structure their work and management
practices to enhance productivity. These countries are operating with different
models of workforce development, with Singapore being a good example of
the 'developmental state' model, where the state is strong, remains autonomous from both business and labour and actively coordinates the demand
and supply of skills (see Ashton, 2001, for more details).

The evidence, marshalled by Machin and Vignoles, shows convincingly
that the effects of training programmes for adults are positive, but there is
little national or international evidence that youth training programmes are
effective, with some researchers even finding a negative impact on wages
from participating in Youth Training Schemes. However, more research has
focused on the impact of training on individuals than on the productivity of
firms. What limited evidence there is suggests that training improves the commitment of employees, fosters a common culture within firms and helps to
attract high-quality workers. Machin and Vignoles argue that if firms are using
training to attract and retain employees, then 'the poaching problem may not
be a major issue for firms' (2001: 14). Poaching by other employers, in fact,
may be a widely accepted excuse for not investing in training. When the two
researchers turn to the benefits of training to the economy and wider society,
they find even less evidence of a direct relationship between training and
economic growth. Their general conclusion is that there are few messages for
policy-makers about the broader social returns from training because of serious shortcomings in the literature.

David Guest, in a comparatively brief paper, concentrates on the flood of
short-lived initiatives which leads to initiative fatigue and to 'behaviour that
is unlikely to tackle the underlying problem at an organisational level and
leaves the cultural institutions that gave rise to the problem in the first place
largely untouched' (Guest, 2001: 5).

Coleman and Keep (2001) produced, however, the most comprehensive
and sharply worded review of the four that were commissioned. The scale
of the problem in the United Kingdom is presented starkly; to give but one
example, data from the 1998 Labour Force Survey recorded that '72% of the
UK employees had received no training in the 13 weeks prior to interview.
Of these, just under half (48%) claimed that they had never been offered any
type of training by their current employer' (Coleman and Keep, 2001: 28).
But these grim statistics – which underline the historical underinvestment in
training by British employers – are not used to support the main plank in official policy, namely, that skills are the only (or the royal) route to increasing

productivity: 'Rather than seeing skills as *the* key to competitive success, it might be more realistic to view upskilling as simply one model vying for senior managers' attention in a market place for ideas' (2001: 10, original emphasis).

In sum, the analysis and synthesis of the existing evidence challenged some of the fundamental assumptions and orthodoxies which have underpinned official United Kingdom policy in this area for a generation. What reception would such views, previously considered heretical by government departments, be given by the PIU team? To move away from a single-minded concentration on increasing the supply of skills requires both a major revision in the way the problems are conceived and a complete overhaul of a confusing battery of policies. In the opinion of the present author, the four academic reviews provide policy-makers with more help with the former than with the latter task. Indeed, most researchers are far better at identifying gaps in knowledge than at explaining the implications of research findings in ways that would enable policy-makers to revise existing policies or devise new ones.

The administrators in the PIU team agreed that policy had indeed become dominated by too many supply-side approaches, not because policy had become permeated with some overarching orthodoxy but because such approaches are the easier policy levers to pull.

Analysing the causes

At the same time as these reviews of the literature were being written by academics, the PIU team was producing successive drafts of the main report which analysed the underlying causes of under-involvement in workforce development, and which outlined a vision of the future with the explicit intention of creating a demand-led system. The scope of the consultations undertaken by the PIU team deserves to be emphasised; for example, it talked to over 150 individuals in a variety of relevant organisations, it commissioned seven focus groups of employers and of individuals, and contacted six teams concerned with the same topic, such as the Department of Trade and Industry's Skills and Education group.[2] In addition, the PIU team was advised by an academic panel of 12 specialists of whom the present author was one; our function was to challenge the ideas for new policy generated by the PIU team.[3] Oversight of the whole project was managed by a group of 15 senior stakeholders from industry, trade unions and government ministries.[4] The work of all PIU teams is also overseen by a government minister and in this case, the sponsor minister was John Healey, the Minister for Adult Skills in England. The role of all these groups was to act as a reality check and to ensure that the team's conclusions were rooted in evidence; but, as Stephen Ball has shown, policies 'privilege certain visions and interests' (1990: 22) and the final selection of recommendations on workforce development is likely to exemplify this point.

By the end of August 2001, the main report, which had by then been posted on the PIU website to elicit further comment, amounted to over 80 pages and five annexes. Evidence-based policy analysis, it can fairly be said, was carried out in an exemplary, open and thorough way and the quality of the main report reflected these extensive consultations. One major task remained: the development of policy options, which were firmly grounded in the analytical conclusions.

Before an assessment of the Analysis Paper is offered, an indication needs to be given of the level of involvement of the present author. All of the commissioned papers and each version of the main report were made available to him, together with other internal working papers and reports. He also took part in the meetings of the academic panel, which on each occasion commented critically on the team's analyses, challenged thinking which was inconsistent with the evidence and offered both orally and in writing alternative interpretations and policy options. An attempt is made throughout to differentiate between ideas presented by the PIU team, suggestions from the Academic Panel and the author's personal commentary.

Processes

The methods adopted by the PIU team on workforce development amount to a transformation of the relationship between policy-makers and researchers, particularly from the time when a junior Minister of Education in a Conservative administration, Eric Forth, claimed: 'We don't need research to tell us what to do, we know that already' (quoted in Kogan, 1999: 11). Within a few years, the climate has changed from one where researchers were totally excluded from policy-making because they were deemed irrelevant, unnecessary and ideologically biased to one where a Secretary of State for Education offered them 'a genuine partnership and interchange between the worlds of policy and research' (Blunkett, 2000: 20). Since 1997, there has been a major change in the value placed upon educational research by politicians and policy-makers: the two most outstanding examples are the establishment of dedicated research centres (e.g. on the Economics of Education and on the Wider Benefits of Education) and a National Educational Research Forum. The PIU report on workforce development provides the latest test of the government's capacity to give serious consideration to difficult findings, especially in an area where powerful interests lobby hard to have their definition of reality accepted.

One of the PIU's advantages, according to Ewart Keep, is that 'it comes to the topic as an outsider, without the accumulated "baggage" that ownership of (and therefore the need to protect) earlier departmental policies tends to bring' (2001: 2). Somewhat to the surprise of the present author, the task (or the pleasure) of asking awkward questions or of thinking the unthinkable was not the sole prerogative of the researchers. Indeed, members of the PIU team took the lead at meetings in challenging some of the fundamental assumptions on which much current policy and practice are based and academics were at times 'pushed hard' to justify or explain inequities or anomalies. Penetrating questions were used to sharpen the group's growing understanding of the complexities of workforce development and to explore the main weaknesses within the field. Three examples are given here: 'If the workforce development system is not performing well, who gets the sack?' 'Are targets the best way of achieving outcomes?' 'How do existing or recommended policies increase the demand for skills?'

These discussions of the analysis of the problems and of policy options were not constrained by any 'no-go areas'. The iterative process of producing draft after draft of the Analysis Paper not only succeeded in involving large numbers of expert commentators but it also served to drive up the quality of the analysis as more and more evidence was assessed and incorporated into the argument. The approach was at all times genuinely open, unrestricted and thought-provoking, although it was evident from the very beginning that the PIU team was nervous about the political implications of the more radical suggestions for policy from the academics. The iterative process also carried the risk of a slow regression to less radical and less controversial policy recommendations.

Outcomes

It is not too exaggerated to claim that the Analysis Paper represents a breakthrough from previous official thinking on workforce development, which had become obsessed with increasing the supply of skills and, in particular, qualifications as a monocausal prescription for economic success. In the Analysis Paper, the causes of the British problem are convincingly identified as a complex mix of economic, social, historical and cultural influences. In particular, a combination of market failures (e.g. 'poaching' of skilled workers, poor information on the benefits of training, etc.) and government failures (e.g. the lack of a national strategy, underinvestment in education and training, the plethora of poorly designed interventions, etc.) have created systemic sclerosis where most British firms are stuck in a 'low-skills equilibrium, in which the majority of enterprises staffed by poorly trained managers and workers produce low-quality goods and services' (Finegold and Soskice, 1991: 215). This thesis was first enunciated by Finegold and Soskice as far back as 1988, when they argued that 'a self-reinforcing network of societal and state institutions ... interact to stifle the demand for improvements in skills levels' (1991: 215). The significance of their argument is that if a set of political and economic institutions is jointly held responsible for the 'low skills equilibrium', then it makes little sense to blame the systemic failure on only one constituent partner – the education and training system – and to attempt to remedy only its deficiencies by introducing new policy initiatives. Further, it makes even less sense to blame individual workers for not investing in their own human capital. And yet, that has been the approach adopted by both Conservative and Labour administrations for over 20 years. All the other institutions and factors that are intimately bound up in Britain's continuing failure to train have until now been omitted from the analysis. These include: the industrial relations system, the financial markets, under-investment in research and development, the political framework, the organisation of work practices within firms, employers' strategies for product innovation and competition, management training and the use of new technologies.

The advance made by the PIU team lies in their explicit acknowledgement that such causal complexity requires a holistic response because it is no longer sufficient to raise the supply of skills. Instead, as they argue, 'Action is needed simultaneously on a number of fronts' (2001a: 23), which includes raising the demand for higher skills through support for innovation and improved management skills. The contrast with previous analyses and prescriptions is encouragingly substantial. We appear to have reached the position where *policy-makers* have become convinced of the need to bring the demand and supply of skills into greater harmony, but *politicians* remain wedded to a dangerously simplistic view: witness the recent claim by Margaret Hodge, the Minister for Lifelong Learning and Higher Education in England: 'If we want to close the productivity gap, we must close the skills gap' (2001). Moreover, some employers have used the new terminology of 'high performance work organizations' to usher in a 'lean and mean' redundancy culture as a way to increase productivity.

The scale of the mismatch between supply and demand for skills has recently been emphasised by a national survey of the skills of British workers. Felstead (2001b) has shown, for example, that there is a gross deficiency in demand from employers at level 3 qualifications. In more detail, almost three million people with either academic or vocational qualifications equivalent to A level (i.e. level 3) held jobs which did not need that qualification. The policy implication is that producing more and more people with intermediate skills is only half of the equation and urgent attention is needed by employers to improve the quality of jobs on offer to such people. It is important to emphasise that the problem is not the low motivation of employees to train but the poor quality of their jobs.

The current battery of government measures has been criticised by the present author in a chapter entitled '101 Initiatives, But No Strategy: Policy on Lifelong Learning in England' (Coffield, 2001) and the following comments represent the views of this ex-adviser.[5] In the field of workforce development alone, the third Annex of the Analysis Paper lists no less than 45 current initiatives – a triumph of creativity over coherence. The list also makes clear that most government funding is devoted to increasing the commitment of individuals to training; for instance, over £1 billion has been spent on the New Deal for Young People, whereas the Council for Excellence in Management and Leadership has received less than £1 million.

The concern is not only the sheer number of initiatives which means that finite resources are severely stretched. Every new initiative has to compete with those already operating in a complex and confusing system that makes evaluation of any one initiative virtually impossible; some of them are mutually inconsistent and contradictory, others are not sustained over time. And the responsibility for assessing their effectiveness is shared among five different ministries, each working through numerous central, regional and local intermediaries. Our short-term political culture also means that ministers want an initiative attached to their names and there have been four Ministers for Lifelong Learning in England in the four years since 1997. A further weakness has been the failure to gather, analyse and act upon feedback on these initiatives from workplaces, especially from smaller firms. Instead of one coherent and easily understood system, policy on workforce development is at present an ill-coordinated accumulation of supply-side initiatives that have not, and will not, release Britain from the low skills trap. At the very least, some coordination and rationalisation of all these government measures on workforce development needs to take place, with priority accorded to those which concentrate on improving the performance of firms.

A more ambitious programme, however, would detail a set of policy options that responded appropriately to the whole range of underlying and interacting causes. In other words, the recommendations for policy should flow from the analysis of the evidence, although it is recognised that other important factors such as cost, feasibility, interactions with other priorities and possible unintended consequences also need to be taken into consideration in the development of new policies. As a result, Hargreaves, in response to criticism, suggests that we should speak of

> evidence-*informed*, not evidence-based, policy or practice. Policy-makers cannot always postpone their decision making until the evidence is in; and even when it is, they are constrained in their decisions by much other knowledge in their possession and by many factors concerned with public perceptions and political consequences
>
> (2001: 204, original emphasis)

In sum, policy-making is a complex brew of possibilities, personalities, presentation, political judgement, cost constraints and 'deliverability'. In this mix, the evidence from research is only one – albeit crucial – ingredient.

The different normative worlds of researchers and policy-makers

Effective change, as Fullan (1991) has argued, takes both time and persistence. Real change also involves altering deeply held beliefs and accepting that previously unquestioned assumptions need to be discarded if found wanting in discussion – slow and painful processes for all concerned. We live, for example, in a culture that celebrates individualism and so it is no surprise that of the 45 initiatives on workforce development currently in operation, most are directed at changing the behaviour of individuals. This cultural and political mindset exerted an enduring influence, even when challenged. For example, at meetings between members of the PIU team and of the academic panel, the latter tended to think they had won the argument in favour of changing the focus of policy from the training of individuals or of firms to government strategies for improving the performance of organisations. Some weeks later, the PIU team would issue an updated version of the analysis paper which was meant to reflect the conclusions of the earlier discussions and the revised vision statement would read 'We should be a society in which employees receive opportunities to develop at their place of work and elsewhere'. The project's vision for workforce development continued, however, to develop and a later version read: 'In 2010, the UK will be a society where Government, employers and individuals will actively engage in skills development to deliver sustainable economic success for all'.

What also became clear at the meetings was that policy-makers and researchers inhabit two separate 'normative worlds' with different goals, constraints and sensitivities, and different timescales, agendas and audiences for their work (see Bell and Raffe, 1991). It was not so much a case of researchers 'speaking truth to power' (Coffield, 1999), nor of researchers possessing 'a superior "truth"; rather they bring a different kind of knowledge to policy-making' (Edwards, 2000: 305). At their worst, researchers exercise an enviable but impotent freedom to float radical, uncosted proposals that could, if acted upon, destabilise the system. At times, they offer generalised advice, which is too remote from the messy world of policy-making to be practically useful; they leave conflicting evidence for policy-makers to wrestle with; and they have been known to argue for different interpretations of the same evidence. At their best, researchers insist on evidence for claims of success, they insist on complex and interactive issues being treated as such, they argue for policies commensurate with the underlying causes, they offer theoretical understanding which can improve the quality of the dialogue between policy-makers and practitioners, and they point to potential pitfalls, e.g. human capital accounting would identify all the costs of training and so may lead to some firms reducing their training budgets rather than increasing them.

Academics also need to appreciate the unwritten 'rules' concerning confidentiality and discretion that administrators adhere to. Modern government operates under intense media interest where leaks are highly prized; no matter how open policy-makers may want to be, they must weigh up carefully the danger of ministerial trust being betrayed. Once that trust is lost, it may be extremely hard, if not impossible, to regain it.

While researchers are able to think and argue for the unthinkable, policy-makers have to work within the parameters set by others. The 'steer' given by politicians or senior officials can be so powerful as to rule out certain options. Policy-makers are in the business of pushing for as much change as they think they can get away with. The danger with the 'strong steer', however, is that policy-makers may try to second-guess the wishes of ministers and so only present what they think is wanted.

In the judgement of the present author, policy-makers find great difficulty in taking seriously 'awkward' findings, which either reveal the superficiality of previous government policies or contradict the prejudices of the current minister. Unwelcome evidence may be heard but not acted upon. The first loyalty of civil servants is to their minister rather than to knowledge: 'The minister is likely to consider these findings unhelpful'. The dedication of the British civil service to ministers and to the public good more generally was, however, clearly shown by the policy-makers in the PIU team, who regularly worked under intense pressure to meet governmental deadlines. Sir Richard Mottram, the permanent secretary at the Department of Transport, in the middle of a political 'crisis' when a civil servant and a political adviser in his department were both forced to resign, described the civil service as follows: 'I always compare it to a rather stupid dog that wants to do what its master wants, and, above all, wants to be loved for doing it. I don't think ministers understand that' (quoted in *The Guardian*, 8 March 2002).

Such unquestioning loyalty at times leads policy-makers to worry about research that produces the 'wrong' finding; in other words, independent researchers may provide sound evidence that does not, however, support some initiative that the minister is determined to introduce. The worry for the scientific community is that civil servants may commission researchers who are already publicly identified with a policy initiative that the minister wants to invest in heavily, and who can therefore be relied upon to come up with the 'right' result. More often administrators are caught in the middle between researchers and politicians, for example, the minister welcomes research findings that are consonant with the general direction in which she/he wants policy to move, but ignores or 'rubbishes' disconfirming findings.

One of the difficulties for researchers who want to establish good working relationships with civil servants arises when their evidence indicates that the minister's shiny new policy is causing more problems than it is solving. The obvious danger for researchers is that by participating in policy-making, they become incorporated and made safe. An alternative approach was successfully adopted in the 1970s by the New Right which redefined, outside of the normal policy channels, what was both thinkable and politically feasible.

Further difficulties confront both researchers and policy-makers; for instance, it is often extremely difficult to work out what the policy implications are of particular research findings. Moreover, there exist so many serious gaps in our knowledge that it is frequently not possible to offer any advice to policy-makers.

In sum, researchers value independence, criticality, open debate, objectivity and holistic approaches to complex problems; but policy-makers have to learn the art of political compromise. Chisholm, who has experience of both trades of research and policy-making, offers two arguments which help to explain the gaps between the perspectives of researchers and policy-makers:

> Science is not politics – the first seeks feasible truths through the systematic interrogation of different positions, the second seeks a workable consensus from the palette of divergent interests. Moreover, policy-making is like teaching and learning – both have to be satisfied with small and incremental steps forward, steps which are frequently only visible in the *longue durée* i.e. as part of a longer-term process.
>
> (Chisholm, 2001: 1)

Final comments

The work so far of the PIU team on workforce development suggests that evidence-informed *analysis* of policy is not only possible but is taking place; this achievement can be attributed to the independence and the methods of the PIU. Whether the considerable advances in official thinking contained in that analysis can now be translated into evidence-informed policy remains to be seen. The real prize to be grasped here is the development of a set of policies that respond appropriately to the analysis of the key weaknesses.

It is, however, worth reflecting on the time it has taken (13 years) for the thesis that the majority of British firms are trapped in a 'low skills equilibrium' to become an accepted part of the government's explanation for Britain's relatively low productivity. The example of workforce development requires a modification of the management cliché that 'change is a process, not an event' (Fullan, 1991: 49). In this instance, changing the understanding of the problem has proved to be an extremely long-drawn-out process and changing policy to match the new understanding is likely to take even longer. The only people who will gain from another decade of dithering are our industrial competitors who watch with increasing incredulity another manifestation of the English 'disease': yet another round of institutional re-structuring without radical reform. This example of research taking 13 years to become accepted should also be noted by those evaluators who seek to assess the impact of research in the months immediately following publication.

The evidence-informed analysis of British weaknesses in workforce development is an important and necessary first step that has now been taken. What, however, are the prospects of a corresponding advance in evidence-informed policy? Three possible outcomes are briefly considered.

First, incisive and comprehensive analysis may still result in blunt and piece-meal policies. The involvement of academics and extensive consultations with interested parties may be used to legitimate a safe set of policy recommendations, where voluntarism remains enshrined, unassailable and non-negotiable. Some limited, incremental progress could be achieved by, for instance, rationalising the current battery of initiatives on workforce development or by targeting particular programmes such as Individual Learning Accounts more accurately at those with few or no vocational qualifications (Owens, 2001). Such a timid approach is, however, very unlikely to pull the United Kingdom economy out of the low skills trap in the foreseeable future.

Second, 10 years ago, when the Training and Enterprise Councils (TECs) were being set up, the present author argued as follows: 'If, for whatever reason, voluntarism is given every chance to succeed and the TECs still fail, then what can voluntarism do as an encore? Will the government be driven to introduce legislation?' (Coffield, 1992: 29). The TECs did in fact fail to secure the commitment of employers to work-force development by voluntary means and that failure was publicly acknowledged in their replacement by the Learning and Skills Councils; and yet voluntarism remains the preferred option of the New Labour government. Those in favour of regulation argue that it is the role of government to stand up to powerful vested interests on behalf of the community as a whole, but it is not widely enough admitted that the opposition from employers' organisations would be formidable. The Confederation of British Industry (CBI) is, for instance, opposed to the government's rather modest proposal to give statutory rights to union learning representatives, warning that such a move would add to the 'regulatory burden' carried by firms (see Rana, 2001). The CBI, representing as it does the big battalions of British industry, is a powerful lobby group; and Wolf has shown how, under Conservative administrations in the 1980s and 1990s, 'civil servants ... showed a consistent tendency to follow CBI recommendations on quite specific matters of policy' (1998: 225). What became established in those years was the unshakeable consensus that 'economic competitiveness was directly and strongly related to education and training levels' (1998: 221). Politics remains the art of the possible and the judgement of the leaders of the New Labour government appears to be that a serious confrontation with employers over regulation may result in more political harm than economic advantage, as well as seriously damaging Britain's reputation as the most flexible labour market apart from the USA. And they may well be right. Conversely, a serious confrontation with 'the monopoly producers' of education and training may be welcomed by the same ministers.

Fortunately, a third way still remains open. In this approach, the government proposes a new national settlement, a historical compromise between itself, employers and trade unions in order to secure for the nation the joint goals of increasing economic prosperity and social inclusion. Instead of a policy of either minimal change (option 1 above which shirks the necessary systemic change) or regulation (option 2 above which is highly likely to lead to protracted public conflict), all policies on workforce development are graded from the least to the most interventionist. Agreement between the social partners (i.e. employers, trade unions and government) is an essential feature of the new settlement and it may be possible to secure a willingness to increase the level of intervention only when less radical measures are shown to be ineffective. The social benefits of such an approach are likely to far outweigh the social costs that could be mitigated by government intervention.

So the least contentious proposals are introduced first (e.g. a rationalisation of existing provision, including current funding systems); then a range of intermediate measures are tried (e.g. fiscal incentives to encourage employers to improve performance). Instead of intervention, the government seeks to influence the debates within firms, for example, by enabling firms to improve performance, to change their product strategies and to view training as an investment rather than as a cost. For their part, employers could use the opportunity to insist on reform of the current, massively complicated assessment of training associated with National Vocational Qualifications. Only if these approaches fail would there be recourse to compulsion. Such a strategy needs an initial acceptance by all the social partners that regulation becomes a legitimate option when all else has been tried and seen to fail. The clear incentive would then exist for those who wish to avoid compulsion to work for the success of other less drastic measures, but the threat of the 'ultimate deterrent' of compulsion may need to exist for significant change to take place. The key ingredients of this third way are high-trust relationships between the social partners, a graded sequence of policy options in increasing order of state intervention and an agreed timetable for action.

The PIU team is proposing to recommend separate policies for the government, employers and individuals so that the rights and responsibilities of each party to the agreement are clear to all and can be separately evaluated. A new strategy for workforce development would also differentiate between policies needed in the *short term* to deal with immediate problems, policies for the *medium term* to cope with emerging trends and policies for the *long term* to indicate the direction the whole system needs to take. The strategy also needs to respond to the heterogeneity of employers and employees and suggest different policies for different sectors (especially given the recent formation of the Sector Skills Councils), with different measures for multinationals, small and medium-sized enterprises and micro-firms; a further dimension that adds to the complexity of the problem is the 'uneven economic performance with marked disparities within and between regions' (Felstead, 2001a: 4). Regional inequalities have increased since 1990, with the demand for skills at work falling in the North East and in the East Midlands.

What lies behind these policy debates are two competing models of Britain's future, the Anglo-Saxon and the European. The Anglo-Saxon neoliberal approach puts its trust in the free, unregulated and flexible market, in ever greater inequalities in income and wealth in order to encourage competitiveness, in mass higher education, some of it of dubious quality, and in welfare to work policies which do not 'distinguish between good and bad jobs' (Tessa Jowell, Minister for Employment, quoted in Westwood, 2001). The Anglo-Saxon model also privileges human over social capital, with low trust in professionals working in the public sector who are subjected to punitive forms of audit.[6] The main features of this model are the presence of a strong business elite, a weak state, weak labour organisations and the market is left to coordinate the supply and demand of skills.

In contrast, the European social model celebrates consensus among the social partners, funds social welfare at higher levels than in the United Kingdom, treats the twin policy goals of employability and active citizenship as equally significant and interdependent and views social exclusion as 'much more than a mere synonym for social disadvantage, much more than a question of the unequal distribution of resources. [For the Europeans, social exclusion] is a multi-dimensional and *structural* phenomenon' (Chisholm, 2001: 3, original emphasis). In brief, the European social model is based on a strong state, collaboration between business and labour, strong institutional arrangements and a regulated market.

Both models provide possible routes out of the 'low skills equilibrium' as both have distinctive strengths. The Anglo-Saxon free market model is more innovative, creates more new jobs and suffers from lower rates of unemployment; it also fosters higher levels of self-employment and inward investment. In contrast, the European social model achieves higher levels of spending on social welfare, is more socially inclusive and has an employment strategy based on high skills and high wages. Critics of the Anglo-Saxon model question the quality of many of the new jobs created, while critics of the European social model point to its inflexibility, higher social costs and higher levels of unemployment.

The policy choices currently being made by the New Labour government in the spheres of education, training and employment indicate that the Anglo-Saxon rather than the European model is being pursued. Certainly, the continuing expansion of higher education will please middle-class voters whose children are the main beneficiaries; but increasing social and economic polarisation, which is a concomitant of the Anglo-Saxon approach, is likely to be rejected by the majority of voters in Scotland, Wales and English regions like the North East. What the United Kingdom needs, however, is neither the Anglo-Saxon nor the European social model but a strategy which incorporates the strengths of both, avoids their weaknesses and responds to our own history, institutions and values.

All of the above was written before the publication on 27 November 2001 of the Pre-Budget Report (HM Treasury 2001) and of the final version of the PIU report (PIU 2001b). The former emphasises the government's determination to bring European economic policy more in line with the Anglo-Saxon model by 'removing unnecessary or over-burdensome regulation ... [and] labour market reforms' (HM Treasury 2001: para. 3:14). The latter is at pains to underline that it is 'a report to the Government about Workforce Development. It is not a statement of Government policy' (PIU 2001b: 3). Instead of proposing a particular set of recommendations, the final version of the PIU report considers the advantages and disadvantages of a wide range of different options that are now to be the subject of consultation inside government and beyond, leading to a second report by the PIU in July 2002. In short, the government has postponed making decisions; it has bought time to win over employers to the notion of a statutory entitlement to paid educational leave by running a series of pilots; and in the meantime, it 'strongly supports' (HM Treasury 2001: para. 3:92) the PIU's conclusion that stimulating demand should be the key objective of a new strategy for workforce development.

The final version of the PIU report, entitled *In Demand: Adult Skills in the 21st Century*, was published in December 2001 and contained some surprises. For instance, the definition of workforce development in the report reads as follows: 'Workforce development consists of activities which increase the capacity of *individuals* to participate effectively in the workplace, thereby improving their productivity and employability' (PIU 2001b: 6, emphasis added).

So at the 11th hour, after the meetings with the academic panel were over and during the period when a presentation of the PIU team's new strategy was made to the Prime Minister, the definition of workforce development changed back from being a structural problem to being an individual one. Two questions cry out for answers: 'why was the definition changed and by whom?'

The report also contains the following definition of education: 'It is ... usually associated – if unfairly – with a very traditional classroom and teacher format and with compulsory schooling, rather than with different forms of learning more generally' (PIU 2001b: 118). Such a definition shows how remote some policy-makers are both from research on teaching and learning and from any understanding of education as transformative.

It has taken years of work by the National Skills Task Force and seven months of intensive effort by the PIU to gain government support for a change to a demand-led strategy. Advances have been made, but the crucial details of the new strategy have still to be worked out. Expectations are low and may be fulfilled. The Prime Minister's recent speech to a CBI conference offers little prospect of radical change: 'there will be no dilution of our essentially flexible labour market. There will be no new ramp of employment legislation taking us backwards to the 1970s. The basic settlement of the last parliament will remain' (Blair, 2001). If these low expectations are fulfilled, then the entrenched pattern of ineffective, individual remedies for intractable, structural problems will be repeated. The only difference this time is that the problems have been more thoroughly diagnosed. It is predicted by the present author that ten years from now yet another round of institutional restructuring and another policy review will be thought necessary.

Notes

1 The PIU team was made up from civil servants (the team leader from the Department of Transport, Local Government and the Regions, two economists from the PIU central economics team, two part-time secondees from the Department for Education and Skills) and six secondees (from Ford, KPMG, the Local Government Association, the Social Market Foundation, the Campaign for Learning, and Worksystems Inc, USA). Of the 11 members, eight were female, including the team leader.

2 The focus group consisted of public and private sector employers, employees from small businesses, and individuals under the age of 35. Fuller details are available in PIU (2001), Annex 5.

3 The Academic Panel consisted of Professor Mike Campbell (Leeds Metropolitan); Professor David Ashton (Leicester); Professor Frank Coffield (Newcastle); Paul Johnson (Director of Analytical Services, DfEE); Mark Corney (MC Consultancy); Professor Steve Machin (University College, London); Geoff Mason (NIESR); Dr Ewart Keep (Warwick); Lorraine Dearden (Institute of Fiscal Studies); Professor Stephen McNair (Surrey); Professor Francis Green (Kent); and Professor David Robertson (Liverpool John Moores).

4 The Advisory Group was composed of the Director and Chief Economist of the PIU; and senior representatives from the Department of Trade and Industry, the Treasury, the Department for Education and Skills and the Learning and Skills Council; from the Council for Excellence in Management and Leadership, the Chartered Institute for Personnel Development and City and Guilds; from the Small Business Service, the Amalgamated Engineering and Electrical Workers Union; and from Ford Europe and Nomura (chair).

5 The figure of 101 initiatives is not a gross exaggeration for effect. It was arrived at by adding the number of initiatives (60+) in the DfEE's White Paper *Schools: Building in Success* (2001) to those on workforce development (45).

6 Maria Slowey made this important point during the discussion following the David Stow lecture in Strathclyde University, given by the author on 21 March 2002.

References

Ashton, D. (2001) The political economy of workplace learning. Paper presented to International Workshop, University College Northampton, 8–10 November.

Ashton, D. and Sung, J. (2001) *Lessons Learnt from Overseas Experience*. London: PIU.

Bell, C. and Raffe, D. (1991) Working together? Research, policy and practice. In G. Walford (ed.) *Doing Educational Research*. London: Routledge, 121–146.

Blair, T. (2001) Blair Soothes Captains of Industry. *Guardian*, 6 November, 2.

Blunkett, D. (2000) Influence or irrelevance: Can social science improve government? In (eds) *Secretary of State's ESRC Lecture*. London: DfEE.

Chisholm, L. (2001) *Learning and Earning, Loving and Living: Transitions and Social Cohesion in Europe*. Institute of Education, Social Benefits of Learning Conference, London, 4 July.

Coffield, F. (1992) Training and enterprise councils: The last throw of voluntarism? *Policy Studies*, 13(4), 11–32.

Coffield, F. (ed.) (1999) *Speaking Truth to Power: Research and Policy on Lifelong Learning*. Bristol: The Policy Press.

Coffield, F. (2001) 101 initiatives but no strategy: Policy on lifelong learning in England. In L. Nieuwenhuis and W. Nijhof (eds), *The Dynamics of VET and HRD Systems*. Netherlands: Twente University, 25–34.

Coleman, S. and Keep, E. (2001) *Background Literature Review for PIU Project on Workforce Development*. London: PIU.

Department for Education and Employment (2000) *Skills for All: Proposals for a National Skills Agenda*. Final Report by the National Skills Task Force. Sudbury: Prolog.

Edwards, T. (2000) All the evidence shows …?: Reasonable expectations of educational research. *Oxford Review of Education*, 26(3/4), 299–311.

Felstead, A. (2001a) Putting skills in their place: The regional pattern of work skills in Britain. In K. Evans, P. Hodkinson and L. Unwin (eds) *Working to Learn*. London: Kogan Page, 163–186.

Felstead, A. (2001b) Using surveys to measure skills at work. Paper presented to International Workshop, University College Northampton, 8–10 November.

Finegold, D. and Soskice, D. (1991) The failure of training in Britain: Analysis and prescription. In G. Esland (ed), *Education, Training and Employment*, vol. 1. Wokingham: Addison-Wesley for Open University, 214–261. First published by *Oxford Review of Economic Policy*, 4(3), 1988.

Fullan, M. G. (1991) *The New Meaning of Educational Change*. London: Cassell.

Guest, D. (2001) *Motivation for Workforce Development: The Role of National Culture*. London: PIU.

Hargreaves, D. H. (2001) Revitalising educational research: Past lessons and future prospects. In M. Fielding (ed), *Taking Education Really Seriously: Four Years' Hard Labour*. London: Routledge Falmer, 197–208.

HM Treasury (2001) *Pre-Budget Report: Building a Stronger, Fairer Britain in an Uncertain World*. London: Stationery Office, Cm 5318.

Hodge, M. (2001) Elitism never made a nation rich. *Guardian Education*, 6 November, 13.

Keep, E. (2001) Researchers on tap but never on top: Working with the cabinet office. *Social Sciences, ESRC Newsletter*, 49, 2 September.

Kogan, M. (1999) The impact of research on policy. In F. Coffield (ed), *Speaking Truth to Power: Research and Policy on Lifelong Learning*. Bristol: The Policy Press, 11–18.

Machin, S. and Vignoles, A. (2001) *The Economic Benefits of Training to the Individual, the Firm and the Economy: The Key Issues*. London: PIU.

Owens, J. (2001) Evaluation of Individual Learning Accounts – Early Views of Customers and Providers: England, DfES Research Brief No 294, September. London DfES.

Performance and Innovation Unit (2000) Mission Statement. Available online: http://www.cabinet-office.gov.uk/innovation/2000/purpose.

Performance and Innovation Unit (2001a) *Workforce Development: Analysis*. London: PIU.

Performance and Innovation Unit (2001b) *In Demand: Adult Skills in the 21st Century*. London: PIU.

Rana, E. (2001) Low skills, low interest. *People Management*, 13 September, 24–30.

Westwood, A. (2001) *Not Very Qualified: Raising Skills Levels in the UK Workforce*. London: Industrial Society.

Wolf, A. (1998) Politicians and economic panic. *History of Education*, 27(3), 219–234.

Chapter 7

Resistance is fertile[1]

The demands the FE sector must make of the next government

Why can British governments not learn from past blunders? Why is no minister ever held to account? This is an edited version of a talk given at a conference for Further Education (FE) staff in March 2015. It catalogues the failures of governments of all colours in dealing with the sector: the abandoned initiatives, qualifications and programmes, major reviews and ministers. We need an independent association like Tutors' Voices to draw upon the craft knowledge and practical experience of those who know most about classrooms and workshops. It lists a series of demands to rectify the injustices inflicted on the sector.

The move from Keele to Durham University involved far more than driving 200 miles to the North East. It wasn't a simple switch from England's newest University after the Second World War to the one claiming to be the third oldest after Oxbridge. Nowhere was the difference more marked than in the contrasting styles of debating in Senate. At Keele, staff openly criticised the plans of senior management, urging them to be withdrawn and re-written. There would follow 'a frank exchange of views' which more often than not led to a compromise that both sides could live with.

In marked contrast, the standard way to get amendments made to official plans in Durham was to adopt the stance of the pre-emptive cringe. 'Warden', for that is a title given there to the Vice Chancellor, 'I'm very impressed with your paper which brilliantly sets out our intentions for the future. May I, however, with respect, suggest one or two minor tweaks to your comprehensive conclusions?' Two wildly contrasting ways of achieving the same end.

Introduction

There is a pressing need for us to use our collective power to defend, deepen and embed our democracy – democracy in education and, in particular, democracy in the FE and Skills sector. We operate at present with a fragile version of democracy where we are treated as consumers and subjects, not as citizens; and we need, in Richard Pring's phrase, 'to acquire the habit of democracy' (2011). He means acting in open, democratic ways with senior

DOI: 10.4324/9781003476146-10

managers, colleagues and students in schools, colleges and universities; and making our students familiar with the democratic history, values and practices of the United Kingdom.

We professionals in education need to stand up for our rights as citizens in a democracy rather than accepting whatever scraps are thrown to us by whatever politicians happen to be in power. We need to make a stand; to make **demands** of the government, ten in all, rather than just accepting the next torrent of reforms being prepared for the sector.

The first of these demands is that we and our professional and union representatives should be equal partners in the formation, enactment and evaluation of any new initiative. There should be no new funding stream; no new qualification; no change in structures, schemes or agencies; and no more Acts of Parliament without comprehensive, open-ended and authentic consultation of the kind enjoyed by equal partners. The present bogus versions of consultation are an insult to our profession and to our democracy.

We need to persist in this struggle to get things changed. One letter to *The Guardian* will not do it, nor will one meeting nor one book. We have to join together in large numbers in a protracted campaign to preserve what we value in education and in this sector. Max Weber's metaphor for political activity is sawing a thick tree trunk: the need to go on and on with the same boring action, which proves effective only in the long run. And he was talking about a world without chainsaws, where trees were felled by hand.

Trying to get politicians or civil servants to alter their thinking or behaviour is hard work. In the words of President Woodrow Wilson: 'If you want to make enemies, try to change something'. There follows a list of ten demands and an explanation of the first demand which will help to usher in the others. Second, a strong, well-founded case will be presented for that change; and then the means by which reform could come about.

Ten demands

In any democracy worthy of the name, we citizens have not only 'the right and duty to ask tough questions' (Hutton, 2015: 28); not only a right and a duty to make requests of our elected representatives; but a right and a duty to demand change to rectify injustices.

1 Teachers' unions and professional bodies to become by law equal partners with government and business in the formation of new policy.
2 Control over professional matters relating to teaching, learning and assessment (TLA) to be returned from the politicians to the teaching profession.
3 Teaching in the sector is to be carried out solely by fully trained professionals. A ban on all unqualified teachers working in any educational institution supported by state funds. Major new investment in the professional learning of all practicing teachers.

4 The £156 million of our money being spent each year on Ofsted is being wasted. Abolish Ofsted – or at least radically transform it – so that it
   behaves as HMI did in the recent past: a body of professional colleagues
   who acted as cross-pollinators of good practice and ideas, dedicated to
   the task of improving teaching and learning. When they uncovered serious failings, HMI offered not only constructive criticism but also the
   help needed to redress them. Inspectors could resume working in collaboration with Local Education Authority advisers to improve provision,
   as well as encouraging self-evaluation and monitored peer review among
   networks of colleges. At present, Ofsted inspectors are acting as the drill
   sergeants of the system; they 'put the stick about' to force tutors to comply
   with government policy.
5 Lifelong learning to become a right of citizenship in a democracy. Abolish
   tuition fees. Why should our children and grandchildren run up debts to
   pay £9k fees per year, which will take them decades to pay off, when our
   generation received generous grants?
6 Create an independent, middle tier of governance to fill the gaping hole
   between central government and individual institutions. No more 'free'
   schools to be opened and all existing ones and academies to be returned
   to the local family of schools, overseen by re-invigorated and democratically elected Local Authorities. It means City Region leaders will have 'the
   long-term freedom to redirect funding where it is actually needed … in an
   increasingly fragmented skills sector' (O'Loughlin, 2015).
7 Resurrect the Tomlinson proposals of 2004 which sought to integrate academic and vocational learning for all 14–19-year-old students by incorporating the best features of General Certificate of Secondary Education
   (GCSEs), A levels and vocational qualifications into a unified set of diplomas. Bipartisan political consensus will be necessary to ensure a decade
   of consistent political support.
8 Ministers will be obliged by law to describe what steps they have taken
   to safeguard the interests of students during the implementation of any
   new initiative. All new interventions to be 'carefully designed, thoroughly
   tested and slowly embedded' (City & Guilds, 2014: 3).
9 End the funding crisis in the sector. Reintroduce Educational Maintenance
   Allowances for disadvantaged students and 'make sixth form colleges ex-
   empt from VAT, like schools and academies' (NUT, 2014: 13). Introduce
   three-year budgets to end year-on-year instability. Simplify and reduce the
   funding streams to enable colleges to plan and provide continuity.
10 The pressures on teachers (from constant government changes; the punitive regimes of accountability and assessment; incessant demands from
   administrators for data; the ever-increasing workloads; targets and performance indicators overriding any concern for the quality of teaching;
   and the recurrent grading of lessons by management acting as 'internal' Ofsted inspectors) are driving some of our best teachers out of the

profession. The strain of working in the state sector has now reached intolerable proportions, with principals, middle managers and tutors scared for their jobs if the test scores of their students do not constantly improve. Change in education is successful when it resembles slow, incremental evolution tailored to the varying abilities and needs of students, not a permanent revolution to accommodate the demands of politicians for quick results.

The first demand needs to be explained in more detail. It challenges the refusal by all the political parties to allow teachers – *the* experts in TLA – to be represented by their unions and professional bodies when governments are introducing reforms: a right which is enjoyed by their counterparts in every civilised country in Europe. In Germany, for example, the education and training system is based on a social contract – a social partnership – which is negotiated at national, regional and local levels between the state, employers, workers, teachers and specialist academics. Such partnerships have proved to be effective in generating social integration as well as a highly skilled workforce.

At present, there is no independent, democratic organisation to represent tutors in this sector. Furthering the professionalism of tutors in the FE and Skills sector may receive a boost with the collapse of the Institute for Learning (IfL) in November 2014 because something more powerful, independent and democratic may take its place. Right from the start, the IfL failed to establish itself as an independent organisation, free from government. It could not even get its own name right. Its core function was to further the development of tutors in FE, so it should have been called the Institute for Tutors or Teaching. That said, it did some good work in offering a new model of professional learning with tutors in charge of it; and this model is explored in the writings of Fiona Mackay and Paul Wakeling (2014); Sue Colquhoun and Jean Kelly (2014); and Andy Boon and Toni Fazaeli (2014).

There is a continuing strength of feeling about IfL within the sector and weaknesses were identified in it: the mandatory nature of membership and the associated fee; the quality of the services provided; and the undemocratic way in which it was run (UCU, 2012). Tutors still need, however, an organisation to represent their views to the government and to hold management to account for providing high-quality professional learning. The sector needs a replacement for IfL that has learned the lessons of IfL; a body established by FE tutors themselves, run on democratic lines and with the professional knowledge to stand up to both government and management: an organisation dedicated to winnowing out what works in TLA, with what students, under what conditions and with what resources and outcomes. Gert Biesta has, however, warned us against the focus on evidence-based practice becoming confined to … 'technical questions – questions about "what works" – while forgetting the need for critical inquiry into normative and political questions about what is educationally desirable ... From the point of view of democracy, an exclusive emphasis on "what works" will simply not do' (2007: 21–22).

The working title, *Tutors' Voices: the professionals in FE and Skills*, has been picked up by a group of tutors in FE, who will launch a new, democratic professional association on 1 May 2015, a highly symbolic date. Members of this new association will, of course, have the final say about its title, remit and funding principles. The immediate task is to get it launched.

Why is reform needed?

Two years ago, at a conference in Guildford, I listed a long catalogue of failures by ministers and senior civil servants at the Department of Education (see Coffield, 2013, 2014). That list of heavily revised or abandoned initiatives included: the National Curriculum, Curriculum 2000, the Open College, Training Credits, Learning Accounts, the University for Industry, Standard Attainment Tests, Employer Training Pilots, the Quality Improvement Strategy, Sector Skills Agreements and the English Baccalaureate.

There have also been eight failed attempts by governments from the main political parties to establish a Development Agency for this sector. The litany of shame reads as follows: the Staff College → FEU → FEDA → LSDA → QIA/CEL → LSIS → FE Guild and on to the present incarnation, the Education and Training Foundation (ETF), which is neither democratic in its constitution nor independent of government. ETF has only a fraction of the staff, resource and clout enjoyed by its predecessor, LSIS. Today, that criticism will be extended by detailing the changes to qualifications, to programmes, to government agencies and to departmental titles which successive governments have inflicted on this sector.

First, qualifications: since the 1970s, the following have been abandoned or changed out of all recognition: the Certificate of FE, the Certificate in Pre-Vocational Education, the Diploma in Vocational Education, BTEC Certificates and Diplomas, National Vocational Qualifications, General NVQs, the Advanced Vocational Certificate in Education, Applied A Levels, 14-19 Diplomas and now Applied General Qualifications and Technical Levels. While the FE and Skills sector responded to each of these changes, the academic route enjoyed the stability provided by well-established and well-resourced institutions (schools and universities) and widely understood and respected qualifications (GCSEs and A Levels). Admittedly, the golden route to success in England has had its own share of constant government intervention to deal with, but in the main, the pathways have remained clear and have been well-trodden, mainly by the children of the middle and upper classes. In contrast, England after more than 30 years of political hyperactivity still does not have a prestigious, vocational path for the 50% of each generation of students who do not go on to university. The Newsom Report of 1963 was entitled *Half Our Future*, and that half has waited for over 50 years for qualifications to rival

A levels and they are waiting still. It is a national scandal which this nation knows next to nothing about and which the national media, even the left-wing media, seem indifferent to.

Second, the changes to programmes. Over the same period, we have had: Youth Training Scheme (YTS), Training Opportunities Programmes (TOPs), Youth Training (YT), Apprenticeships, Traineeships, Train to Gain (T2G), Entry to Employment (E2E), Skills for Life (SfL), Adult Basic Skills, Educational Maintenance Allowances (EMAs), Centres of Vocational Excellence (COVEs), Centres of Excellence in Training (CETs) and Employer Ownership of Skills.

Third, the list of arms-length, government agencies established to run the sector runs as follows: the Manpower Services Commission (MSC), the Training Commission (TC), the UK Commission for Employment and Skills (UKCES), the Training Agency (TA), Training and Enterprise Councils (TECs) Regional Development Agencies (RDAs), Government Offices in the Region (GOR), Local Enterprise Partnerships (LEPs), the Further Education Funding Council for England (FEFC), the Learning and Skills Council (LSC), Lifelong Learning UK (LLUK), Learning and Skills Network (LSN), Local Learning and Skills Council (LLSC), the Young People's Learning Agency (YPLA), the Skills Funding Agency (SFA), the Education Funding Agency (EFA), the Sector Skills Council (SSC) and the Sector Skills Development Agency (SSDA).[2]

Next, the changes in the name of the Department of Education itself: the Department of Education and Science (1964–92); the Department for Education (1992–95); the Department for Education and Employment (1995–2001); the Department for Education and Skills (2001–07); the Department for Children, Schools and Families (2007–10); and now back to the Department for Education (2010–present). The economic costs of these changes – in stationery, signage and brass plates – are as of nothing compared with the human cost in smashed careers, redundancies and enforced early retirements.

The list of the major reviews of the sector includes: Dearing, Kennedy, Beaumont, Cassels, Tomlinson, Foster, Leitch, Wolf and Richards. In the 34 years since 1981, there have been 28 pieces of legislation on education, training and skills. The report of the City and Guilds Group – on three decades of skills and employment policy – discovered that 'there is no central repository of past policies, reviews and evidence' for policy makers to access … they suffer from 'collective amnesia' (2014: 3). This condition is self-induced by the dysfunctional churning of ministers and civil servants.

Let us examine one scheme – individual learning accounts (ILAs) – in a little depth. According to Anthony King and Ivor Crewe, the ILA scheme 'in conception, design and execution … was a well-nigh perfect example of a policy blunder' (2013: 127). Within a year of being launched, the Department had 'received 4,300 complaints, mainly of mis-selling, aggressive marketing, poor value for money and the blatantly low quality of some courses' (ibid: 135). At least £97 million was siphoned off by fraudsters, but more important damage was inflicted: 'it failed miserably to reach the vast majority of those it

was meant to help: disadvantaged people lacking any sort of vocational qualifications' (ibid: 139). And yet the Department had been warned by representatives of the FE sector about 'the risks to quality of having an unregulated
market, but their warnings were dismissed as self-interested and protectionist'
(Ibid: 132). This case study soon reached the level of farce because 'many
holders of individual learning accounts simply did not exist. They were fig-
ments of the criminal imagination … In one case, 6,000 learners turned out to
live at the same residential address. In another, the names in which learning
accounts had been opened were not proper names but Hindi swear words'
(ibid: 137). Neither the ministers who devised this scheme nor the permanent secretary at the time were called to give evidence to the parliamentary
enquiry. Ministers and senior civil servants continue to hail success as a personal triumph, but failure is attributed to collective 'errors of judgement' for
which no one is held accountable.

I could add the changes to the inspectorate, to ministerial responsibility for
this sector and to the myriad funding streams, but the main point has been
made. This sector has suffered failure after failure in most areas of policy. The
image that occurs to me is a ritual slaughterhouse where agencies, like sacrifi-
cial animals, have a life expectancy of no more than 3/4 years. What has held
the sector together is both the resilience of our FE colleges to absorb change
of this volume and intensity and the commitment of staff to keep the show on
the road for the sake of the students.

A conclusion can be drawn from the work of the playwright, David Hare,
who wrote recently:

> Commentators write glibly about the public's increasing contempt of poli-
> ticians, and yet what goes unremarked, and is equally damaging, is politi-
> cians' growing contempt for us.
>
> (2015: 3)

The evidence just reviewed reveals the contempt held by the political and
civil service classes in this country for this sector. Witness what Vince Cable,
the Liberal Democrat Minister for Business, Innovation and Skills, said last
October: 'I could have taken the advice we had from the civil servants who
said "why don't you just effectively kill off FE? Nobody will really notice"'
(BBC News, 2014).

King and Crewe offer a sophisticated explanation composed of 12 factors
for the propensity of the British political system to make appalling mistakes.
They argue that it should not be viewed as 'a sequence of unrelated episodes
but as a **pattern**' (2013: 397, my emphasis). Of the 12 factors they include in
their diagnosis, four seem particularly pertinent to FE. First, they cite 'cultural
disconnect', by which they refer to politicians and senior civil servants dealing with 'values, attitudes and whole ways of life that are not remotely like
their own' (2013: 244).

Second, they introduce the term 'operational disconnect' to describe the politicians' belief that the formation of policy (their task) is hard, but its implementation (the task of tutors) is easy. The reverse is more accurate. Third, King and Crewe point to a 'lack of accountability', whereby ministers who are responsible for failures are simply moved to another department where they are free to commit another set of blunders. Fourth, they point to a 'deficit of deliberation'. New initiatives are neither carefully considered, designed nor tested; and the experts in the field – classroom teachers - are excluded from the process.

Governments seem to be convinced of the efficacy of Student Voice in improving TLA. Why, then, have they set their faces against listening to the voices of tutors? Tutors should not be held responsible for failed interventions which they had no part in devising or evaluating.

Getting what we want

Martin Kettle makes the pragmatic point that 'knowing what you want is utterly useless unless you know how to get it' (*The Guardian*, 23 January 2015). To turn any one of the ten demands into practice will require collaboration, political nous and the stomach for a prolonged struggle.

First, we need to establish a strong, independent association like Tutors' Voices which gains the support of thousands of staff in the sector; and it must be their concerns which become the rallying points for the movement. We also need to build a coalition of support by forming alliances with the main players, the most important of whom are our students and with whom we need to make common cause by supporting the campaigns of the National Union of Students. Then, we must seek help from governors, parents, unions and business leaders, many of whom will be supportive because they are surprised that they are invited by the government to develop curricula and then find that the curriculum experts – the tutors – are not sitting around the table.

There are also some politicians sympathetic to the cause of devolving powers from Whitehall to communities. Politicians like Liz Kendall and Steve Reed argue that:

> ... the key to making lasting change lies in giving people real power and control over the decisions that affect their lives ... People are no longer prepared to be the passive recipients of whatever is offered to them. They want, and they deserve, the right to be involved in decisions taken about them ... directing change from the centre without realising how taking control over people's lives and communities can leave them incapacitated and weak.
>
> (2015: xv)

Kendall and Reed are here referring to clients of social work or housing departments, but their reflections on New Labour's performance in government apply with equal force to the teaching profession. Listening to Tutors' Voices will improve the quality of TLA in colleges because it means drawing upon the craft knowledge and the practical experience of those who know most about classrooms and workshops. The intention is to do what no government has succeeded in doing so far, namely, release the creativity of all those working in the sector.

Instead of tutors still feeling 'as if policy is being done to them' (Sedgmore, 2015), the first demand is about changing the present process of developing, enacting and evaluating policy to enable information, ideas and feedback to flow sweetly from practitioners to policy-makers and from policy-makers to practitioners. Students and tutors have to show that they can learn; but the *system* itself has to demonstrate that it is also willing to learn. If this demand continues to be resisted, the Department for Education, which is in charge of the learning of millions of students and thousands of teachers, will remain a prime example of a non-learning organisation.

The powers of the Secretary of State for Education in England have grown enormously over the last 30 years, by as many as 2,500, according to some estimates (Brighouse, 2011). Such powers are excessive, go largely unchallenged and urgently need to be curtailed. How? Government ministers need to be subjected to greater scrutiny. Those who are so keen to hold others to account should themselves be made responsible, not only for any misuse of public resources but also for any blunders. It is, however, the unusual politician who voluntarily gives away power.

One further obstacle is that the FE sector is, in comparison with Oxbridge or the Russell group of universities, relatively isolated from the key players who exercise political power in this country. Researchers like Michael Woolcock (1999) think there are three basic dimensions of social capital that are necessary for sustainable improvement – bonds, bridges and linkages. FE has strong bonds as can be seen daily in the collaboration of colleagues, within and across institutions; it also has useful channels or bridges into local communities and businesses; but what it lacks are influential linkages which forge 'alliances with sympathetic individuals in positions of power' (1999: 8).

Final comments

This story is one of blunder upon blunder committed by governments in our name and with our money. The weight of the evidence has forced the conclusion that the biggest problem we face is government policy (see Coffield, 2008). The case for the prosecution was presented above, but the case for the defence has still to be put. Please consult the book I wrote with Bill Williamson, which offers a considered balance sheet of the strengths and weaknesses in educational reform since 1988 (2011: 34–45).

Other sectors of education – schools and universities – have also suffered from the depredations of the government. Ron Glatter describes the coalition's record on schools as 'a breathtaking catalogue of failures' which has left a 'ramshackle infrastructure that ... cannot underpin a 21st century school system' (2015: 2). Education has suffered at the hands of the coalition government, but FE has suffered the most. It has borne the brunt of the education cuts. No politician would have dared to inflict the permanent revolution in qualifications, programmes and agencies suffered by FE on those 'no-go' areas in education policy-making, private schools and Oxbridge.

Within the FE sector, the prevailing mood can be judged by the remark made by a senior government agent to college managers after a poor Ofsted report: 'The Minister wants a head on a stick'. This comment quickly went the rounds and fear was sent coursing through the bloodstream of the system. Performance management relies on fear to do its dirty work: education relies on trust to foster better human beings. Performance management seems to attract cold, unfeeling and authoritarian personalities.

The first annual report of the FE Commissioner, whose role – briefly – is to assess the governance and leadership of those colleges, deemed inadequate by Ofsted or by the SFA. The report runs to only 30 pages, but includes key performance indicators, benchmarking of performance with peers, annual appraisals, SMART targets, dashboards, resignations of principals and vice-principals, 'refreshing' the governing body, significant redundancy costs, structured teaching and learning observation programmes, tough action, a functional skills audit of vocational staff, reducing staffing and salaries in line with sector norms, the reluctance to hold 'difficult conversations', Post Inspection Action Plans, Structure and Prospects Appraisal, Strategic Options Reviews, quantitative success criteria, year milestones, stocktake assessments and SFA attending Board meetings as observers (DBIS, 2014). There is, however, no discussion of teaching and learning; quality is 'evidenced by student success rates' (2014: 15); and the report's language, values and concepts are more applicable to the inspection of garages, restaurants or supermarkets than they are to FE colleges which are supposed to be educational institutions. The current system of inspection and enforcement seems incapable of appreciating that tutors are moral agents working to improve the lot of those less fortunate, not disposable units of production to be thrown on the scrapheap the moment 'business' has no further use for them.

The national system of education belongs to us all – to students, parents, teachers, governors, employers and all citizens – and we should demand a greater say in it. It is not the personal possession of whoever happens to be Secretary of State, but it has become so. The democratic right of tutors to be involved in reform as equal partners has been denied and that right has to be enshrined in law. It will be necessary for the teachers' unions and professional bodies to offer something in return; to demonstrate, for example, their commitment to raising the achievement of all students and to becoming a fully research-informed profession.

There are colleges which, through no fault of their own, are already in financial difficulties and further cuts could spell closure for them as well as the death of hope for a better future for millions of working-class people. If we want to avoid that calamity, then we need to work collectively over the next few weeks to let our voices – Tutors' Voices – be heard loud and clear, voices of protest, voices of resistance, voices demanding a more just, more educational and properly resourced future for the people we serve.

Notes

1 I am grateful to Maire Daley and Joel Petrie for allowing me to use their engaging phrase as the title of this chapter, see Daley et al. (2015).
2 The City and Guilds Report (2014: 64) requires a whole page to explain 68 acronyms used in the governance of the FE and Skills sector, and that list is not comprehensive.

References

BBC News (2014) Officials want to axe FE colleges – Vince Cable, www.bbc.co.uk/news/uk-politics-29496475. Accessed 9 March 2015.

Biesta, G. (2007) Why 'what works' won't work: Evidence-based practice and the democratic deficit in educational research. *Educational Theory*, 57(1), 1–22.

Boon, A. and Fazaeli, T. (2014) Professional bodies and continuing professional development: A case study. In Crowley, S. (ed) *Challenging Professional Learning*. Abingdon: Routledge.

Brighouse, T. (2011) Decline and fall: Are state schools and universities on the point of collapse? Oxford: Oxford Education Society, Annual Lecture, 16 September.

City and Guilds Group (2014) *Sense and Instability: Three Decades of Skills and Employment Policy*. London: City and Guilds.

Coffield, F. (2008) When the solution is the problem … University and College Union Magazine, 8–10 October.

Coffield, F. (2013) Can we transform classrooms and colleges without transforming the role of the state? Keynote address at a New Bubbles conference, Guildford, 22 March. Copies available from paultully@newbubbles.com.

Coffield, F. (2014) *Beyond Bulimic Learning: Improving Teaching in Further Education*. London: Institute of Education Press.

Coffield, F. and Williamson, B. (2011) *From Exam Factories to Communities of Discovery: The Democratic Route*. London: IOE.

Colquhoun, S. and Kelly, J. (2014) Interpreting professional learning: The trouble with CPD. In Crowley, S. (ed) *Challenging Professional Learning*. Abingdon: Routledge.

Daley, M., Orr, K. and Petrie, J. (2015) *Further Education and the Twelve Dancing Princesses*. London: Institute of Education Press.

Department for Business, Innovation and Skills (2014) *Further Education Commissioner: Annual Report 2013/14*. London: DBIS.

Glatter, R. (2015) This ramshackle education framework cannot underpin a 21st century school system. *Times Education Supplement*, 25 February.

Hare, D. (2015) Justice v Money. *The Guardian Review*, Saturday 31 January.

Hutton, W. (2015) Unions should pioneer profit sharing and employee share ownership. *The Guardian*, 11 February, 28–29.

Kendall, L. and Reed, S. (2015) Let it go: Power to the people in public services. In Kendall, L. and Reed, S. (eds) *Progress*. London: Local Government Association, Labour Group.

Kettle, M. (2015) Cromwell the fixers' fixer: A role model for our times. *The Guardian*, 23 January.

King, A. and Crewe, I. (2013) *The Blunders of Our Governments*. London: Oneworld.

Mackay, F. and Wakeling, P. (2014) Leading and learning in challenging circumstances. In Crowley, S. (ed) *Challenging Professional Learning*. Abingdon: Routledge.

NUT (2014) *A Manifesto for Our Children's Education*. London: NUT. www.teachers. org.uk/manifesto.

O'Loughlin, L. (2015) Supporting local priorities through devolution. http://www.aoc. co.uk/blog/2015/03/05.

Pring, R. (2011) John Dewey. Talk at a conference on *Radical education and the common school: a democratic alternative*. Institute of Education, 18 March.

Sedgmore, L. (2015) If we attempt to stifle satire, the joke's on us. *Times Education Supplement Magazine,* 6 February.

UCU (2012) *Initial Submission to the Independent Review of Professionalism in the FE and Skills Sector*. London: UCU.

Woolcock, M. (1999) *Managing Risks, Shocks and Opportunity in Developing Economies: The Role of Social Capital,* World Bank Group, www.worldbank.org/poverty/ scapital/library/woolcock.htm.

Part 4

Enhancing education

Chapter 8

Breaking the consensus

Lifelong learning as social control

Socrates taught me that knowledge would set me free; Peter Mandelson tells me its modern function is to make employers rich. This article (from the *British Educational Research Journal*, 25(4), 1999, 479–499) rejects the powerful consensus in the United Kingdom that lifelong learning is a won-der drug which, on its own, will solve a wide range of ills. Ten key prob-lems with the consensus are listed and this prompts the question, if the thesis is so poor, why is it so popular? Alternative visions of lifelong learn-ing are then presented, including a sceptical version of lifelong learning as social control, which treats lifelong learning not as a self-evident good but as contested terrain between employers, unions and the state. This helps to explain why lifelong learning became a transient phenomenon, as the article predicted. The definition of social control is Stan Cohen's: 'the organized ways in which society responds to behavior and people it regards as deviant, problematic, worrying, threatening, troublesome or undesirable' (1985: 1).

Most of us have thought of the perfect reply when it's too late. Once, at a conference, I was due to follow Michael Portillo, who began his talk by speaking wittily about losing his seat in Parliament on election night in 1997. Or as he phrased it: 'having a bucket of shit poured over my head, live on telly, while thousands rejoiced'. He went on to describe how many of his contemporaries from his sixth form had gone on to either Oxford or Cam-bridge. What I should have asked him was: do you know how many went on to any of the other 125 universities in this country? How many went on to FE colleges or colleges of Art? Would he have known? Conservatives tend to be interested in those they call 'the elite', with the rest of us called 'the masses'. But there's no such thing as 'the masses', only ways of treating people as if they were 'the masses'.

Only once in my career have I thought of an appropriate response. My first lecturing post was at Jordanhill College of Education in Glasgow, where I gave lectures to a lively class of graduate Art students. I became irritated by one student who every week swept late into the room, looking like the

DOI: 10.4324/9781003476146-12

famous poster of Aristide Bruant by Henri de Toulouse-Lautrec. The class would then watch as he ostentatiously took off his black cloak and trilby hat, unfurled his red scarf, and immediately asked me a question. One Friday, having arrived particularly late, he interrupted me by saying: 'Sorry, Mr Coffield, but to my virgin mind...' I shot in to ask: 'Does that mean a thought has never entered it?'

Introduction

This article, like Roman Gaul, in three parts divided is. First, reasons will be advanced to reject the powerful consensus which has been developed over the last 30 years to the effect that lifelong learning is a wonder drug or magic bullet which, on its own, will solve a wide range of educational, social and political ills. It will be argued that this consensus is naive, limited and ambiguous as well as being deficient, dangerous and diversionary. This analysis prompts the question if the thesis is so poor, why is it so popular? Second, alternative visions of the learning society and of lifelong learning will be presented and the relevance to policy of viewing lifelong learning as social control will be stressed. Third, an attempt will be made to answer Lenin's great question, what is to be done? It is incumbent, I think, on researchers funded by the public purse to address policy, where appropriate.

Wherever possible, the findings from the Economic and Social Research Council's (ESRC) *The Learning Society Programme* will be drawn on, but it is important to emphasise that neither the ESRC nor any of the 50+ researchers in the 14 projects within the Programme should be held responsible for what follows; they are guilty only by associating with the author in public.

I have one further introductory comment. The consensus is *not* a straw man, whose demolition may delight the reader but be of little significance beyond that; instead, it constitutes a central plank in the policy of many Western governments in the field of education, training and employment. It is time, however, to move beyond this cosy consensus and develop more ambitious policies for creating economic prosperity and social justice.

The consensus criticised

The following critique has three objectives: to encapsulate the main features of the consensus in a few central tenets and to demonstrate its influence by means of a few representative quotations; then to list the problems with it; and then to explain its popularity and resilience in the face of criticism. For the sake of variety, the consensus will also be called, interchangeably, the thesis, the orthodoxy, the regime or the settlement.[1]

Central tenets of the consensus

The prevailing orthodoxy within the United Kingdom contains the following elements:

- A nation's competitiveness in global markets ultimately depends on the skills of all its people.
- The new economic forces unleashed by globalisation and technology are as uncontrollable as natural disasters and so governments have no choice but to introduce policies to 'upskill' the workforce.
- Education must be modernised and become more responsive to the needs of employers. In some formulations, education becomes the mere instrument of the economy, e.g. 'Education is the best economic policy we have', as the Prime Minister expressed it (Blair, 1998: 9).
- The responsibility is passed to individuals to renew their skills regularly to ensure their employability.
- The model for educational institutions to follow is that of British business.

Each of these propositions is problematical and each deserves critical analysis. Here, there is space to deal only with the fifth commandment, namely, 'Thou Shalt Covet the Practices of Business'. Two objections suggest themselves immediately. First, the Treasury's *Pre-Budget Report* argued that 'the UK has a productivity gap with the United States of around 40% and around 20% with France and Germany. In most sectors of the economy the UK is far short of the best in the world' (HM Treasury, 1998: 28). The Treasury Report also produced evidence which showed that 'over the past decade the aggregate amount of R and D conducted by UK firms has continued to lag our international competitors' (p. 32) and that 'The Government believes that at the root of much of the productivity problem in the UK lies a long history of underinvestment … For decades, the UK has invested less than our major contributors' (p. 37).[2]

Given this evidence, the exhortation for education to emulate British business seems perverse, unless we in education are supposed to learn from comparative failure rather than from comparative success. Second, the government has recognised the urgent need to modernise both business and education, but there the similarity ends. Legislation upon legislation and a punitive form of regulation are deemed necessary to modernise education, but the Prime Minister argues in his foreword to the Department of Trade and Industry's (DTI) White Paper on *Our Competitive Future* that in relation to business, 'old-fashioned state intervention did not and cannot work' (1998a: 5). The voluntary framework for employers, inherited from the previous Conservative Government, is reconfirmed and strengthened in the DTI White Paper, where the only legislation proposed is to 'change the law to give businesses in difficulties more chance to turn things round' (1998a: 62). Perhaps the government would care to explain why policies acknowledged to have failed when dealing with business are still thought appropriate for education. This issue will be picked up again in the final section, but the consensus as a whole needs to be dealt with first.

The policy of upskilling the workforce is a simplified version of the theory of human capital, which came to dominate debates about the importance of education in promoting economic development after the publication of the ideas of Theodore Schultz (1961) and Gary Becker (1964/1975). In the subsequent 30 years, the original reservations of the proponents have been forgotten and a degraded version has assumed the status of conventional wisdom. It is this degraded version of human capital theory that is being criticised here. Gary Becker, for instance, emphasised that 'the attention paid to the economic effects of education and other human capital ... is not in any way meant to imply that other effects are unimportant, or less important than the economic ones' (1975: 11). Unfortunately, those other factors have all but vanished from consideration and need to be reintroduced into the debate.

It would also be easy but tedious to show how this consensus enjoys the support of politicians of the left, centre and right (in most anglophone countries), of policy-makers, industrialists and trade unionists, and of economists and educationists. Instead of quoting chapter and verse for all these groups, three representative quotations are given.

The first comes from an influential report[3] from the Confederation of British Industry (CBI) in 1989, *Towards a Skills Revolution*, which helped to persuade the Conservative Government of the time to establish National Targets for Education and Training:

> Individuals are now the only source of sustainable competitive advantage. Efforts must be focused on mobilising their commitment and encouraging self-development and lifetime learning.
>
> (CBI, 1989: 9)

This focus on individuals was repeated in each of the three reports on *Competitiveness*, published by John Major's government in 1994, 1995 and 1996 and resulted in the establishment of an Individual Commitment to Learning Division within the Department for Education and Employment.

The second quotation is taken from the first White Paper produced by the new Labour Government of 1997, *Excellence in Schools*, and shows an unbroken continuity in thinking between Conservative and Labour administrations. This is an example of that indolent cliché of modern politics 'joined up government':

> Investment in learning in the 21st Century is the equivalent of investment in the machinery and technical innovation that was essential to the first

great industrial revolution. Then it was physical capital; now it is human capital.

(Department for Education and Employment [DfEE], 1997a: 15)

The idea that modern manufacturing by Nissan or British Aerospace does not crucially depend on technological innovation and physical capital is, of course, ludicrous.

The final quotation comes from the Labour Government's first Minister for Lifelong Learning, who, ironically, held the post for only 1 year:

> If we do *not* create a learning society-if we do not find the means of gen-erating the appropriate skills and craft and expertise, then we will fail to develop our most important resource-our people-and we will fail as an economy in this increasingly globalised market.

(Kim Howells, 1997, original emphasis)

The inflated claims in these quotations have become *the* conventional wisdoms at education and business conferences. They need to be cut down to size.

Problems with human capital theory

The orthodoxy has become a set of unquestioned articles of faith by, for instance, the Blair[4] and Clinton[5] administrations despite being subjected to continuous criticism. The reasons for its apparent invulnerability will be explored in the following section; here, the main criticisms that have been levelled against it will be briefly rehearsed.

  i *The thesis is diversionary.* In 1997, Jerome Karabel and Chelly Halsey concluded at the end of an extended review that human capital theory did not 'provide an adequate framework for understanding the relationship between education and the economy' (p. 15), as it was seriously flawed both theoretically and empirically. Moreover, because the theory was used to explain that individuals, communities and whole nations were poor because their human capital had not been developed, it diverted attention away from structural failures and injustices and blamed victims for their poverty.

  In a similar manner, the two flagship initiatives of the government's strategy for lifelong learning – the *University for Industry* and *Individual Learning Accounts* – welcome as they are, both transfer responsibility for remaining 'employable' onto *individuals*, who do not have the power to remove the structural barriers which prevent them learning. The research projects in the ESRC's *Learning Society Programme* provide many examples of such structural barriers, but there is space here to describe only one. A study of the National Health Service by Jenny Hewison, Bobbie Millar and Therese Dowswell examined the shift towards regarding training as an individual responsibility to be completed in the employee's own time. The implications for staff with young children are serious, because not taking the opportunity to train is interpreted as evidence of a lack of commitment: 'By these means, structural inequalities in access are turned into attributes of individuals' (Hewison *et al.*, 1998).

ii *It overshadows social capital*, and other forms of capital (e.g. cultural and material). The overconcentration on individual human capital leads to a corresponding neglect of social capital, which means the social relationships and arrangements (e.g. strong social networks, shared values and high trust) needed to support learning. Again, within the *Learning Society Programme*, John Field and Tom Schuller have been studying the interaction between human and social capital in Northern Ireland and Scotland and one of their arguments is pertinent here: 'investment in human capital by an employer or by society requires the appropriate social context in order to be realised effectively' (Schuller and Burns, 1999).

iii *The empirical basis of the theory is highly disputable*. Henry Levin and Carolyn Kelley conducted another review of the research in the USA and found, just like Karabel and Halsey, that 'test scores have never shown a strong connection with either earnings or productivity' (Levin and Kelley, 1997: 241). The notion that the competitiveness of the USA can only be sustained by American students outperforming their counterparts abroad in scores on achievement tests is, according to Levin and Kelley, 'naive and hardly supported by the overall empirical data' (1997: 243). Moreover, cross-sectional studies of earnings tend to overstate the longitudinal impact of education. And, thanks to Ivar Berg, we have known for 20 years that personal characteristics and job conditions are more important determinants of work performance than educational attainments (Berg, 1973).

iv *The theory is seriously incomplete*. Levin and Kelley (1997) also point out that, for education to be effective, it is crucially dependent on complementary inputs such as new investment, new methods of production and organising work, new technologies, industrial relations based on trust, sufficient customers able to buy high-quality goods and services and new managerial approaches. At its most obvious, highly educated and trained personnel need jobs commensurate with their abilities if they are to boost productivity.

v *It is dangerous*. The danger lies in employers 'being reinforced in their beliefs that the main obstacle to their success is the poor education of the workforce' (Levin and Kelley, 1997: 245). The overconcentration on one factor – improving standards in education – distorts both industrial and educational policy in ways that are unlikely to improve competitiveness and delays the advent of more comprehensive strategies.

vi *It ignores polarisation*. Human capital theory has nothing to say about the sharpening polarisation in income and wealth both internationally (see Manuel Castells, 1998) and within the United Kingdom (see Joseph Rowntree Reports in 1995 and 1998). This polarisation is being exacerbated by performance indicators in education such as the school league tables. The pass rates at the General Certificate of Secondary Education (GCSE) examinations in 1998 revealed two trends: a rising number failing to obtain any passes; and a widening gap between this group at the bottom and those achieving average or high grades. Let us examine the data in more detail at both a national and a local level. Peter Robinson and Carey Oppenheim studied GCSE grades in England and Wales over the period 1991–97 and concluded (see Table 8.1) that the top 10% of pupils had increased their average score by nearly nine points, while the bottom 10% had shown hardly any improvement at all. The outcome of providing teachers with incentives to concentrate on those pupils capable of obtaining five or more higher grade GCSE (A*-C) has been that those students with few or no qualifications have been correspondingly neglected. Robinson and Oppenheim (1998: 19) have provided hard evidence 'of how key indicators can distort incentives in a way which can have undesirable consequences'.

To bring this argument home, the figures of the highest and lowest scoring schools at GCSE in Newcastle in 1998 have been extracted and are presented in Table II. Such raw scores have been rightly criticised on a variety of counts by other commentators, but the point to be made here is different. It does not take a detailed knowledge of social class in Newcastle to be able to identify the first four as schools from the private sector; and the bottom four as schools serving seriously deprived areas. No one is arguing for equality of outcome, but such extreme *inequalities* of outcome, repeated year after year, are the mark of a society which is becoming dangerously polarised. These figures speak eloquently of an educational 'apartheid' in this and other cities throughout the country;

Table 8.1 School performance in Newcastle

% of five GCSEs			
Schools	A*-C	No. with SEN	Total no of pupils
I	98	Nil	906
2	97	31	501
3=	96	4	440
	96	nil	1,056
16	25	243	810
17	14	17	1,198
18	10	164	561
19	6	300	1,396

Source: DfEE (1998a, 1998b), *Performance Tables* (London, DfEE).

the emotive phrase is used by George Walden (1996: 1) to describe the two segregated systems of education within this one country. The policy of publishing such tables, for all their unwelcome consequences, may still prove to be of value, *provided* it results in robust policies to tackle such unjustifiable, unacceptable but remediable inequality.

Manuel Castells has produced extensive evidence to show how new forms of capitalism are creating 'a sharp divide between valuable and non-valuable people and locales' (Castells, 1998: 161) and 'a fundamental split in societies all over the world: on the one hand, active, culturally self-defined elites ... on the other hand, increasingly uncertain, insecure social groups, deprived of information, resources and power, digging their trenches of resistance' (1998: 340).

vii *It ignores the sexual division of labour.* Human capital theory treats skill as a measurable attribute of individuals, but Jill Blackmore (1997) argues that it is better viewed as a relational concept whose meaning shifts over time depending on, for example, the perceived status of particular tasks; the supply of and demand for skilled people; and the ability of the skilled to exclude others. In other words, skills are not neutral, technically defined categories but are socially constructed by, for example, trade unions negotiating higher pay rates for their male members, or employers redefining skill levels to reduce costs. For Blackmore, human capital theory has no sense of history and has ignored 'the maintenance of particular gendered power relations in the workplace' (Blackmore, 1997: 233). To David Ashton and Francis Green, 'the fundamental weakness of the theory ... is that in regarding human capital as a 'thing' to be acquired and utilised alongside other factor inputs, it misses the social context of skill and of technology' (Ashton & Green, 1996: 17).

viii *It has created a new moral economy*, where some people are treated as more 'desirable' than others (see Stephen Ball *et al.*, forthcoming – another project team within *The Learning Society Programme*). The government's stated aim is 'to rebuild the welfare state around work' (Department of Social Security, 1998: 23) and paid employment is seen as the best means of averting poverty and social exclusion. But if people are to be treated first and foremost in relation to their potential contribution to the economy, then a market value is attached to each individual according to that contribution. So people with learning difficulties may come to be seen as a poor investment, more expensive to train, less flexible and less employable. In such a moral climate, it becomes possible for an industrialist to question whether public money should be wasted on research into adults with learning difficulties.[6] Sheila Riddell, Stephen Baron and Alistair Wilson's project within *The Learning Society Programme* makes clear that, if learning is made the central organising principle of society, those with learning difficulties may well be excluded (see Baron *et al.*, 1998).

In this way, the language of one research area within economics has hi-jacked the public debate and the discourse of professionals so that education is no longer viewed as a means of individual and social emancipation, but as either 'investment' or 'consumption', as having 'inputs' and 'outputs', 'stocks' which 'depreciate' as well as 'appreciate', and it is measured by 'rates of return', an approach which produces offensive jargon such as 'overeducated graduates' and 'monopoly producers'. The discourse which has been sidelined as a result and which must now be brought centre stage is the discourse of social justice and social cohesion.

ix *Other options may be more appropriate.* Ewart Keep and Ken Mayhew (1998) have argued that, instead of upskilling their workforce, companies have a range of competitive strategies to choose from, including seeking protected markets, growing through takeover, shifting investment abroad, developing monopoly power and cutting costs. Evidence for the cost-cutting strategy can be seen in the proliferation of retail outlets in the high streets of the United Kingdom with names like Aldi, Poundstretcher and Superdrug, where competitive advantage is based on low prices and bulk purchases. As Keep and Mayhew contend, 'many employers are pursuing perfectly rational training policies because their competitive strategies do not necessarily require them to upskill their entire workforce' (1998: 8).

x *Upskilling creates credential inflation.* The upskilling debate is conducted as though all skills and qualifications are equally valued in the labour market. But the value of educational credentials begins to fall as a higher percentage of each generation achieves graduate status, when there is no corresponding expansion of elite jobs. Moreover, the new graduates from the expanded higher education system expect the same benefits from their university qualifications as those qualifications brought to their predecessors from the much smaller elite system. In such an inflationary spiral, selection is intensified and the class of degree (first vs. lower second), the subject (physics vs. media studies), the level (undergraduate vs. postgraduate) and the awarding institution (Oxbridge vs. ex-polytechnic) form the basis of a more steeply graded hierarchy of prestige.[7] Ralph Fevre (1997), studying patterns of participation in education in South Wales as part of The Learning Society Programme, predicts that, as a result of policies designed to increase our investment in human capital, we run the serious risk that 'the UK will veer towards the US model of higher participation rates but with much education and training being of dubious value', because students will increase their credentials rather than their understanding (Fevre, 1997: 15).

If the thesis is so poor, why is it so popular?

The list of weaknesses could be extended (e.g. input-output models ignore the processes of education), but sufficient damage has been inflicted to add force to the question, if the thesis is so poor, why is it so popular? Each of the criticisms on its own makes a substantial dent in the theory of human capital; taken together, they damage its credibility beyond repair as the sole justification for policy. And yet the consensus continues to be referred to reverentially on public platforms as though it contained articles of unquestionable faith. Four main reasons are advanced to explain this invulnerability to criticism.

i *It legitimates increased expenditure on education.* According to Karabel and Halsey (1997), human capital theory flourished in the USA because it offered 'quantitative justification for vast public expenditure on education' (1997: 13). It continues to be used by Secretaries of State for Education as a means of prising open the coffers of the Treasury in favour of increased spending on education; a considerable argument in its favour, but if the policy fails, there may well be a backlash.

ii *It provides politicians with the pretext for action.* 'Politicians', argued Tony Edwards (1998), 'exalt educational reform because they believe they see in it unusual opportunities for acting both decisively and nationally. They then tend to greatly overestimate the problems which more effective schooling would alleviate or solve' (1998: 144). It will prove difficult to wean politicians off an idea which is so readily translatable into the kind of short-term initiatives on which their careers depend.

iii It deflects attention from the need for economic and social reform. Legislation to change the behaviour of individuals and educational institutions diverts attention away from more fundamental causes of low productivity, such as the short-termism of British financial institutions, which denies manufacturing the long-term investment it depends upon. Another attraction of the theory for politicians is that it converts deep-seated economic problems into short-lived educational projects.

iv *It offers the comforting illusion that for every complex problem, there is one simple solution.* To many politicians and policy-makers, 'the seductive appeal' of this approach at a time of economic uncertainty 'offers the illusion of control and of managerial solutions' (Hodkinson *et al.*, 1996: 138).

To sum up, we shall not create a learning society in the UK by investing all our hopes in a single policy of expanding human capital. The Treasury's *Pre-Budget Report*, for instance, lists four historic weaknesses in the UK's economy; improving the skills base is the fourth and last. The three factors considered more important causes of the UK's relative economic decline are: the absence of a culture celebrating innovation and enterprise; the failure of capital markets to provide sufficient investment; and the need for more competition in business to tackle vested interests and 'to expose management to international best practice' (HM Treasury, 1998: 42). These are challenges to which education has a distinctive contribution to make, but the main onus of change falls squarely on British business. In a logical world, there would now be an end to treating education as the whipping boy for the country's economic ills, which has been the sport of politicians from all parties since James Callaghan's Ruskin College speech in 1976.

Alternative visions of a learning society and of lifelong learning

The full title of the ESRC research programme is 'The Learning Society: knowledge and skills for employment', which might suggest that researchers were being invited to study lifelong learning in the service of the national consensus, which has been so severely criticised above. In practice, the project directors and the director of the programme have, from the very beginning, sought to examine changes in the labour market in the context of broad notions of citizenship, social justice and the quality of life. One of our objectives was to explore critically the concept of the learning society and the various versions of it proposed so far, as a necessary prelude to addressing that vital question: what is to be done?

For example, two researchers within *The Learning Society Programme*, Teresa Rees and Will Bartlett (1999), have suggested that the term can be viewed in three contrasting ways, which help to make sense of the myriad uses to which the phrase is put. The first version is the human capital thesis, which they call *the skill growth model*. They too consider the assumed link between upskilling and economic prosperity to be dangerously oversimplified and deterministic and therefore introduce a second approach – *the personal development model*, which argues for 'an increase in capacities to achieve individual self-fulfilment in all spheres of life, not just in economic activities' (Rees and Bartlett, 1999: 21). Again, those critics who think it unlikely that a learning society will ever be established by developing *individuals* offer a third model – social learning – which celebrates social as well as human capital and which emphasises 'the role of institutions of trust and co-operation in promoting economic growth on an equitable basis' (Rees and Bartlett, 1999). These three models are a convenient device for making sense of the research and policies on lifelong learning. Other projects within *The Learning Society Programme* have, however, developed different models[8] of a learning society (e.g. Michael Young, Ken Spours, Cathy Howieson & David Raffe, 1997), and it has also been suggested that, instead of treating the learning society as a future destination which the UK may or may not reach, it may be preferable to use the concept reflexively to enable this society to learn about itself and to evaluate progress (Coffield, 1997a).

In a similar fashion, lifelong learning appears in the literature and in political discourse in a bewildering number of different guises. For instance, it is an instrument *for* change (in individuals, organisations and society) and a buffer *against* change (see Darmon *et al.*, 1999); it is a means of increasing economic competitiveness and of personal development; it is a social policy to combat social exclusion and to ease the re-entry of the unemployed into the labour market; it is a way of promoting the professional and social development of employees and of acquiring new knowledge through the labour process; and it is a strategy to develop the participation of citizens in social, cultural and political affairs. But there is also a sceptical version of lifelong learning which has received little attention in this country, namely, that it has become a form of social control and has the potential to become so ever more powerfully (see Malcolm Tight, 1998). We are clearly not dealing with an unambiguous, neutral or static concept, but one which is currently being fought over by numerous interest groups, all struggling for their definition.

The insight that lifelong learning has become a moral obligation and a social constraint came from projects within the ESRC Programme with a strong comparative dimension and from contacts with researchers like Walter Heinz at Bremen University (1999). To our European counterparts, it is obvious that both the state and employers throughout Europe are using the rhetoric of lifelong learning first and foremost to make workers more flexible and more employable. In the words of the Tavistock research team within *The Learning Society Programme*:

> This new discourse on flexibility and employability legitimates the already well-advanced shift of the burden of responsibility for education, training and employment on to the *individual*, and implicitly denies any notion of objective structural problems such as lack of jobs, and the increasing proportion of poorly paid, untrained, routine and insecure jobs.
>
> (Darmon *et al.*, 1999; original emphasis)

The Tavistock team describes in detail the settlements which France and Spain are formulating in response to the challenges of the global market and technological innovation, compared with which the British consensus is seriously out of kilter. The French social compromise, for instance, seeks to *limit* flexibility by, *inter alia*, issuing regulations to make firms more socially responsible (e.g. the same working conditions for part-time, fixed contract and full-time staff). Meanwhile, in Spain, in 1992, the social partners agreed to a new training tax on employers and employees, which devotes 50% of all the funds to the training of the unemployed in accordance with the principle of solidarity. What all three countries (France, Spain and the UK) have in common is that trade unionists are reluctantly accepting increased flexibility in return for training to improve employability. But the researchers consider such deals not 'so much a trade off as a trap' (Darmon *et al.*, 1999), particularly in view of the estimate of more than 25% redundancies over the next 10 years. The term 'employability' also disguises the tension between training workers to meet the short-term needs of employers and the preparation for frequent changes of job for which high-level general education may be more useful.

In short, in the rest of the European Union, lifelong learning is not a self-evident good but contested terrain between employers, unions and the state. Lifelong learning is being used to socialise workers to the escalating demands of employers, who use: *'empowerment'* to disguise an intensification of work-loads via increased delegation; *'employability'* to make the historic retreat from the policy of full employment and periodic unemployment between jobs more acceptable; and *'flexibility'* to cover a variety of strategies to reduce costs which increase job insecurity. Such a critical approach exposes both 'the fiction that workers and management are on the same team', and the 'new structures of power and control' introduced by flexibility, such as 'the discontinuous reinvention of institutions' (see Richard Sennett, 1998: 47).

From an employer's perspective, the ideal *'portfolio'* workers of the future are those who quickly internalise the need for employability, who willingly pay for their own continuous learning and who flexibly offer genuine com-mitment to each job, no matter how short its duration or how depressing its quality. There is more chance of Scotland winning the World Cup. A more likely and more rational response from employees would be to show loyalty in the future only to their own careers. But the rhetoric of that mythical beast, *the learning organisation*, requires total commitment from all workers, who in return are likely to be treated as totally expendable by footloose employers such as Siemens and Fujitsu. The equation does not add up and this conflict at the heart of the concept of *the learning organisation* helps to explain why so few, if any, organisations are worthy of the title.

Such views may be dismissed as the morbid anxieties of German soci-ologists from the unreconstructed Left. Consider, in that case, the recently expressed views of Alan Tuckett, Director of the National Institute for Adult Continuing Education and vice-chair of the government's National Advisory Group for Continuing Education and Lifelong Learning:

> I find to my surprise that I have been thinking about compulsory adult learning … In the information industries continuing learning is a necessary precondition to keeping a job, and your capacity to keep on learning may affect the job security of others. Learning is becoming compulsory. And if it is true for people in some sectors of industry, why not for people who might want to rejoin the labour force later?
>
> (Tuckett, 1998)

It is not too difficult to detect in this quotation not only the voice of moral authoritarianism which Walter Heinz (1999) believes to be the hidden agenda behind the rhetoric but also mounting frustration among liberal educators who, after 20 years in the political wilderness, have now become policy advisers and are confronted with the same, seemingly intractable statistics on low levels of participation in lifelong learning by certain groups. Within a short time, however, genuine social concern to widen the social base of participation appears to be turning opportunities to learn into impositions to be obeyed. Ivan Illich and Etienne Verne (1976) predicted such an outcome when they argued that lifelong learning would become 'not the symbol of our unfinished development, but a guarantee of our permanent inadequacy' and would constantly reassign learners to their place in a meritocracy (Illich and Verne, 1976: 13). Compulsory emancipation via lifelong learning is a contradiction in terms.

Please also take into consideration the British Government's policy framework on competitiveness, which is set out for the next 10 years in the DTI's White Paper on *Our Competitive Future* (1998a). This document is so one-sided it could have been written by the Institute of Directors; for example, it claims that the 'DTI will ... champion business needs in government' (1998a: 61). Surely it is the role of government to champion the public good and the national interest, which is frequently in conflict with the short-run needs of business. Moreover, the White Paper contains no discussion of the fundamental changes in the labour market *as they affect workers*, such as the move to core and peripheral workforces, i.e. the simultaneous growth of longer working hours for some and of many more casual, part-time, temporary and insecure jobs for others. In higher education, for example, the proportion of staff on fixed-term contracts is increasing (41.1% of the total in 1996–97), while the proportion on permanent contracts is declining. No measures are included in the White Paper to protect workers from galloping flexibility, but it does list no less than 75 commitments, many of which are *designed 'to reduce the burdens of unnecessary regulation'* on business (DTI, 1998b: 21).

Seventy-five proposals for government action suggest that 'old-fashioned state intervention' is still popular with politicians. And the introduction of a national minimum wage, the signing of the Social Chapter and the implementation of the Working Time Directive (a limit of 48 hours of work a week) are welcome examples of positive action by this government, which are detailed in the White Paper, *Fairness at Work* (DTI, 1998b). The Prime Minister explains, however, in his Foreword to the White Paper that these proposals 'put a very minimum infrastructure of decency and fairness around people in the workplace' (DTI, 1998b). But if redundancies, contracting out, delayering, casualisation, mergers and shifting investment overseas intensify, workers, their families and communities will need more protection than that provided by 'a very minimum infrastructure'. Moreover, *Fairness at Work* takes an uncritical and complacent view of what are called the two 'keys to securing efficiency and fairness ... employability and flexibility', with the latter being talked up as follows: 'By enabling business success flexibility promotes employment and prosperity' (1998b: 14).

According to Peter Mandelson, the former Secretary of State for Trade and Industry, in an article introducing *Our Competitive Future*, 'the starting point for the Government's analysis is that knowledge and its profitable exploitation by business is the key to competitiveness' (Mandelson, 1998). So knowledge which is created by universities with public funds is to be transferred to British firms who will then 'exploit' it for private profit. No hint appears in the White Paper that this proposal creates moral, financial and logistical problems. Socrates taught me that knowledge would set me free; Peter Mandelson tells me that its modern function is to make employers rich. It is time to turn from the pleasures of criticism to the pain of creation.

So what is to be done?

What follows are some reflections on possible ways forward, reflections which have been shaped by 5 years of working for the ESRC's[9] *Learning Society Programme* and by the findings produced so far by the 14 projects. The earlier disclaimer needs to be repeated – no one but the author should be held responsible for these recommendations for action, which are offered as a constructive contribution to the public debate.

A more detailed plan of action will come later and will tackle such issues as the changes which need to be made to the curriculum. The intention here is to present parts of a skeleton, to use feedback to produce some solid flesh and then, given a favourable wind, to breathe life into what is admittedly only an idiosyncratic selection of four disconnected bones.

A historical caveat is appropriate here. In 1972, Edgar Faure, the former French Prime Minister, as Chairman of an international Commission established by UNESCO, published a report, *Learning To Be*, which proposed 'lifelong education as the master concept for educational policies in the years to come' (Faure, 1972: 182). It has not happened; instead, flexibility has become the master concept in Western societies and Faure's enlightened and democratic vision of lifelong learning has been largely and unfairly forgotten (see Roger Boshier, 1997). *Education Permanente* proved to be a rather transient phenomenon and the same fate may befall lifelong learning.

Although the consensus remains the dominant discourse, alternative visions of the learning society are beginning to be articulated, especially by the ESRC Programme. Such creative dissent is healthy in a democracy, but we have in the UK no forum where the positive qualities of all these possible futures begin to coalesce into one policy. Let us be clear about the importance of the issue. In discussing various versions of the learning society, we are talking about the present and future shape of British society and how our systems of education, training and employment can help us to realise the type of society we want to create. It is also worth considering why the ESRC decided to commission research into the learning society rather than, say, 'the socially just society' or 'the competitive society'. What is being developed in the UK is best described as a *flexible society*, fit for the global market. And the most appropriate slogan for the National Campaign for Learning should, in my opinion, be 'Lifelong learning: your flexible friend for your flexible future'. The education system is to be modernised, but some of the worst features of modernity (e.g. the dark side of the market principle, polarisation, and 'the concentration of power without centralization of power' [Sennett, 1998: 55]) are being built into it.

Whatever vision is finally decided upon, it will have to deal directly with capitalism, which is now the only show in town. In Anthony Giddens's words, 'No one any longer has any alternatives to capitalism - the arguments that remain concern how far, and in what ways, capitalism should be governed and regulated' (Giddens, 1998: 43–44). But Richard Sennett (1998) argues powerfully that the aim of curbing the destructive aspects of the new capitalism should have a rationale beyond restraint: 'it must ask what value is the corporation to the community, how does it serve civic interests rather than just its own ledger of profit and loss?' (1998: 137). Armed with this insight, let us examine the Training and Enterprise Council [TEC] National Council's call for 'a competitive society which succeeds in achieving a dynamic equilibrium between wealth creation and social cohesion, between competitiveness and social inclusion' (1997). This appears to be an astute compromise, but the government has inherited a serious disequilibrium and the UK needs more than social cohesion; it also needs a renewal of democracy, citizenship and social justice.

Preference is therefore accorded with the stance of Martin Carnoy and Henry Levin, who argued that 'the relationship between education and work is dialectical – composed of a perpetual tension between two dynamics, the imperatives of capital and those of democracy in all its forms' (1985: 4). For over 20 years, the economic imperative has dominated the democratic imperative and it will take a long, hard and concerted struggle to redress the imbalance. What is needed is a new consensus but, as Isabelle Darmon and her colleagues have shown, 'the nature and workability of these compromises very much depend on the relative strength of the institutional actors' (Darmon et al., 1999: 40). New 'terms of engagement' between the main players also need to be introduced and that issue is addressed now.

A new social contract between the state, business, trade unions and education

The present framework for developing policy and the current consensus, shot through as it is with economic values, have failed this country. As argued earlier, our productivity gap with our major trading competitors is substantial and is not closing, and the deprived continue to receive a deprived education, which is both socially unjust and economically inefficient. The most important lesson we could learn from Europe is that this divided society could begin the process of healing by developing jointly agreed plans for our future through *social partners*. What is needed is nothing less than a new social contract (please not a *'strategic partnership'*[10]) between the state, business, trade unions and education, each of which should be treated as equal and respected partners.

The government is right to insist that a fundamental change in culture is needed in both education and business, but the government must take the lead by showing itself capable of such change. There is little prospect of developing a culture of lifelong learning in the UK if the government itself does not become a model of learning. Similarly, we need a government which routinely uses research (including disconcerting findings) in the formation of policy, a government which welcomes constructive criticism, a government which is not only prepared to tolerate dissent but one which recognises and uses the innovative potential of dissenting voices. In a knowledge-driven economy, the government must take the lead by showing how it incorporates the latest knowledge, namely research findings, into its thinking and policies.

The consultations which the DfEE engaged in over the goals and priorities of the department (DfEE, 1997b) are evidence of a welcome change in style from the *dirigiste* approach of the previous administration. But a major change of heart has still to take place right across government: can departments, for instance, desist from claiming that their latest initiatives are instant successes before any independent evaluation has even begun? Such ministerial claims of instant success are as satisfying as instant coffee. Given the departure of Peter Mandelson, the DTI's 1998 White Paper on *Our Competitive Future* will also have to be set aside and a new start made with a new Secretary of State who should produce a White Paper acceptable not only to the CBI but also to the other social partners.

Education also needs to improve upon its usual negotiating stance (that of the pre-emptive cringe) and make demands of its partners in the new social contract. Just as industrialists have realised that education is too important to be left to teachers, so we in education must argue that British business is too important to be left to employers and politicians. For example, if the Shell Oil Company can be pushed into establishing a Social Responsibility Committee (in response to the vigorous protests of consumers to the Brent Spar incident), then all major firms could be positively encouraged to act likewise. Learning at work has also become so significant in the creation and management of knowledge (see Coffield, 1997b) that a statutory framework is needed to prompt employers:

- to establish learning committees with representatives from management and workers;
- to develop in conjunction with unions learning agreements which lay out the rights and responsibilities of both parties;
- and to account for their investment in the learning of all their staff (full-time, fixed-term and part-time) in annual reports. (See Trade Union Congress [TUC], 1998, for detailed proposals for the union card to become an access card to learning.)

Furthermore, British financial markets should be exhorted to invest in new businesses (see Gerald Holtham, 1998) not in Malaysia, Morocco or Manitoba but in Middlesbrough, Manchester and Motherwell. The ownership and location of major industrial enterprises *does* matter and, for all that the arrival of Nissan has been beneficial to the North-East, the profits of the work of over 4,000 North-easterners are still transmitted to Japan; and the North-East remains a branch plant economy, with the key decisions about its future being taken in Japan, USA and London. It will, however, take determined action by a supra-national power (e.g. the European Union) to protect the rights of workers and their communities in dealings with multinationals whose main loyalty is to the maximisation of profits.

The Faure report rightly predicted that industry and commerce would develop extensive educational functions and that education would need 'to work hand in hand with industry' (1972: 199). Education should further develop the many types of productive relationships which have been formed over the intervening years with business, provided it remembers that 'the primary concern of the schools should not be with the living that [the students] will earn with but the life they will lead' (Halsey *et al.*, 1961, foreword). The tensions come from the multifaceted role of education, which seeks to develop participating citizens, wise parents and discriminating consumers, sceptical thinkers and decent human beings and lovers, as well as creative workers. But an unofficial hierarchy of types of learning is being created with *'learning for earning'* at its apex. What must be resisted are the great moral purposes of education being reduced to serving the needs and demands of business. To quote the DTI White Paper yet again, 'The Government wants to help businesses get the skills they want and to get the best out of education and training providers' (1998a: 31). With friends like that in high places, education should publicly reaffirm its broader mission. It also needs to be surer of the professional contribution it brings to the new social contract; that issue is dealt with next.

Put a new theory of learning into the learning society and into lifelong learning

There is a large hole in the heart of the government's policies for lifelong learning and the same fatal weakness can be detected in the rhetoric about the learning society: plans are afoot to create a new culture of lifelong learning without either any theory of learning or a recognition that a new *social* theory of learning is required. Briefly, a *social* theory of learning argues that learning is located in social participation and dialogue as well as in the heads of individuals; and it shifts the focus from a concentration on individual cognitive processes to the social relationships and arrangements which shape, for instance, positive and negative 'learner identities' which may differ over time and from place to place (see Lave and Wenger, 1991; Rees *et al.*, 1997).

Such a social theory also criticises the fashionable eulogising of learning and the denigration of teaching by treating teaching and learning not as two distinct activities but as elements of a single, reciprocal process. Moreover, this social theory is transforming the study of the transfer of knowledge (see Yrjo Engestrom, 1998).

To ask a politician, a civil servant or a professional specialising in education what their theory of learning is and how it helps them improve their practice tends to produce the same kind of embarrassed mumblings that result from a direct question about their sexual orientation. Teaching and learning remain, even for many experts in education, unproblematical processes of transmission and assimilation, but no learning society can be built on such atheoretical foundations. It is to be hoped that the new ESRC Programme in *Teaching and Learning* will help plug the hole.

Within *The Learning Society Programme*, the theoretical advances made by Michael Eraut et al. (1998) on non-formal learning, implicit learning and tacit knowledge; the research by Gareth Rees et al. (1997) into the central significance (still largely unrecognised) of informal learning and of the widening contexts for learning; and the project by Pat Davies and John Bynner, describing the spectacular success in London of the credit system of learning in attracting non-traditional adults (e.g. ethnic minorities and unemployed adults) into learning are just three examples of the many contributions being made to put the learning[11] into the learning society.

Informal learning was not the central focus of any of the 14 projects within *The Learning Society Programme*, but it quickly became clear to a number of project directors that it represents a largely neglected aspect of lifelong learning. Both policy and academic discourse on access to, provision of, and achievement in lifelong learning concentrate heavily on formal education and training. And yet the latter constitutes only a small part of work-based learning, which was 'non-formal, neither clearly specific nor planned. It arose naturally out of the demands and challenges of work – solving problems, improving quality and/or productivity, or coping with change – and out of social interactions in the workplace with colleagues, customers or clients' (Eraut et al., 1998: 1). This finding, which was replicated by other projects, requires us to reassess our conventional understanding of lifelong learning as exclusively concerned with target-setting, formal courses and qualifications. The policy implications of this finding are also significant: the need to appoint and educate managers who know how to develop their staff by creating a climate which promotes informal learning.

The concept of lifelong learning also needs to be rescued from all those pressure groups who have adopted this wide-ranging term to pursue their sectional interests in a particular phase within education. For example, there are adult educators who argue in a self-interested way that no further resources should be spent on initial education because it would 'puff up a front-loaded system to new dimensions rather than fostering a system of lifelong learning' (e.g. Schuller, 1996: 2). It makes more sense, however, to prevent thousands of young people leaving school unprepared to compete for jobs in a knowledge-driven economy than to build extensions to the system to cope with failure. What is also required is a new cadre of professionals who owe their loyalty to lifelong learning and not to a particular phase.

Use an appropriate model of change

The same task of creating a change in culture confronts the three sectors under discussion – government, business and education – but the model of change thought appropriate for education now varies to an extreme degree from those employed in the other two areas. Since 1988, a powerful hold on education has been taken by the state via legislation (e.g. a national curriculum backed by national testing; the market principle to encourage competition among parents, students and institutions; and a quality control system to enforce compliance), but in stark contrast, 'the Government believes that it is for business itself to consider how ... it can achieve the best results' (DTI, 1998a: 48).

Increased powers for ministers are proposed in the most recent White Paper from the DfEE to restructure the teaching profession (e.g. 'a contractual duty for all teachers to keep their skills up-to-date' and 'a national Code of Practice for training providers and a new inspection programme' [DfEE,, 1998c: 8]). Paul Black's strictures on the debacle over the introduction of the National Curriculum and assessment should be remembered: 'in the management of educational change, our national approach has been clumsy to the point of incompetence' (Black, 1995: 8). Yet little appears to have been learned from these failures. The Labour Government is attempting to transform the teaching profession on which it depends to implement its reforms, but it has already squandered much of the goodwill of the profession, despite devoting an additional £19 billion to education and introducing a whole raft of welcome new measures. The crass tactic of 'naming, blaming and shaming' schools thought by the Office for Standards in Education (OFSTED) to be failing has been dropped, but the reappointment of the Chief Inspector of Schools signalled to the profession that the Prime Minister still thinks teachers are part of the problem rather than part of the solution. The government urgently needs a new model of change to release the creativity and commitment of teachers, but the more teachers' professional practice is hollowed out by top-down change, the less the likelihood of developing independent-minded and enterprising young people who know how to learn throughout their lives.

How many of us believe, for example, that if a clear majority of the teaching profession rejects the proposals for performance-related pay, they will not be implemented? If the proposals are to be introduced irrespective of the reasoned objections of the profession, then the consultation exercise is a dishonest sham. Teachers' leaders should not only be consulted (receiving information and submitting their own ideas) but should also be involved in the decision-making process (forming the policy and influencing the final decision). Twenty-five years ago, the Faure report described governmental attempts at reforming education:

> The aim appears to be to act *on* teachers - for them, possibly, but rarely with them. This technocratic paternalism is based on distrust and evokes distrust in return. Teachers, on the whole are not against reforms as much as they are offended at the way they are presented to them, not to mention imposed on them.
>
> (Faure, 1972: 181, original emphasis)

Hence, the importance of governments showing they can learn from past mistakes by involving teachers from the beginning in their plans for reform as well as encouraging teachers' ideas for reshaping the system to bubble up from below.

Tackle inequalities and structural barriers

The findings of projects within *The Learning Society Programme* confirm a longstanding, brutal and awkward truth: the roots of educational disadvantage lie beyond education in our social structure and so beyond the remit of the DfEE (see, for example, Gorard *et al.*, 1998 and Ball *et al.*, 1999). Concerted action by the government as a whole will be needed, for example, to respond to the 9 million adults in Britain living in poverty (below 50% of average income after housing costs) or the 2.2 million children in a family receiving Income Support (see the Acheson Report, 1998: 34). Contrary to the government's beliefs, structure is separable from standards, but education is *not* the best economic policy we could have. Educational policy needs to be integrated with an industrial strategy and with a well-resourced, community-focused, anti-poverty campaign.

Revealingly, the government has announced that it will publish the 'Competitiveness Index – to track British performance and guide policy development' (DTI, 1998a: 8), but has been slower to respond to the demands for an annual poverty and social exclusion report (see Catherine Howarth *et al.*, 1998, who have produced a model of what such a report should cover). And Tom Schuller and Caroline Bamford (1998) have called for the 'annual publication of a state of the nation report on lifelong learning', part of which could be devoted to an account of the action taken to combat unjustifiable inequalities and structural barriers in education.

There remains, of course, a powerful but secondary role for education to play. Having reviewed the mounting evidence on educational polarisation, of the kind referred to in Newcastle earlier, the Acheson report comments 'Logic and equity argue that children most in need should receive increased resources for their education' (Acheson, 1998). It specifically recommends that 'The Revenue Support Grant formula and other funding mechanisms should be more strongly weighted to reflect need and socio-economic disadvantage' (1998: 39). But instead of continually pleading for extra help to be extended to the casualties of the system, it would be preferable to mainstream equality, that is, 'integrate equal opportunities into all structures and systems, and into all policies, programmes and projects' (1998: 39). (See Teresa Rees, 1998 for further explanation.)

It is also not difficult to find examples of structural barriers which militate against the interests of a lifelong learning culture and which need to be swept away: the 16-hour rule which controls the amount of time the unemployed can devote to study; the indefensible differential in the funding of part-time and full-time students; output-related funding which encourages 'cream skimming' (i.e. the concentration on those most likely to obtain a qualification); and the remorseless drive in all sectors of education and training to demand more for less.

The scale of the task facing policy-makers can be gauged from one of the conclusions of the project within *The Learning Society Programme*, directed by Gareth Rees *et al.* in South Wales. They argue that removing barriers to participation, such as costs, time and lack of childcare, will have only a limited impact because:

> those who failed at school often come to see post-school learning of all kinds as irrelevant to their needs and capabilities. Hence, not only is participation in further, higher and continuing education not perceived to be a realistic possibility, but also work-based learning is viewed as unnecessary.
> (Rees and Bartlett, 1999: 11)

Moreover, as Secretary of State for Education and Employment, David Blunkett should seize the historic opportunity, missed by Sir Ron Dearing, to replace the divisive binary line between further and higher education with a *tertiary* system that celebrates diversity. Students would not only move from further to higher education but also, as happens in the Community Colleges in the USA, from higher to further education for postgraduate vocational training. Running prestigious, high-level courses of continuing professional development for British scientists and engineers (e.g. master degrees while at work) would help to raise the status of further education colleges and of the *University for Industry*, which runs the risk of becoming associated primarily with basic skills courses for the unemployed – important though these courses are. The learning society needs to be underpinned by multiple learning opportunities at every age, at every stage and at every level of achievement.

All of these inherited problems could be rectified, but there would still remain significant obstacles such as the lack of high-quality jobs in the labour market. This point reinforces the general argument that there are strict limits to an *educational* solution to creating a learning society. And addressing both the inequalities and the barriers means, of course, redistributing income and wealth via increased progressive taxation.

Notes

1 Avis *et al.* prefer the term settlement because it 'extends beyond that of consensus in providing for the possibility of inconsistencies and contradictions. Settlements are based upon superficial consensus and, though prone to rupture and disintegration, are marked by their capacity to hold diverse interests together within an unstable equilibrium which has to be continually reworked and remade' (1996: 5). On the other hand, Richard Sennett plumps for 'regime' because 'it suggests the terms of power on which markets and production are allowed to operate' (1998: 55).

2 The charts on the productivity gap, the R and D gap and on underinvestment in the United Kingdom are to be found in The Treasury's Pre-Budget Report (1998), on pages 29, 33 and 37, respectively.

3 Alison Wolf describes how successful the CBI has been as a lobbying organisation for the large corporations: 'Thanks to its activist policies-the promotion of NVQs, the development of training targets-it has seen off the threat of compulsory levies' (Wolf, 1998: 13).

4 The first report of the National Skills Task Force explains its vision in the following terms: 'To compete effectively on the world stage, employers need access to the best educated and best trained workforce; to compete effectively in a dynamic labour market, individuals must acquire the skills needed; while education and training providers and Government must be responsive to those requirements' (DfEE 1998b: 11).

5 In a major speech on education in 1992, Bill Clinton argued that 'In the 1990s and beyond, the universal spread of education, computers and high-speed communications means that what we earn will depend on what we can learn and how well we can apply what we learn to the workplaces of America' (quoted by Halsey et al., 1997: 8).

6 At a conference for researchers within *The Learning Society Programme*, an industrialist, who deserves to remain nameless, was invited to comment on the shape and objectives of the programme as a whole. The inclusion of a project on 'The Meaning of the Learning Society for Adults with Learning Difficulties' was, he thought, an inappropriate use of scarce research resources.

7 See the research of Geoff Whitty, Sally Power and Tony Edwards (1998) for data on the very close connection between the status of the university attended and the type of job (and size of salary) obtained. Graduate unemployment varies considerably across pre- and post-1992 universities according to data from the Higher Education Management Statistics group.

8 These researchers distinguish four models: the *schooling* model which aims at high levels of participation; the *credentialist* model which prioritises qualifications; a model which stresses improving *access*; and a *reflexive* model which 'prioritizes learning as a major feature of all social relationships' (1997: 534).

9 I should like to thank the ESRC publicly for the opportunity to carry out the most exciting and the most demanding job I have ever had and the researchers in the 14 projects for teaching me so much.

10 As I have written elsewhere (Coffield, 1990), 'strategic partnerships' are the kind of weasel words used by bureaucrats when they wish to disguise a major shift in power or resources; for example, the DfEE currently recommends a 'strategic

partnership' because it wishes to transfer part of cost for lifelong learning to employers and individuals.

11 The phrase is Michael Eraut's (forthcoming) and it deserves to be repeated and spread abroad.

References

Acheson, Sir D. (1998) *Independent inquiry into inequalities in health.* London, Stationery Office. Cheltenham: Edward Elgar.

Ashton, D. and Green, F. (1996) *Education, Training and the Global Economy.* Aldershot: Edward Elgar.

Avis, J., Bloomer, M., Esland, G., Gleeson, D. and Hodkinson, P. (1996) *Knowledge and Nationhood: Education, Politics and Work.* London: Cassell.

Ball, S. J., Macrae, S. and Maguire, M. (1999) Young lives at risk in the 'futures' market: Some policy concerns from on-going research. In Coffield, F. (ed) *Speaking Truth to Power: Research and Policy on Lifelong Learning.* Bristol: Policy Press, 30–45.

Baron, S., Stalker, K., Wilkinson, H. and Riddell, S. (1998) The learning society: The highest stage of human capitalism? In Coffield, F. (ed) *Learning at Work.* Bristol: Policy Press, 49–59.

Becker, G.S. (1975) *Human Capital: A Theoretical and Empirical Analysis, With Special Reference to Education* (1st edition 1964). Chicago, IL: University of Chicago Press.

Berg, I (1973) *Education and Jobs: The Great Training Robbery.* Harmondsworth: Penguin.

Black, P. (1995) *Ideology, Evidence and the Raising of Standards.* London: Second Education Lecture, King's College, London, 11 July.

Blackmore, J. (1997) The gendering of skill and vocationalism in twentieth-century Australian education. In Halsey, A.H., Lauder, H., Brown, P and Wells, A.S. (eds) *Education: Culture, Economy and Society.* Oxford: Oxford University Press, 224–239.

Blair, T. Rt Hon (1998) Quoted in Department for Education and Employment, *The Learning Age: A Renaissance for a New Britain.* London: Stationery Office, Cm 3790, 9.

Boshier, R (1997) *Edgar Faure after 25 Years: Down but Not Out. Conference Paper, Lifelong Learning: Reality, Rhetoric and Public Policy.* University of Surrey, Department of Educational Studies, 4–6 July.

Carnoy, M. and Levin, H.M (1985) *Schooling and Work in the Democratic State.* Stanford: Stanford University Press.

Castells, M. (1998) *End of Millenium,* Vol. III. Oxford: Blackwell.

Coffield, F (1990) From the decade of the enterprise culture to the decade of the TECs. *British Journal of Education and Work,* 4(1), 59–78.

Coffield, F. (1997a) The concept of the learning society explored. *Journal of Education Policy,* 12(6), 449–558.

Coffield, F. (Ed.) (1997b) *Learning at Work.* Bristol: Policy Press.

Cohen, S (1985) *Visions of Social Control.* Cambridge: Policy Press.

Confederation of British Industry (1989) *Towards a Skills Revolution.* London: CBI.

Darmon, I., Frade, C. and Hadjivassilliouh, K. (1999) The comparative dimension in continuous vocational training: A preliminary framework. In Coffield, F. (ed) *Why's the Beer up North Always Stronger? Studies of Lifelong Learning in Europe.* Bristol: Policy Press, 31–42.

Department for Education and Employment (1997a) *Excellence in Schools.* London: Stationery Office, Cm 3681.

Department for Education and Employment (1997b) *Living and Working Together for the Future.* Sudbury: DfEE Publications.

Department for Education and Employment (1998a) *The Learning Age: A Renaissance for a New Britain*. London: Stationery Office, Cm 3790.

Department for Education and Employment (1998b) *Towards a National Skills Agenda*. First Report of the National Skills Task Force, London: DfEE.

Department for Education and Employment (1998c) *Teachers: Meeting the Challenge of Change*. London: Stationery Office, Cm 4164.

Department of Social Security (1998) *A New Contract for Welfare: New Ambitions for Our Country*. London: Stationery Office, Cm 3805.

Department of Trade and Industry (1998a) *Fairness at Work*. London: Stationery Office, Cm 3968.

Department of Trade and Industry (1998b) *Our Competitive Future: Building the Knowledge Driven Economy*. London: Stationery Office, Cm 4176.

Edwards, T (1998) A daunting enterprise? Sociological enquiry into education in a changing world. *British Journal of the Sociology of Education*, 19(1), 143–147.

Engestrom, Y. (1998) Transfer of knowledge. Conference Paper at COST *All Conference* at the University of Newcastle, 28 November.

Eraut, M. (forthcoming) Non-formal learning, implicit learning and tacit knowledge. In Coffield, F. (Ed.) *The Necessity of Informal Learning*. Bristol: Policy Press.

Eraut, M., Alderton, J., Cole, G. and Senker, P (1998) *Development of Knowledge and Skills in Employment*. Brighton: University of Sussex, Institute of Education, Research Report No. 5.

Faure, E. (Ed.) (1972) *Learning To Be: The World of Education Today and Tomorrow*. Paris: UNESCO.

Fevre, R (1997) *Some Sociological Alternatives to Human Capital Theory and Their Implications for Research on Post-Compulsory Education and Training*. Cardiff: University of Cardiff, School of Education, Working Paper 3.

Giddens, A (1998) *The Third Way: The Renewal of Social Democracy*. Cambridge: Polity Press.

Gorard, S., Rees, G., Renold, E. and Fevre, R (1998) *Family Influences on Participation in Lifelong Learning*. Cardiff: University of Cardiff, School of Education, Working Paper 15.

Halsey, A. H. *et al.* (1961) *Education, Economy and Society*. New York: Free Press.

Halsey, A.H., Lauder, H., Brown, P. and Wells, A. S (1997) *Education: Culture, Economy and Society*. Oxford: Oxford University Press.

Heinz, W. (1999) Lifelong learning-learning for life? Some cross national observations. In Coffield, F. (Ed.) *Why's the Beer Up North Always Stronger? Studies of Lifelong Learning in Europe*. Bristol: Policy Press, 13–20.

Hewison, J., Millar, B. and Dowswell, T. (1998) *Changing patterns of training provision: Implications for access and equity*. Swindon: Economic and Social Research Council, end of award report.

HM Treasury (1998) *Pre-Budget Report: Steering a Stable Course for Lasting Prosperity*. London: Stationery Office, Cm 4076.

Hodkinson, P., Sparkles, A. C. and Hodkinson, H (1996) *Triumphs and Tears: Young People, Markets, and the Transition from School to Work*. London: David Fulton.

Holtham, G. (1998) Lie Back, think of South Korea, *The Guardian*, 3 August.

Howarth, C., Kenway, P., Palmer, G. and Street, C (1998) *Monitoring Poverty and Social Exclusion: Labour's Inheritance*. York: New Policy Institute and Joseph Rowntree Foundation.

Howells, K. (1997) Howells Welcomes Kennedy Report to the Further Education Debate. *Department for Education and Employment Press Release*, 1 July.

Illich, I. and Verne, E (1976) *Imprisoned in the Global Classroom*. London: Writers and Readers Publishing Cooperative.

Joseph Rowntree Foundation (1995) *Inquiry into Income and Wealth*. York: Joseph Rowntree Foundation.

Joseph Rowntree Foundation (1998) *Income and Wealth: The Latest Evidence*. Edited by John Hills, York: Joseph Rowntree Foundation.

Karabel, J. and Halsey, A.H (1997) *Power and Ideology in Education*. New York: Oxford University Press.

Keep, E. and Mayhew, K (1998) *Was Ratner Right? Product Market and Competitive Strategies and Their Links with Skills and Knowledge*. London: Employment Policy Institute.

Lave, J. and Wenger, E (1991) *Situated Learning: Legitimate Peripheral Participation*. New York: Cambridge University Press.

Levin, H. M. and Kelley, C. (1997) Can education do it alone? In Halsey, A.H., Lauder, H, Brown, P. and Wells, A. S. (eds) *Education: Culture, Economy and Society*. Oxford: Oxford University Press, 240–251.

Mandelson, P. (1998) We are all capitalists now. *The Daily Telegraph*, 17 December.

Rees, T (1998) *Mainstreaming Equality. Inaugural Lecture*. Bristol: University of Bristol, School for Policy Studies, 15 October.

Rees, T. and Bartlett, W. (1999) Models of guidance services in the learning society: The case of the Netherlands. In Coffield, F (ed) *Why's the Beer up North Always Stronger? Studies of Lifelong Learning in Europe*. Bristol: Policy Press, 21–30.

Rees, G., Fevre, R., Furlong, J. and Gorard, S (1997) *Notes Towards a Social Theory of Lifetime Learning: History, Place and the Learning Society*. Cardiff: University of Cardiff, School of Education, Working Paper 6.

Robinson, P. and Oppenheim, C (1998) *Social Exclusion Indicators*. London: Institute for Public Policy Research.

Schuller, T (1996) *Building Social Capital: Steps Towards a Learning Society*. Inaugural Lecture, Centre for Continuing Education, University of Edinburgh.

Schuller, T. and Bamford, C (1998) *Initial and Continuing Education in Scotland: Divergence, Convergence and Learning Relationships*. Edinburgh: Centre for Continuing Education, Edinburgh University.

Schuller, T. and Burns, A. (1999) Using social capital to compare performance in continuing education. In Coffield, F. (ed) *Why's the Beer up North Always Stronger? Studies of Lifelong Learning in Europe*. Bristol: Policy Press, 53–61.

Schultz, T. W. (1961) Investment in human capital. *American Economic Review*, 51, 1–17.

Sennett, R. (1998) *The Corrosion of Character: The Personal Consequences of Work in the New Capitalism*. New York: W. W. Norton.

Tight, M (1998) Lifelong learning: Opportunity or compulsion? *British Journal of Educational Studies*, 46(3), 251–263.

Trade Union Congress (1998) *Union Gateways to Learning: TUC Learning Services Report*. London: Trade Union Congress.

Tuckett, A. (1998) Recruits conscripted for the active age. *Times Educational Supplement*, 22 May.

Walden, G. (1996) *We Should Know Better: Solving the Education Crisis*. London: Fourth Estate.

Whitty, G., Power, S. and Edwards, T. (1998) Education and the formation of middle class identities. Paper given at ECER Conference, Ljubljana, Slovenia, 19 September.

Wolf, A. (1998) The training illusion. *Prospect*, August/September, 12–13.

Young, M., Spours, K., Howieson, K. and Raffe, D (1997) Unifying academic and vocational learning and the idea of a learning society. *Journal of Education Policy*, 12(6), 527–537.

Chapter 9

Learning styles

Time to move on

The bandwagon of learning styles turned into a hearse. David Moseley, Elaine Hall, Kathryn Ecclestone and I carried out a systematic and critical review of the 13 most influential learning styles, which found them to be unreliable, invalid and of negligible impact on practice. We concluded that the field of learning styles is theoretically incoherent and conceptually confused. Overblown claims about success with all age groups and all types of students only served to give the field a bad name. This article first appeared as an opinion piece, published by the National College for School Leadership in 2013.

Dr John Brennan, then CEO of the Association of Colleges, made the best introduction to a conference I have ever heard. He began by explaining that, after finalising his opening remarks, he turned to his wife and said: 'Darling, did you ever in your wildest dreams imagine that one day your husband would open a conference with more than a thousand delegates?' 'John', she replied, 'in my wildest dreams, you don't ever appear'.

Introduction

Whatever your views on Ofsted – and mine are unequivocal that the millions the government devotes each year to this organisation would be far better spent on staff development for teachers within a rigorous system of peer review – I have to admit that the recent changes it has made to inspection have at last turned teaching and learning (henceforth T&L) into the number one priority for schools and colleges. For someone like myself who used *Just suppose teaching and learning became the first priority* ... as a title of a publication in 2008, such a change should have sounded like Mozart to my ears, but I have reservations as I shall explain.

All teachers from the newest entrant to aspiring heads and principals are acutely aware that from now on no school will be judged 'outstanding', unless T&L in that school are considered outstanding. A further innovation is that the leadership of T&L will now be evaluated by Ofsted, whose new chief considers that such leadership consists of four features: a passion for T&L; a commitment to high-quality professional development; effective monitoring

DOI: 10.4324/9781003476146-13

of T&L; and robust (a typical, hectoring adjective) performance management (Wilshaw, 2012).

I'd like to suggest that *the* most essential feature is missing from that list of managerial concerns, namely, a solid, extensive and constantly updated base of knowledge about T&L on which to build a culture of learning in every school. The new demand that headteachers and principals become not just efficient business managers but *inspirational educational leaders* will require them to be (or become) experts in T&L. Senior leaders will have to be comfortable, for example, about being asked what is their theory (or theories) of learning and how they use it (them) to evaluate and improve their practice and that of their colleagues. To be more specific, they will need to have considered views, informed by up-to-date evidence, on current debates and controversies within T&L; for example, what interventions have been shown to have the biggest impact on students' learning? How can we most efficiently introduce change into complex, social institutions like schools? Are synthetic phonics the best way to teach children to read? Is dyslexia just a label used by pushy parents to get their children extra help or a genuine learning disability? How effective is the teaching of 'emotional' intelligence or thinking skills? How do we get students at all levels of ability to become better at learning? And, to come finally to the topic of learning styles, are they more of a hindrance than a help?[1]

Evidence on learning styles

I have been studying the research literature on learning styles since 2003 and have written up my findings in a series of publications, aimed at practitioners (2004a, 2005, 2012) and academics (2004b, 2012). The four most important limitations of the LS approach can be stated very briefly here, but readers who want access to detailed evidence and arguments are referred to the full reports.

First, the literature on learning styles is theoretically incoherent and conceptually confused; for example, endless, overlapping and poorly defined dichotomies such as 'verbal' v 'auditory' learners; 'globalists' v 'analysts'; and 'left brainers' v 'right brainers' for which there is no scientific justification. I counted 29 such confusing dichotomies in the literature and they are listed in Coffield (2012).

Second, not all learning styles questionnaires are alike, some are better than others. That said, of all of the 13 most popular models which we examined in detail, only one met the four minimal standards for a psychological test and it was designed for use, not in education, but in business.

Third, the questions posed in learning style tests are devoid of any particular context, as though learning was a free-floating skill which is independent of the subject or problem being studied. It is not possible, for instance, to learn to become a hairdresser or a plumber by using the same learning style. In plumbing, it is usual for an apprentice to learn by trial and error how to bend a copper pipe with a blow torch, but that kinaesthetic approach is likely to lead to some seriously singed heads in the salon.

Interestingly, the German-speaking educational world has rejected the notion of learning styles because their strong pedagogical tradition objects fundamentally to the notion of styles of teaching and learning which are generalised and divorced from content and context. The learning styles movement has unwittingly led to a devaluing of knowledge and Stephen Johnson, in his searching critique of thinking skills, has argued that 'appropriate, detailed, subject-specific knowledge renders thinking skills redundant' (2010: 27). I would contend that the same applies to learning styles.

Fourth, to answer the question that is of most interest to practicing teachers, I found no hard evidence that students' learning is enhanced by teaching tailored to their learning style. A comprehensive American study concluded in 2009 as follows:

> ... there is no adequate evidence base to justify incorporating learning styles assessments into general educational practice ... limited education resources would better be devoted to adopting other educational practices that have a strong evidence base
>
> (Pashler et al., 2009: 105)

And there are plenty of such practices to choose from (e.g., Wiliam, 2011). So it comes as no surprise that within John Hattie's recent, monumental survey of 150 factors which affect students' learning, matching teaching to the learning styles of students was found to have an insignificant effect, a little above zero (2012: 79).

Practice of learning styles

For some years now, the research evidence has been clear, consistent and convincing: learning styles are invalid, unreliable and have a negligible impact on practice. How, then, am I to explain the fact that in virtually every school or college where I have given a talk on T&L, I have found at least one classroom with posters challenging students to discover whether they are visual, auditory or kinaesthetic learners? Elsewhere (e.g. Coffield, 2012), I have offered a variety of possible explanations (e.g., intuitive appeal; simple but spurious solutions to complex problems of T&L; need to differentiate and classify) for this curious paradox. But on re-reading my comments, I realise that I have omitted the most obvious and likely reason: most practicing teachers and senior leaders become steadily more and more remote from the research literature as they get further away from initial teacher education.

A recurrent programme of professional updating is urgently required to keep staff acquainted with that literature, which is, admittedly, often couched in the most off-putting jargon, although the best of it is not. We are back to the argument I made earlier about the need for all teachers, and especially those whose job it is to exercise leadership on T&L, to have a firm knowledge base on the subject. Without such a knowledge base, leadership becomes little more than 'the blind choice of one route over another and the confident pretence that the decision was based on reason' (Harris, 2004: 5). One of the principal criteria of a profession is that it possesses a body of specialist knowledge which it uses, together with the craft knowledge derived from practice, to improve.

What is unprofessional in my view is to administer a learning style questionnaire to all new students at the beginning of the term, analyse the results, inform the students of their preferred learning style, file the forms away in a drawer and then continue teaching as before without any further reference to learning styles. To act in such a way raises and dashes students' expectations, leaving some of them (whom I have met) with the erroneous idea that, as they believe themselves to be 'kinaesthetic' learners, the whole curriculum should be presented to them kinaesthetically.

Coda

The Roman Emperor Hadrian, who ordered the construction of the Pantheon in Rome as well as the wall from the Solway Firth to Tynemouth, was once described as follows: 'In one and the same person [he was] stern and cheerful, affable and harsh, impetuous and hesitant, mean and generous, hypocritical and straightforward, cruel and merciful and always in all things changeable' (Historia Augusta, 1921). Instead of building on these insights to explain the complexities, inconsistencies and apparent contradictions of human beings known to the ancients and to the greatest dramatists and novelists like Montaigne, Shakespeare, Dickens and Tolstoy, learning style theorists have developed simplistic, self-report tests. They are devoid of context and force the takers of these tests to choose between predetermined categories such as 'pragmatists' or 'theorists'. The tests do not allow you to be a pragmatic theorist or a theoretical pragmatist. It is high time that the teaching profession moved on from these pre-scientific instruments which carry the real danger of labelling and trapping students into fixed categories which have little or no research evidence to back them.

Note

1 There is a vibrant research literature on all these topics and a useful introduction to these controversies and many others can be found in Adey and Dillon (2012).

References

Adey, P. and Dillon, J.(Eds.) (2012) *Bad Education: Debunking Myths in Education.* Maidenhead: Open University Press.

Coffield, F. (2005) *Learning Styles: Help or Hindrance?* Research Matters, No 26, Autumn. Institute of Education, National Schools Improvement Network, www.nsin.org.

Coffield, F. (2008) *Just Suppose Teaching and Learning Became the First Priority ....* London: LSN.

Coffield, F. (2012) Learning styles: Unreliable, invalid and impractical and yet still widely used. In Adey, P. and Dillon, J. (eds) *Bad Education: Debunking Myths in Education.* Maidenhead: Open University Press, 215–230.

Coffield, F., Moseley, D., Hall, E. and Ecclestone, K. (2004a) *Should We Be Using Learning Styles? What Research Has to Say to Practice.* London: Learning and Skills Research Centre, LSDA.

Coffield, F., Moseley, D, Hall, E. and Ecclestone, K. (2004b) *Learning Styles and Pedagogy in Post-16 Learning: A Systematic and Critical Review.* London: Learning and Skills Research Centre, LSDA.

Harris, R. (2004) *Pompeii.* London: Hutchinson.

Hattie, J. (2012) *Visible Learning for Teachers: Maximising Impact on Learning.* London: Routledge.

Historia Augusta (1921) *The Life of Hadrian.* London: Heinemann: Loeb Classical Library.

Johnson, S. (2010) Teaching thinking skills. In Winch, C. (ed) *Teaching Thinking Skills.* London: Continuum, 1–50.

Pashler, H., McDaniel, M., Rohrer, D. and Bjork, R. (2009) Learning styles: Concepts and evidence. *Psychological Science in the Public Interest,* 9(3), 105–119.

Wilshaw, M. (2012) High expectations, no excuses. Speech on 9 February, Ofsted.

Wiliam, D. (2011) *Embedded Formative Assessment.* Bloomington, IN: Solution Tree.

Chapter 10

Coffield's learning or teaching styles questionnaire (CLOTS 2008)™

I produced this spoof questionnaire to counter the seemingly unstoppable progress of learning styles. At a conference where I had used the evidence presented in Chapter 9 to urge teachers to stop using learning styles, one teacher told me she would go on using them as she had printed out hundreds of copies. A student then said he had stopped attending his maths classes at the university because the staff had refused to present the curriculum to him kinaesthetically. He had been convinced at school that this was the only way he could learn. The questionnaire was first published as Appendix 2 of Frank Coffield (2008) *Just suppose teaching and learning became the first priority ...* London: Learning and Skills Network.

At Keele University, Phil Robinson and I were awarded a research grant to study Sir Keith Joseph's notion of Transmitted Deprivation. I was then invited to Suningdale Civil Service College to give a talk on our research proposal in front of Sir Keith and the Permanent Secretaries of the relevant ministries. As a young lecturer, I was daunted by the prospect, but thankfully the ice (and there was a distinctly icy atmosphere in the room) was broken by Professor Basil Bernstein who spoke before me.

He began by writing on the blackboard the word 'heirarchy' (sic). Before he could correct himself, Sir Keith intoned: 'You've made a mistake there, Professor'. Basil spun around, threw the chalk up in the air, caught it and asked 'You pay me a lousy £100 for this lecture and you expect spelling as well?'

I got to know Basil over that weekend and so invited him to give the same talk to students at Keele. At that time, he was such a towering figure in education that he attracted a crowd of students and staff from local colleges of education as well as from the university. He walked to the front of the lecture hall, claimed (improbably) to be nervous before such a large audience and pleaded for someone to throw down a cigarette. Within minutes, the floor was littered and he began to sift through the offerings. 'Capstan Full Strength? Not bad. Sobranie? Better still. Ah, my favourite, Gauloises. But who's had the nerve to offer me Embassy Six?' He threw that fag back into the crowd, while explaining that he'd just given an example of hierarchy and off he launched

DOI: 10.4324/9781003476146-14

into his lecture. As he spoke, he filled an empty cigarette packet with his choice of the fags on the floor.

Coffield's learning or teaching styles questionnaire (CLOTS, 2008)™

Write your name, sex and maternal grandmother's favourite colour in the space I've forgotten to provide.

1 **I learn best by:**
   a internalising the wit and wisdom of Homer Simpson on TV ☐ V
   b listening to myself talk ☐ A
   c throwing the books at the wall ☐ K
   d rubbing the bumps on my forehead (sorry, pre-frontal cortex) ☐ T
   e following the clear, simple instructions of the IT staff ☐ O
   f listening to boring speakers and working out why
      I disagree with them. ☐ !

2 **My brain hurts when:**
   a I see students being labelled 'pragmatists' or
      'theorists' after a 10-minute questionnaire. ☐ V
   b I listen to politicians making vacuous speeches
      on education based on only the evidence they like. ☐ A
   c I forget to take a glass of Côte de Rhone with every
      glass of sparkling Buxton water. ☐ K
   d I compare the very tangible benefits for those attending a
      City Academy against the damage done to other local schools. ☐ T
   e I try to make a connection between answering 10 daft
      questions and how I learn or teach. ☐ O
   f I'm completely VAKT. ☐ !

3 **I've worked out the incredibly sophisticated theory behind this questionnaire, so I'm tempted not exactly to cheat or lie but to apply a little spin. I am:**
   a Tony Blair ☐ XPM
   b Howard Gardner ☐ Prof
   c Brain Jim ☐ CLPTRP
   d Alistair Campbell ☐ BGSTNRD
   e Ruth Kelly ☐ WHO?
   f Chris Woodhead ☐ RTWLR

4 **I learn best with:**
   a a fag in my mouth ☐
   b a glass of 25-year-old Macallan in my hand ☐

c a double espresso stiffened with a little pill ☐
d a wet towel round my head ☐
e without a theory or definition of learning; I just 'suck it and see' ☐
f all of the above, while listening actively to my partner ☐

5 I learn best after:
a hearing of my team's latest 1-0 annihilation of Man U ☐
b two weeks in the Bahamas ☐
c organising our early retirement ☐
d reading deeply about theories of learning ☐
e the spontaneous joy felt on hearing about
   the government's latest initiative this week ☐

6 I'd describe my teaching style as:
a modelled on Gradgrind ☐
b fuelled by Mogadon ☐
c better than those who can only inspect ☐
d good enough ☐
e student centred; I give the little buggers equal respect ☐

7 The metaphor which best describes my teaching style is:
a subject seller ☐
b young people's friend ☐
c government apparatchik ☐
d controller of the untamed ☐
e socratic ☐

8 As a tutor, I'm able to take only one of the following. I would choose:
a a 10% pay cut ☐
b weekly meetings with the parents of all
   my students who present difficulties ☐

(No, you must tick one box)

9 I differentiate my class into:
a one group ☐
b two groups ☐
c three groups ☐
d four groups ☐
e what's differentiation? ☐

10 Learning, like child rearing, is always fun. I've most fun when:
a teaching Level 1, Basic Maths revision ☐   S-M
b watching my team lifting the Cup ☐   NCL (hope springs eternal)
c clubbing 'til 4 am ☐   HDNST

d   I take my clothes off and …   ☐   NYM
e   in staff meetings we revise our   ☐   BRWNSE
    Mission Statement yet again

TECHNICAL DATA

RELIABILITY   : zero
VALIDITY   : no tests carried out
IMPACT ON PRACTICE   : nil
But please, don't let these findings   © Frank Coffield, 2008
    deter you from using it.

Chapter 11

Rolling out 'good', 'best' and 'excellent' practice

What next? Perfect practice?

Gwendolen in *The Importance of Being Ernest* resists the suggestion that she is perfect as that would leave no room for development. Sheila Edward and I, in an article for the *British Educational Research Journal, 2009* (35(3), 371–390), explored the government's strategy for developing the education system by identifying and disseminating 'good practice'. 'Good practice', however, is no longer good enough, nor is 'best practice'. The requirement now for post-compulsory education and training is nothing less than 'excellent practice for all'. This article critically examines these significant shifts in the rhetoric of policy, finds them wanting and argues that we need to face up to the complexities involved in deciding not only what is 'excellent practice' but also in working through all the stages which would be needed to transmit it throughout the sector. We attempted to explain the frenetic activity of politicians and policy-makers in this sector, and ended by moving from critique to construction by considering what can be rescued from the inherently contestable notion of 'good practice', and, in doing so, drawing heavily on the work of Robin Alexander.

When studying for an MEd degree at Glasgow University after completing an undergraduate degree in Classics, I was astounded when the Professor of Education, Stanley Nisbet, wrote on the board the equation 'Plato = Hitler'. I'd read Plato's Republic in the Greek Department, but no member of staff had ever thought to discuss its contents. Stanley Nisbet's equation was his way of introducing Sir Karl Popper's The Open Society and its Enemies, which I quickly devoured.

Some thirty years later, I noticed that Sir Karl was due to give a public lecture, the title of which, 'Darwin's Theory of Evolution Disproved', intrigued me. This ninety-year-old hobbled on to the stage with the aid of sticks and spoke with a thick Viennese accent. I can remember his whole lecture as it consisted of only these sentences: 'I've used my notion of falsifiability to test Darwin's theory and I've failed. End of lecture. Any questions?' The first questioner expressed his surprise that he'd even tried to disprove a theory that was backed by so much evidence. Popper broke in to say: 'You are surprised, Professor? Imagine the veritable shock I had when I first thought of the idea'.

DOI: 10.4324/9781003476146-15

Introduction

The 'Champion of the Agenda for Change' at the Learning and Skills Council (LSC),[1] who is a seconded further education principal, described recently how he was spending much of his time visiting further education colleges and private training providers up and down the country 'looking at best practice and publicising it' (Dowd, 2006). That statement prompts the following questions: how does he know that what he looks at is best practice? What criteria or norms is he using to make these judgements? How does he deal with the immense diversity and complexity of local contexts? Will best practice be used by other tutors just because it has been so labelled and publicised? And what are the implications for the quality of teaching and learning in colleges if he is wrong?

The identification and dissemination of 'good', 'best', or 'effective' practice are not minor, technical matters, but a central part of the government's strategy 'to radically change the whole of the post-16 landscape' (Rammell and Haysom, 2006: 2). These three adjectives are used interchangeably in official texts, although one might have expected a qualitative difference between 'good' and 'best' practice; after all, did not Voltaire argue that the best is the enemy of the good?

In England, centrally determined policy seeks to 'drive' the improvement of teaching and learning in the post-compulsory sector. Hence the stream of policies and initiatives from the Department for Education and Skills (DfES) which aim to put 'teaching, training and learning at the heart of what we do by establishing a new Standards Unit (SU) to identify and disseminate best practice' (DfES, 2002: 5). Our research project on the impact of policy on learning and inclusion in the postcompulsory sector[2] suggests that perhaps the reverse approach should at least be considered: the processes of teaching and learning are the heart of the enterprise and should therefore be a major influence on policy. The main mission of the sector, *pace* the Foster Report (2005)[3] and the White Paper on Further Education (EE) (2006),[4] is *not* employability, which proposes an individual solution to a systemic problem, but raising the quality of teaching and learning in general, vocational and adult education.

The first task is to appreciate the implications of the complexities of teaching and learning in specific localities and only then to devise policies to respond to those implications. We need an approach that constructs policy, based on a deep understanding of the central significance of what happens in classrooms, for example, by first assessing the needs of learners, tutors and institutions, the demands of practice, the conditions of local labour markets and how these (and many other) factors interact differently and dynamically in particular areas.

A high-profile example of centralised policy making in this sector is the focus on 'good' or 'best' practice, which has recently been intensified into a concentration on excellence; or as the White Paper on FE boasts: 'we will eliminate failure' (DfES, 2006: 56). This article critically examines these highly significant shifts in the rhetoric of policy, finds them wanting and suggests that we need to face up to the complexities involved in deciding what is 'good practice' and how it can be transmitted. Much research has been published on the difficulties of transfer, from the pioneering research of Edward Thorndike (1913) to the model of transfer as a learning process proposed by Michael Eraut, but there remains 'profound ignorance of the nature and amount of the [new] learning involved' in transferring knowledge from one setting to another (Eraut, 2004: 201).

What is at the heart of the sector?

Confusion reigns within official circles and even within the same policy text as to what constitutes the heart of post-16 learning. For instance, the White Paper on FE confidently states on its first page that 'the needs and interests of learners and employers [are] at the heart of the system' (DfES, 2006: 1). Only five pages later, the needs and interests of learners have been forgotten and the government shows its true colours by claiming, 'we will put the economic mission of the sector at the heart of its role' (p. 6). On page 41 of the same document, 'qualification reform' has become 'the heart of our strategy', but five pages later comes another change of heart, so to speak: 'a continued drive for quality improvement is at the heart of this White Paper' (p. 46). *Either* the sector has one enormous, all-embracing heart and no head, *or* it has four separate hearts, or different civil servants draft different chapters within the same text without reference to each other, *or* the government, desperate to transform the sector quickly, is uncertain which of its myriad proposals is the most important and hopes that some combination of measures will magically prove to be effective. Whatever the explanation, the result is sloppy thinking, which sends out contradictory messages.

Our own view, formed from studying 24 learning sites (12 in the North-East and 12 in London) in FE colleges, Adult and Community Learning (ACL) centres and work-based learning (WBL) providers,[5] is unequivocally that the relationship between tutor and student is, or should be, at the heart of the sector. The emphasis should be placed *neither* on learning alone, *nor* on teaching by itself, but on the interactive processes of teaching and learning, which should be viewed as the two inseparable sides of the same coin. When teacher and learner are engaged in some shared activity, 'the teacher is a learner, and the learner is, without knowing it, a teacher – and upon the whole, the less consciousness there is, on either side, of either giving or receiving instruction, the better' (Dewey, 1961: 160). We particularly wish to oppose the modish celebration of students' learning, as if it could somehow be dissociated from the teaching of their tutors or the assessment of their work. If we are right, then the main policy questions become: what are the characteristics of effective teaching and learning relationships? What pedagogy (or pedagogies) is most suitable for the wide variety of subjects taught in vocational education? What educational, social and financial arrangements will best promote such relationships? And what institutional and political climates and strategies help or hinder such relationships? The role of this article, however, is to explore the government's attempt to reform the sector by, in part, disseminating 'good', 'best' and now 'uniformly excellent' practice.

From 'good' to 'best' practice

Government policy in this sector operates like a ratchet screwdriver with no reverse movement allowed; only constant forward progression is acceptable, e.g. 'all provision must be consistently good and continuously improving' (DfEE, 1999: 43). In the rest of the world, the learning curves of students acquiring a new skill, understanding or ability, as studied by psychologists, typically show: sudden bursts of improvement, an occasional plateau where nothing new is apparently being learned but consolidation may be taking place, and also dips in performance, which can be deep and prolonged, where learners appear to forget what they had previously provided evidence of acquiring. No such 'normal' deviance from a smooth upward curve is tolerated by politicians and policy-makers, who insist on nothing less than continuous improvement by all providers and learners. The 'normal' patterns of learning are a serious obstacle to steady upward progression, so they are ignored, if they were ever known, by those who demand that ever more 'stretching' targets are met.

In January 2003, the Standards Unit (SU) was established as part of *Success for All*, which sets out the government's strategy to transform the sector in order to 'identify and disseminate good practice' (DfES, 2002: 12). Later in the same document, the job of the SU has become the identification of 'best practice' in the four areas of 'delivery' methods, assessment, content and teaching and training techniques (p. 31). The terms 'good' and 'best' practice are apparently interchangeable and unproblematical; they are also undefined, but somehow their meaning is considered to be widely understood and agreed. The difference between 'delivery methods' and 'teaching and training techniques' is also left unexplained. The SU was required to produce for each of these four areas 'the key deliverables' of: guidance to practitioners, an intensive face-to-face training programme, revised initial teacher training, an 'ongoing support programme' and teaching materials (p. 31). These materials are to be 'incorporated directly into lesson plans' (Association of Colleges, 2005: 8). Little is being left, it appears, to the skilled judgement of professionals.

A DfES research project into *Factors Influencing the Transfer of Good Practice* criticised governmental assumptions that 'good practice' can be so easily identified and transferred. It commented: 'The concept of a common decontextualised practice may be nothing more than a delusion' (Fielding *et al.,* 2004: 58). Two of the key findings of this study (e.g. that talk of transfer marginalises the importance of developing new ways of working which fit the different professional setting of the partner who has to learn the 'good' practice; and the need for extended periods of time for 'joint practice development') present considerable difficulties to the model of transfer chosen by the SU. By autumn 2005, the SU had produced Teaching and Learning Frameworks in eight curriculum areas from Construction to Health and Social Care. Each framework contains 'a teacher guidance book, a range of learner resources, teacher-training resources including training videos and DVDs (where appropriate) and guides and a CD-ROM, illustrating the approaches and containing support materials and session plans' (www.successforall.gov. uk [accessed 15 July 2005]).

The main criterion for success, as always with such curriculum materials, will be how extensive is the take-up among those practitioners who were not part of the trials and pilots. The SU's approach was to invite each post-16 learning organisation in England to nominate a 'subject learning coach' for each of the eight priority curriculum areas, with the intention of training 3,000 of these coaches by March 2006. In what were rather insensitively called 'master classes', the 'best demonstrated practice' which had been observed in particular pilot sites was offered as a resource to practitioners in a wide variety of colleges or private training firms (see Cousin, 2004).

One difficulty for this approach is that it is of little help to practitioners to talk in generalities about 'good practice', as Office for Standards in Education (Ofsted) reports tend to do. For example, in their report *Evaluating mathematics provision for 14–19-year olds,* the inspectors claim that the strongest and most inspirational teaching in numeracy programmes:

- Conveyed enthusiasm for mathematics
- Stemmed from robust subject knowledge
- Showed excellent classroom skills
- Embedded the work in compelling and relevant vocational contexts (2006: 11).

Good maths teachers and competent heads do not need visits to 26 schools, sixth-form colleges and FE colleges to reach such obvious conclusions. What practitioners want is, for example, help with teaching Business Finance as part of the Edexcel GNVQ (General National Vocational Qualification) course to Level 2 students, who range from able, female immigrants from Somalia with little English to indigenous working-class lads with a long history of failure in maintained schools. The general point is well summarised by *Brown et al.*: 'knowledge is situated, being in part a product of the activity, context and culture in which it is developed and used' (1989: 32).

At the time of writing (in March 2007), there was no evidence available from national evaluations of the self-styled 'Transformation Programme', as the sources cited by the Quality Improvement Agency (QIA) (2006: 25)[6] proved, on request, to be interim studies not deemed by the DfES to be sufficiently rigorous to be placed in the public domain.[7] That leaves a study by Liz Browne which is descriptive rather than critical; nor is it strictly independent, as her data were collected by a consultancy firm 'acting on behalf of the Standards Unit' (2006: 276). Moreover, her response categories were restricted to 'Too soon to tell' and 'A little/some/significant impact' with no opportunity for the 17% of people who responded to record 'no impact' or even 'negative impact'.

The notion of spreading 'good' or 'best' practice is, however, fraught with further problems, which may help to explain why it happens so seldom. First, as David Hargreaves has pointed out:

> The term itself is ambiguous and flabby. Often 'good practice' and 'best practice' are treated as synonyms, although clearly 'best practice' suggests a practice that has been compared with others and has proved itself better than other 'good' practices.
>
> (2004: 72)

'Best practice' also implies that there is only one approach which, if used, will solve any difficulties. The notion of a single, optimum solution to a wide range of complex problems has also been seen by some commentators as the beginning of the slide into authoritarianism (see Scott, 1998).

'Excellent' practice could be interpreted as a more liberal term than 'best' practice, since excellent practices could be flourishing in many colleges across the country, just as there are plenty of excellent football teams in the Premier League but only one 'best' team. But in the official texts, 'excellent' is clearly meant to be an improvement on 'best', so it carries from 'best' the implication that there is One True Model, which only needs to be discovered and disseminated for standards to rise.

Those who consider that judgement exaggerated may care to consider the suggestion in the Prime Minister's Strategy Unit document on reforming public services that 'the best response may be for government to simply take a top down approach and to require the adoption of best practice' (PMSU, 2006: 58). The detailed example given is where 'the government has made a commitment to make synthetic phonics the prime method of teaching reading across the country' (58). The research referred to by the PMSU is not, however, sufficiently robust to support such a universal change in practice.[8]

Second, 'good practice' is always contingent on the professional judgement of particular tutors working with particular groups of students with varying needs in particular settings and is rarely based on any research evidence.

The critical questions remain: how do tutors form such judgements? What factors, values and local conditions do they consider? What counts as 'good' or 'best practice' varies from one learning site to another, and this is certainly the conclusion of the largest ever research project into FE. Their cultural approach helped them to see that 'the improvement of learning cultures always asks for contextualised judgement rather than for general recipes' (James and Biesta, 2007: 37). They argue that 'both "improvement" and "good practice" are terms that imply consensus or common-sense agreement, but which may *conceal* quite fundamental tensions' (original emphasis: 144).

Third, if a practice is labelled 'good' or 'best', then it is incumbent on the labeller to specify explicitly the basis for that judgement; this is rarely, if ever, done and is not done by the SU.

So any claim that a particular method or resource is 'good' or 'best practice' needs to be met with the following questions: Who says so? On what evidence? Using what criteria? 'Best' for whom? Under what conditions? With what type of students? If what is officially promoted as 'best practice' turns out to be bad practice, will the learners be compensated?[9] As Rice and Brooks argued, in relation to teaching dyslexic adults in the Skills for Life (SfL) initiative:

> Even if the judgment [about 'best practice'] is backed by an appropriate theoretical background and teaching experience, it remains a judgment and one likely to be challenged by the next professional with similar background and experience.
>
> (2004: 86)

We need a much firmer basis for deciding what constitutes 'good practice'. After considering the views from practitioners we have interviewed, in the final section below, we will try to provide it.

Views from practitioners

The tutors we interviewed in colleges, adult and community learning and work-based learning sites were almost unanimous in identifying the needs of learners as the most important influence on their practice. They explained 'good practice' in relation to identifying and responding to the needs of the particular groups of learners we were studying, on Level 1 and Level 2 courses in colleges, or adult basic skills learners in the other sites. Many of those learners had been unsuccessful in their previous experience of education in school, and lacked confidence. A college tutor, talking about dealing with Level 1 nursery nurses, expressed succinctly a recurring theme in interviews with basic skills and subject tutors across all our sites:

> We have got to get them to that point where they believe in themselves.
>
> (AITI/2)

While few would have disagreed with that, the differences lay in the ways that they would help learners with widely differing needs get to that point: some focus on confidence building and showing learners that they are valued:

They need spoon-feeding until they get a bit of confidence up.

(B2Tl/3)

Others talked about team-building and encouraging mutual respect with a Level 1 group in order to foster inclusion and stifle bullying; about breaking down assignments into very small sections, to give learners tasks they could succeed in; or about the provision of learning support in the classroom and learning mentors. One course leader described how Level 1 childcare learners who had achieved that qualification but were not well equipped to cope with Level 2 would be steered towards a progression route which suited them, in, perhaps Art or Small Animal Care. Each solution could be seen as 'good practice' in achieving the professional goal of enabling learners *in a specific context* to believe they could succeed. The need for self-belief was universal; the means of achieving it differed between sites, and even between learners in the same site.

Were staff looking for handbooks of 'good practice' to guide them? Staff in two of our colleges had been involved in the work of the SU, producing materials and appearing in videos, and others had looked at the materials and thought they would be a useful source of new ideas. Some of those who did use them did so selectively:

They have got a Health and Social Care pack and there are bits in there that I have used, on Health and Safety and a bit on Child Protection and there is a little bit in about professional development, but there is nothing for us [in Childcare]. But we have got quite a lot. I make a lot of my own resources … I am quite imaginative with resources.

(A2Tl/4)

Another tutor had tried them, but used them selectively, having found they did not fit the needs of a particular group:

There are certain of the Standards Unit materials which I won't use. I think they are too-maybe set up for the 14-16 year-olds. There is a card game and I tried that on the apprentices, and for a few minutes they were interested, but they would rather see it on [the whiteboard].

(A2Tl/4)

This tutor possessed two sets of SU materials, one of which was still wrapped in cellophane, and the other had been opened but nearly all the contents were still in their original wrappers. His manager was a fan of the materials, but admitted that there was a reluctance on the part of tutors to use other people's materials:

> I think it's a natural reluctance that people always think that their material is better, but it's changing. What we say to people when we are doing best practice, we say: 'Here's ours. Have a look at it-do what you like with it'.
>
> (A2MI/2)

In District College, a Health and Social Care tutor reported that a Learning Coach had been trained and was providing training in incorporating games into teaching, which was seen as particularly valuable for tutors who had not been teaching for long. In Business Studies there, the manager thought the materials were being sampled, was not sure how widely they were being used, but believed that a 'joined up' approach involving both the materials and input from learning coaches might

> raise awareness and generate a bit of this innovation ... or you could adapt those materials to get across as a teacher what you want to deliver.
>
> (D2M2/5)

Another manager saw the potential for the SU materials to help both with teaching quality and financial constraints:

> What the Standards Unit is doing is teaching us to deliver in a different way and using a variety of methods and actually showing that it doesn't have to be expensive.
>
> (DIMI/5)

While the SU materials were aimed at college staff, Skills for Life teaching materials had been produced for basic skills tutors. In this context too, we found staff who, without being critical of the content of these materials, were very aware of the limitations of over-reliance on them by inexperienced tutors in some settings:

> People are giving [learners] out the workbooks-so you're no longer getting the toys, the play games, the bits that we have lying around: all you're get-ting now is, for ease and for speed and for keeping up with where you are, all you're getting is, 'It tells you to look at workbook 2. Here is workbook 2. If you get stuck, just come and see me: I'll be in the corner'.
>
> (MTI/2)

The overall message is that 'good practice' materials may only lead to crea-tive teaching if they are used imaginatively by a tutor who knows the needs of the particular group of learners and who has the experience and confidence to adapt them to that end.

If the 'secrets' of 'good practice' cannot be discovered by using pre-prepared materials, can they be distilled from the various elements which tutors identified, when asked what changes they were making to improve learning, and what they considered 'good practice' in their area? Regrettably, we think not. The list would be too long, and include individual traits, such as commitment, empathy with the learners, patience, skill in explaining expectations of learners and in providing challenging feedback, flexibility and willingness to work long hours on lesson preparation, assessment and administration; characteristics and cultures of course teams, such as sharing ideas and resources, ensuring a consistent approach in dealing with learners, planning together, sharing a professional background and knowing the needs of the employers in the sector learners are preparing to enter; and factors in management and organisational culture, such as ensuring that staffing levels are adequate, that the conditions for staff to remain lifelong learners exist, and that staff feel valued stay motivated, and share the vision of the organisational leadership.

The list could be longer, but the problem is that we could never claim that the list was exhaustive, nor that it could do justice to even one of the 24 learning sites we visited, unless that context were discussed in exhaustive detail. It would also contain internal contradictions: for example, a very cohesive team of childcare tutors, all formerly nursery nurses, were justly proud of their closeness to employers and excellent knowledge of the sector their learners would work in; but to suggest that such conditions become an essential prerequisite for 'good practice' would be to devalue the efforts of tutors working with less collegial support, in less clearly defined vocational areas, such as Business Studies, but still providing excellent teaching and support, and working long hours at nights and weekends to ensure that their learners achieved.

At managerial level, the list would highlight differences between managers who valued stability, motivation and commitment in their teaching teams, others whose focus was mainly on responding to policy levers and driving up numbers for retention and achievement, and others who still wish to encourage innovation in teaching methods. One manager described 'good practice' in terms of compliance and keeping up with changes deriving from government policy, to maximise funding:

> I suppose a year of consolidation would be nice, but it's not likely to happen ... If we're told basically, 'This is what you do: this is what we suggest you do and your funding depends on it', then is that not what we do?
>
> (B2M3/5)

Another, intent on raising achievement through close monitoring and teaching focused primarily on students' assignments, declared candidly:

> I don't care about the staff, to be honest. If they want to leave, I'll get more.
>
> (C2Ml/2)

Unsurprisingly, that did prove necessary. Our point here is that meanings of 'good practice' are contested, both within and between levels of staffing in organisations, and, if we look across all 24 learning sites, these differences multiply. We are also mindful that our sample of sites is tiny in comparison with the 6 million learners in the learning and skills sector (LSS), and that we were originally directed towards that sample by college or LSC managers who identified them as examples of 'good' or interesting practice.

From 'best practice' to 'excellence'

In early 2006, the government rationalised all the agencies involved in quality improvement and accountability; it established the Quality Improvement Agency (QIA) and a single inspectorate, the Adult Learning Inspectorate being amalgamated into Ofsted. These moves are part of the constantly changing architecture of organisations in the post-compulsory sector. The arrival of new bodies with new Chief Executives also allows Ministers not just to continue but to intensify policy: the number of priorities is increased, the criteria for the success of the new organisation become more numerous and explicit and, in the case of the QIA, 39 'key deliverables' for nine areas of work are listed on three pages (see Annex C, Grant Letter to QIA, Kelly, 2006). So, according to Andrew Thompson, the new Chief Executive of QIA, its job is to move the sector 'from a culture of improvement via compliance to a culture of excellence' (Thompson, 2006). No mention is made of the fact that 'the culture of compliance' was and remains a rational response by providers to the plethora of policy initiatives from government.

The QIA has already spawned a set of new acronyms, for it has produced a three-year Quality Improvement Strategy (QIS), engaged with a Quality Improvement National Advisory Group (QINAG) and worked with the LSC to establish Regional Quality Improvement Partnerships (RQIPs). The QIA will be closely controlled by the DfES, not only by the most detailed and challenging of remits but also by an annual review of progress and by 'Ministerial reviews ... held on a quarterly basis from July 2006 onwards' (Kelly, 2006: 4). In short, the QIA is a Non Departmental Public Body in name only, and it will be micro-managed by the DfES, which seems unable to wean itself from a culture of command and control, as recommended by the Foster Report (2005).

A central part of the QIA's remit is 'the drive for excellence' (QIA website, www.qia.org.uk [accessed 23 May 2006]). Some of its earliest tasks were to define excellence, articulate a vision of it and 'assist the sector to build excellent organisations with the capacity for self-improvement' (QIA website, www.qia.org.uk [accessed 23 May 2006]). In March 2006, the DfES published the first ever White Paper on FE and emphasised the same broad themes. The sector is charged, for example, with 'ensuring that the quality of teaching and learning is uniformly excellent' (DfES, 2006: 18) and warned that the government will take 'decisive action to eliminate failure' (p. 55). These phrases may well return to haunt the department, which in a year or two will need a new form of exhortation, as it seeks 'deliberately and significantly [to raise] the bar of quality and performance' (p. 24). But how do you improve on 'uniform excellence'? Can the demand for ubiquitous perfection be far behind? Such unattainable objectives could only have been written by politicians and policy-makers who are seriously remote from the realities of teaching Level 1 students in FE colleges, or adults with learning difficulties in ACL centres, or employees in WBL who have never received an hour's training in over 20 years of work.

Another worrying feature of this intemperate rhetoric is its implicit model of learning and of learners. Nowhere in the official texts are the differences between 'good', 'best' or 'excellent' practice defined; so their meaning remains implicit, as if we all understood and agreed on what they mean. Similarly, the government is silent about what it means by learning, but a close reading of the texts suggests that a narrowly conceived 'acquisition' model of learning is favoured where learning is thought of 'as gaining possession over some commodity' (Sfard, 1998: 6). For instance, the QIA has to provide 'appropriate packages of support to teachers and trainers' and 'ensure effective transfer within the provider network' (Kelly, 2006: 3 and 8). The intensely complex processes of learning and transfer are thought of as a simple matter of delivering packets of 'good practice' to professionals, who apparently digest them without difficulty and then pass them on to colleagues who absorb them with similar ease. Those who have researched transfer explain why it happens so rarely:

> What is transferred is not packages of knowledge and skills that remain intact; instead, the very process of such transfer involves active interpreting, modifying and reconstructing the skills and knowledge to be transferred.
> (Thomi-Gröhn et al., 2003: 4)

Michael Eraut conceptualises transfer in terms of no less than five interlocking stages which are briefly described here:

- Potentially relevant knowledge has to be recognised and extracted from the practice identified as 'good' or 'best'.
- The different social contexts of the 'old' and of the 'new' situation have to be understood, a process that often depends on informal social learning.
- The knowledge and skills relevant to the new situation have to be recognised.
- They have then to be transformed to fit the particular features of the new context.
- Finally, the relevant knowledge and skills have to be combined into an integrated, holistic performance that allows the professional to think, act and communicate effectively in the new, improved practice.

These are not simple processes which can be learned quickly, and they do not appear anywhere in official accounts of sharing best practice across the system. Is it any wonder that Eraut concluded by claiming 'that traditional thinking about transfer underestimates the learning involved by an order of magnitude' (2004: 220)?

It is time we took Bourdieu's advice about 'the restitution of the complexity of problems' (1998: 106) and restored to policy discussions and documents a recognition of the complexities involved in teaching, say, disaffected young people who have come to see themselves as unworthy human beings and as incompetent learners after 11 years of formal schooling.

This article will explore these complexities below; but first, new strategies have been published by the government in 'the drive for excellence'.

The pursuit of excellence

In June 2006, the QIA issued for consultation the first draft of the QIS, called *Pursuing excellence: an outline improvement strategy for consultation*; and a month later, the LSC published a complementary document, entitled *Framework for excellence: a comprehensive performance assessment framework for the further education system*. In January 2007, the QIA produced the first ever National Improvement Strategy for further education (QIA, 2007). The dawn of the age of excellence has truly broken. The texts from the QIA are concerned with the quality of teaching and learning in classrooms and that from the LSC with the performance of institutions.

What, however, is the scale of the problem to which these two new strategies are the response? The White Paper on FE describes the extent of the problem:

> 2% of colleges are currently assessed by inspectors as inadequate, 20% of colleges have at least one curriculum area regarded as unsatisfactory, and 5% of leadership and management in colleges is unsatisfactory. Inspection results for work-based learning … indicated that 12% of providers were inadequate.
>
> (DfES, 2006: 15)

Moreover, the QIS indicates (2007: 6) that success rates have exceeded, by 3 percentage points and two years early, the target of 72% set by *Success for all* (DfES, 2002).

So this is not a sector in crisis and yet it is to be subjected to a new set of intensive performance indicators because of some, admittedly serious, problems at the margins. Government ministers and senior civil servants appear to have formed a deficit model of the whole sector and now propose to scrutinise all institutions and professionals within the LSS by applying, as we shall see, a new panoply of regulatory measures. Pressure from the media, which will follow the publication of college league tables, and which has done such damage to primary and secondary schools via 'naming and shaming', will now be unleashed on the LSS, which seems incapable of learning from experience in other educational sectors.

The documents from the QIA and the LSC are clearly inspired by a genuine concern to improve the quality of learning and skills (the word 'education' is, however, systematically avoided) in the sector, but they both contain the same fundamental weaknesses and other specific faults.

First, both begin with brief political rationales for the new wave of reforms being introduced, rationales which are naive, insulting and inaccurate. Naive, because government ministers from both the main parties have for over a generation peddled the myth that improving the skills base will on its own create economic prosperity. Insulting, because the professionals and commentators working in the sector realise that other factors are equally, if not more, important, such as investment in physical capital, in research and development and in innovation; moreover, employers need to improve the quality of jobs, goods and services via training, but they are left by the government to train or, as happens so frequently in the UK, *not* to train their workers (Keep, 2007). Inaccurate, because the economic returns to investment in skills are declining, as more and more young people graduate and face competition from well-educated and professionally trained graduates from Eastern Europe and the Far East (Brown, 2006).

Second, the documents aim to transform the sector by providing 'excellence for all' and yet neither has an explicit model of change nor a theory of learning. To have no view of learning could be considered a serious deficit in a Learning and Skills Council, and similarly, one would expect a QIA to have a model of change.

Third, both strategies contain unrealistic expectations: 'All colleges and providers should be able to perform to excellent standards' (Rammell and Haysom, 2006: 2). Moreover, the QIS has as one of its objectives that success rates should 'become equally outstanding for learners from different backgrounds' (2007: 9). They list in great detail the desired benefits of their proposals, but neither contains an assessment of their perverse and unintended consequences. Unintended they certainly are, 'but unforeseeable they are not' (Arrowsmith, 2006). The LSC's *Framework for Excellence*, for instance, proposes seven new 'key performance indicators', but each of these is divided into several constituent measures, making up a minimum of 27 new indicators in all (see Annex B, LSC, 2006: 16). And yet the LSC believes the new regulatory framework will require 'the minimum of additional work' (p. 11). It would be laughable if it were not so serious.

There is also one serious anomaly in the new arrangements because the QIS will apply to school sixth forms, but the LSC's Framework will not; how, then, will the government be able to make comparisons across post-16 learning if different sections are to be judged by different performance measures?

Let us now turn to each document in turn as each merits serious consideration. The draft QIS, for instance, was not so much a strategy as a series of lists, suggesting it had been written by a committee and numerous partners, without strong editorial control. So it consisted of 11 characteristics of excellence; five characteristics of successful colleges; four 'principles for enabling transformation' (p. 4), which don't amount to a model of change; three aims later broken down into 14 priorities and 33 action points; eight key partners and 12 others consulted; five functions of the QIA; at least 10 measures of performance; and 18 questions for respondents to answer. The final version of the QIS follows the same pattern but is somewhat more restrained, consisting as it does of: three aims, 11 objectives, 12 priorities, five principles, 23 new targets and indicators of success and 34 responses to the final report of the Leitch review of skills. It is clear from this list what will dominate official thinking in the coming years – the move to a demand-led system.

In a similar vein, the DfES has produced a list of the qualities expected of teachers who are appointed to the 'Excellent Teacher Scheme'. The list runs to 87 characteristics, including the ability to 'show a consistent record of parental involvement and satisfaction' and to 'ensure successful learning by all pupils' (DfES, 2005a: 13). Such unrealistic standards amount to a counsel of perfection.

The draft QIS began by offering a definition of excellence: 'We believe that excellence means developing, maintaining and delivering to the highest standards of responsiveness, effectiveness and efficiency' (2006: 9). There are two serious problems with this definition. First, *what* is to be developed, maintained and 'delivered' to the highest standards? Second, the three big criteria by which the success of the strategy is to be measured are responsiveness, effectiveness and efficiency, but equity is not considered to be as important. So the FE sector would be judged a success by QIA if it could demonstrate that it was responsive, effective and efficient, even if it remained inequitable or were to become even more inequitable than it currently is. Certainly, the text went on to explain in more detail some of the main characteristics of its 'Pursuit of Excellence' and in seventh place, it argued that 'equality of opportunity is actively promoted' (p. 10). That, however, seriously demotes equity, which, ironically, is given unequal status to that of the three big criteria of responsiveness, effectiveness and efficiency. By page 19, the document was claiming that 'our notion of 'excellence' fully incorporates equality and diversity', but no detail was given of what that might entail.

The draft QIS also helpfully included in Annex D a list of definitions of 'learners', 'national partners' and so on. As discussed above, however, it contained no definition of learning or of 'good' or 'best' practice. Without such definitions, the sector is likely to flounder in a morass of unexamined and untestable empiricism. Interestingly, the final version of the QIS omits the definition of excellence, Annex D and any mention of equity.

The second text is the LSC's *Framework for Excellence*, which is part of the government's aim to 'develop an FE system that is responsive to the needs of our economy and our society' (Rammell and Haysom, 2006: 2); but neither the Minister of State for Lifelong Learning, Further and Higher Education nor the Chief Executive of the LSC are prepared to concede that the needs of the economy and of society are frequently in conflict; when, for example, business and industry create greater inequalities and social exclusion.

The LSC also wastes no time in withdrawing its iron hand from its iron glove. Systems of performance management are to be 'robust' (Foreword); standards will be 'demanding' (p. 6); a new category of 'underperforming' will be introduced (p. 6); intervention may consist of 'formal notice to improve or the removal of funding' (p. 6) and the process of self-assessment is to be 'rigorous and robust' (p. 7). It is not clear who will decide whether the self-assessment by colleges and providers is sufficiently 'rigorous and robust' – the colleges themselves, peers or perhaps Ofsted? What does this mean for self-regulation?

We have also been led to believe that the reshaped LSC wishes to establish new relationships with colleges and providers based on trust, and yet the Framework for Excellence warns:

> Chairs, Principals and Chief Executives will be expected to make a signed statement in annual reports to the effect that the performance ratings are an accurate reflection of the college's or provider's performance.
>
> (LSC, 2006: 11)

What happens if a principal refuses to sign? What if he or she considers that the statistics produced by the performance ratings seriously misjudge the qualitative work of his or her organisation? And what will such a requirement do for the relationships between the regulators and the regulated?

This framework is a concerted attempt to pin down the providers. It is also overwritten in what looks like a desperate attempt to placate the politicians; for instance, it talks of 'precise quantitative definitions' (p. 3) for the key performance indicators and twice claims 'the Framework deals with *absolute* standards rather than relative assessment' (LSC, 2006: 14 and 15, emphasis added). The idea that the work of a large city college with 20,000 students and 2,000 staff can be assessed under the seven headings of 'delivery against plan' (a euphemism for responsiveness to government), responsiveness to learners and to employers, quality of provision and of outcomes, and financial health against '*absolute* standards' betrays a failure to understand assessment and its limitations. All assessment fundamentally is based on judgements, and claims by the LSC that it can allocate funds based on 'absolute' judgements are spurious. The LSC is trying to judge quality and levels of achievement and is not measuring physical properties like the size of head or length of hair.

The tyranny of momentum

How are we, however, to explain the frenetic activity of politicians and pol-icy-makers in this sector, as they constantly increase the pressure on practi-tioners to move from 'good' to 'best' practice and now on to 'excellence for all'? They are driven in part by the need for quick results before the next gen-eral election in order to demonstrate that manifesto pledges have been kept. Peter Hyman, in his account of his time as chief speech-writer to the Prime Minister, shows the importance in modern politics of being in control of the media and of seizing the agenda: 'Momentum is essential or politicians are accused of drifting. This meant constantly coming out with initiatives, talking points, speeches, nuggets of policy' (2005: 384).

The culture of permanent restructuring, which particularly affects the LSS, also needs explaining. For Ewart Keep, state control of the English education and training system is akin to playing with the biggest train set in the world, where 'the cycle of intervention takes place to a pace and tempo dictated by the internal dynamics of the political process rather than the real needs of the education and training system and those who work within it' (2006: 55). It is difficult to resist the conclusion that such constant turbulence takes place in the LSS because the sector remains invisible to most politicians, academics and commentators, as, with very few exceptions, neither they nor their chil-dren have ever passed through it (see Coffield, 2007).

Politicians and policy-makers no longer concern themselves solely with strategic issues such as funding, targets and performance indicators, but with professional topics such as how students should learn, how tutors should teach and what methods they should use. Behind these simple-sounding but treacherous questions, however, lies a far deeper question, which the Nuffield Review of 14-19 Education and Training poses as follows: 'what counts as an educated 19 year old in this day and age?' (Nuffield, 2006: 1). It is an excel-lent question, but 19-year-olds and, for that matter, adults of all ages, today need more than a good, general education; they also need vocational training and a job worthy of a human being.

From critique to construction

So far, this article has probed and questioned the educational assumptions be-hind both existing policy and future proposals. It is time to consider whether anything positive and practical can be rescued from the inherently contest-able notion of 'good practice'. What follows is highly dependent on the work of Robin Alexander (1997), who has neatly dissected the term 'good practice' in relation to primary education. We have converted his analysis into the lan-guage and concerns of post-compulsory education, added to and re-ordered some of his analysis, but the original conception remains his and we are try-ing to build on his pioneering work.

Alexander proposed that there are five main dimensions of 'good practice', which he listed as:

- *political*, e.g. what practices does the SU (or other powerful groups) suggest I use?;
- *evaluative*, e.g. what practices do I most value or which best fit with my values?;
- *empirical*, e.g. what practices has research shown to be most effective?;
- pragmatic, e.g. what practices work for me and which do not? and
- *conceptual,* e.g. how do I marry my answers to the questions above to the essential elements of practice? What conceptions do I have of good teaching and good learning? This examination of 'good practice' necessarily leads us to scrutinise what we mean by 'practice'.

In post-16 learning, there are at least nine elements of practice that need to be considered:

- The context, e.g. what localities do teachers and students come from and how should that impinge on my practice (see Jephcote *et al.,* 2006)?
- Knowledge, e.g. how is the 'codified' knowledge learned in college to be related to the 'situated' knowledge of the workplace (see Guile and Young, 2003)?
- Curriculum, e.g. what selection of knowledge should be presented to these students?
- Pedagogy, e.g. do my teaching methods dovetail with the subject I'm teaching?
- Assessment, e.g. what is the backwash effect of the assessment criteria on my teaching and students' learning?
- Management, e.g. how do I plan, sequence and evaluate my practice? And what constraints have been imposed on my teaching by government policies as they have been translated into institutional practice by senior management?
- Students, e.g. what are their needs, capabilities and understandings?
- Professional training, e.g. what more do I need to know about teaching and learning?
- Society, e.g. what influence are local labour markets or particular employers having on my students, the college and its courses?

This is an illustration of what was meant earlier by restoring the complexity of the problems involved in deciding what constitutes 'good practice'; moreover, all of the above topics need to be addressed simultaneously as well as separately.

We are now in a position to put these two frameworks (the five dimensions and the nine elements) together in an attempt to answer the question: what

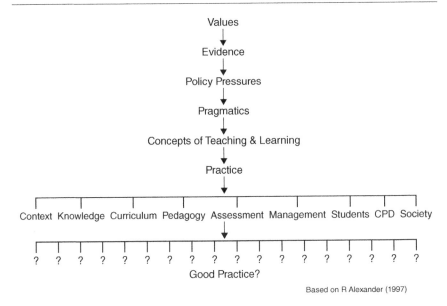

Figure 11.1 What is good practice?

is 'good practice'? Figure 11.1 sets out a typical intellectual journey which skilled and experienced practitioners are likely to follow in their own inimitable and probably implicit way. Most tutors are likely to agree that the five dimensions are not all equally important, and there is likely to be considerable debate about what order they should be placed in. Figure 11.1 presents one possible way of proceeding.

In this example, questions of value are addressed first, then research evidence is consulted, the advice of the SU is considered, practical considerations are weighed up, ideas about effective teaching and learning techniques are drawn into the planning and finally the nine elements of practice are reviewed. For example, what jobs are available for my students and what knowledge, understandings and skills do local employers currently require of new recruits? What recent training can I draw on to help me construct my lesson plans? And what stages are my students at in their understanding of this part of the curriculum? When all these factors have been taken into consideration and a lesson plan drawn up, then some examples of 'good practice' *may* be the outcome in this classroom, with these students, studying this particular topic, with these methods, at this particular moment in time and in this locality. Alexander sums it up well: 'good practice, created as it is in the unique setting of the classroom by the ideas and actions of teachers and pupils, can never be singular, fixed or absolute, a specification handed down or imposed from above' (1997: 287).

Typically, however, professionals do not decide what constitutes 'good practice' on their own. In the work of Etienne Wenger, for instance, practice is the source of coherence in a community, because through it, members of a 'community of practice' are mutually engaged, they are involved in a joint enterprise and they develop a shared repertoire of routines, stories and concepts. 'Such communities', he argues, 'hold the key to real transformation – the kind that has real effects on people's lives', because of their 'engagement in action, interpersonal relations, shared knowledge, and negotiation of enterprises' (1998: 85).

Unfortunately, these insights are not part (although they could become so) of the government's implementation plan for 14-19 Education and Skills, which will 'require profound changes throughout the system' (DfES, 2005b: 7). The mechanisms for creating change throughout the nation's schools and colleges are the establishment in every area of a 14-19 partnership and a programme of learning visits, 'through which we will support people to examine and experience some of the most effective existing practice' (DfES, 2005b: 8). There is no acknowledgement in any of these plans of the new learning that is required to convert the knowledge and practices of tutors in one setting into personal knowledge and skilled routines that could be used in a different school or college, as Michael Eraut has convincingly demonstrated.[10]

Finally, 'good practice' is not just a professional concern of individual tutors, 'communities of practice' or 14-19 partnerships: a vibrant democracy needs an open-ended approach to 'good practice', which remains within the control of reflective and learning professionals, which remains sensitive to constantly changing local contexts and which provides the resources to deal appropriately with the complexities involved in its identification and dissemination. In sum, the political emphasis on momentum, increasing pressure for improved performance and innovation need to be matched by continuity for institutions, stability for students, professional autonomy and adequate funding.[11]

Notes

1 The LSC was established in 2001 to bring together into a single learning and skills sector in England (excluding higher education) learning opportunities in further education, community and adult learning and work-based learning for young people and adults.

2 The researchers wish to acknowledge the funding of this project by the Economic and Social Research Council-reference number RES-139-25-0105. Its full title is 'The impact of policy on teaching, learning and inclusion in the new learning and skills sector' and it ran from January 2004 to July 2007.

3 Sir Andrew Foster was invited to review the future role of further education colleges in England. Part of his remit was to consider 'systems to disseminate best practice' (2005, p. 109).

4 The White Paper on Further Education sets out the government's response to the numerous recommendations made by the Foster review.

5 For a fuller account of the research project and our methodology, see Edward and Coffield (2007).
6 The QIA was set up in 2006 to speed up the pace of improvement in the lifelong learning sector by focusing on continuous improvement and creating a quality improvement strategy (QIS).
7 And yet the QIS claims very specifically that 'Evaluation of the national teaching and learning change programme found that success rates increased by 2.8% in the phase 1 pilots' (QIA, 2006, p. 25).
8 A systematic review of the research literature on the use of phonics found that the Clackmannanshire research of Johnston and Watson (2004) contained two experiments, the first of which contained such design faults that it had to be excluded. The second experiment was included in the review which concluded that: 'There is currently no strong random controlled trial evidence that any one form of systematic phonics is more effective than any other' (Torgerson et al., 2006, p. 49). A subsequent study by Johnston and Watson (2006), although it made substantial claims for synthetic phonics, had no control group, used different tests to measure progress and used outdated tests at that, such as the 1952 Schonell and Schonell.
9 This is not a hypothetical question. The DfES, for example, has for years promoted the use of learning style instruments which were neither valid nor reliable nor had beneficial impacts on practice (DfES, 2004).
10 The first official acknowledgement of the difficulties inherent in spreading 'good practice' is to be found in the final version of the QIS: 'sharing that practice is not easy, as it takes time, can be expensive and requires particular skills' (2007, p. 7). This is a welcome development.
11 We wish to thank our colleagues Ian Finlay, Maggie Gregson, Ken Spours and Richard Steer for their useful comments on an earlier draft. We are also grateful to the two anonymous referees whose constructive criticisms helped to improve this article.

References

Alexander, R. (1997) *Policy and Practice in Primary Education: Local Initiative, National Agenda* (2nd ed.). London: Routledge.
Arrowsmith, R. (2006) Look back in anger. *Education Guardian*, 8 August.
Association of Colleges (AoC) (2005) *Good Practice in the Development of Subject Learning Coaches*. London: AoC.
Bourdieu, P. (1998) *Contre-Feux*. Paris: Liber, Raisons d'Agir.
Brown, J., Collins, S. and Duguid, P. (1989) Situated learning and culture of learning.. *Educational Researcher*, 18, 32–42.
Brown, P. (2006) Education and the competition for a livelihood. Paper given at *British Educational Research Association Conference*. Warwick University, 8 September.
Browne, L. (2006) Teaching and learning national transformation programme. *Research in Post Compulsory Education*, 11(3), 267–276.
Coffield, F. (2007) *Running Ever Faster Down the Wrong Road: An Alternative Strategy for Education and Skills*. London: Institute of Education, University of London, Inaugural Lecture.
Cousin, S. (2004) *National Roll-out of Teaching and Learning Frameworks*. London: DfES Standards Unit.
Dewey, J. (1961) *Democracy and Education: An Introduction to the Philosophy of Education*. New York: Macmillan.
Department for Education and Employment (DfEE) (1999) *Learning to Succeed: A New Framework for Post-16 Learning*. Cm4392. London: Stationery Office.

Department for Education and Skills (DfES) (2002) *Success for All: Reforming Further Education and Training: Our Vision for the Future*. London: DfES.

Department for Education and Skills (DfES) (2004) *Learning Styles. Unit 19 of Pedagogy and Practice, Teaching and Learning in Secondary Schools*. London: DfES.

Department for Education and Skills (DfES) (2005a) *Excellent Teachers*. Sherwood Park: DfES Publications.

Department for Education and Skills (DfES) (2005b) *14-19 Education and Skills: Implementation Plan*. Annesley: DfES Publications.

Department for Education and Skills (DfES) (2006) *Further Education: Raising Skills, Improving Life Chances. CM 6768*. London: The Stationery Office.

Dowd, R. (2006) What we really really want. *Education Guardian*, 5 September.

Edward, S. and Coffield, F. (2007) Policy and practice in the learning and skills sector: Setting the scene. *Journal of Vocational Education and Training*, 59(2), 121–135.

Eraut, M. (2004) Transfer of knowledge between education and workplace settings. In H. Rainbird, A. Fuller and A. Munro (eds) *Workplace Learning in Context*. London: Routledge, 201–221.

Fielding, M., Bragg, S., Craig, J., Cunningham, I., Eraut, M., Gillinson, S., Home, M., Robinson, C. and Thorp, J. (2004) *Factors Influencing the Transfer of Good Practice*. London: DfES Publications, RR615.

Foster, A. (2005) *Realising the Potential: A Review of the Future Role of Further Education Colleges*. London: Department for Education and Skills.

Guile, D. and Young, M. (2003) Transfer and transition in vocational education: Some theoretical considerations. In T. Thomi-Grohn and Y. Engstrom (eds) *Between School and Work: New Perspectives on Transfer and Boundary-Crossing*. Oxford: Elsevier, 63–81.

Hargreaves, D. H. (2004) *Learning for Life: The Foundations for Lifelong Learning*. Bristol: Policy Press for the Lifelong Learning Foundation.

Hyman, P. (2005) *1 Out of 10: from Downing Street Vision to Classroom Reality*. London: Vintage.

James, D. and Biesta, G. (Eds) (2007) *Improving Learning Cultures in Further Education*. London: Routledge.

Jephcote, M., Salisbury, J. and Rees, G. (2006) Locality, learning and identity: teachers' constructs of students and their learning. Paper presented at the Annual Conference of the *British Educational Research Association*, Warwick University, September.

Johnston, R. S. and Watson, J. E. (2004) Accelerating the development of reading, spelling and phonemic awareness skills in initial readers. *Reading and Writing*, 17(4), 327–357.

Johnston, R. S. and Watson, J.E. (2006) *A Seven Year Study of the Effects of Synthetic Phonics Teaching on Reading and Spelling Attainment, Insight 17*. Edinburgh: Scottish Executive Education Department.

Keep, E. (2006) State control of the English education and training system-playing with the biggest trainset in the world. *Journal of Vocational Education and Training*, 58(1), 47–64.

Keep, E. (2007) Both Leitch and Gordon Brown are over-optimistic about what skills and education alone can deliver. *Adults Learning*, 18(5), 15. January.

Kelly, R. (2006) *Quality Improvement Agency Grant Letter 2006-07*. London: Department for Education and Skills.

Learning and Skills Council (LSC) (2006) *Framework for Excellence: a Comprehensive Performance Assessment Framework for the Further Education System*. Coventry: LSC.

Nuffield Review of 14-19 Education and Training (2006) *Curriculum for the 21st Century*. London: Nuffield.

Prime Minister's Strategy Unit (PMSU) (2006) *The UK Government's Approach to Public Sector Reform - A Discussion Paper*. London: Cabinet Office.

Quality Improvement Agency (QIA) (2006) *Pursuing Excellence: An Outline Improvement Strategy for Consultation*. Coventry: QIA.

Quality Improvement Agency (QIA) (2007) *Pursuing Excellence: The National Improvement Strategy for the Further Education System*. Coventry: QIA.

Rammell, B. and Haysom, M. (2006) *Foreword to Framework for Excellence: A Comprehensive Performance Assessment Framework for the Further Education System*. Coventry: Learning and Skills Council.

Rice, M. and Brooks, G. (2004) *Developmental Dyslexia in Adults: A Research Review*. London: National Research and Development Centre for Adult Literacy and Numeracy.

Scott, J. C. (1998) *Seeing Like a State: How Certain Schemes to Improve the Human Condition Have Failed*. New Haven, CT: Yale University Press.

Sfard, A. (1998) On two metaphors for learning and the dangers of choosing just one. *Educational Researcher*, 27(2), 4–13.

Thomi-Gröhn, T., Engeström, Y. and Young, M. (2003) From transfer to boundary-crossing between school and work as a tool for developing vocational education: An introduction. In T. Thomi-Gröhn and Y. Engström (eds) *Between School and Work: New Perspectives on Transfer and Boundary-Crossing*. Oxford: Elsevier, 1–15.

Thompson, A. (2006) *The Quality Improvement Agency for Lifelong Learning*. Standards Unit Conference, Newcastle Racecourse, 27 January.

Thorndike Edward, L. (1913) *The Psychology of Learning*. New York: Teachers College, Columbia University.

Torgerson, C. J., Brooks, G. and Hall, J. (2006) *A Systematic Review of the Research Literature on the Use of Phonics in the Teaching of Reading and Spelling*. Research Report 711. London: Department for Education and Skills.

Wenger, E. (1998) *Communities of Practice: Learning, Meaning and Identity*. Cambridge: Cambridge University Press.

Chapter 12

If there's no such thing as 'best practice', how can we improve teaching?

Government policies created a culture of mistrust where fear became the driving force for change. This chapter argues for the notion of 'best practice' to be dropped in favour of Joint Practice Development, where professionals jointly (J) share their practice (P) in order to develop it (D). This has led to a new, more effective model of professional learning based on trust and collaboration. The chapter, taken from my edited book *Beyond Bulimic Learning: Improving Teaching in Further Education* (Coffield, 2014), ends by discussing how to develop and audit levels of trust.

When I first arrived in Durham, I was invited by the Head of Department to lunch at Castle, the first college of the university founded in 1832. There he introduced me as his 'junior colleague' as we sat down at High Table to a meal that was worse than any school dinner I'd ever eaten. It was, however, being described by the mainly bachelor residents of the college as if it was the latest in 'cordon bleu' cooking. Afterwards, as we walked back to the School of Education, the senior professor said to me: 'I'll not be putting you up for membership of the Senior Common Room at Castle'. Inwardly, I sighed with relief. 'You see', he continued, 'Castle is a gentlemen's club and you come from Glasgow'.

Years later, I learned that after the war, at the same High Table in Castle, the then Vice Chancellor, Sir James Duff, had addressed a newly arrived tutor in Geography, Bill Fisher, as follows: 'Is it true that your real name is Wilhelm Fisher, that you are a German Jew and that you have anglicised your name to pass yourself off as English?' Bill Fisher replied, 'Sir James, have you ever thought of putting –er at the end of your surname?'

Introduction

'I hope I die during an in-service session because the transition between life and death would be so subtle'. Teacher quoted by Helen

Timperley (2011: 1)

DOI: 10.4324/9781003476146-16

It is a standard finding of educational research amounting almost to a cliché that it is extremely difficult to change the classroom practice of teachers. It is not, however, a problem confined to the teaching profession; indeed, the inability or unwillingness to change affects us all and no group more than those who are always badgering the rest of us to change: I refer in particular to senior politicians. Take, for example, Tony Blair's recent vision for the future: he would have us believe that '... the case for fundamental reform of the post-war state is clear ... how do we take the health and education reforms of the last Labour government to a new level ...?' (2013: 27). There is not a scintilla of doubt anywhere in his article: all his policies, in his view, ushered in huge improvements. So no change there, nor any prospect of change.

I want to begin this chapter with a pertinent example of reluctance to change from the world of FE and Skills, which will serve as an introduction to the main themes of this chapter. In 2009, Sheila Edward and I wrote a long, highly critical article on one of the strategies being used by the government and Ofsted to effect radical reform of the education 'system'. In more detail, we found serious fault with the simplistic notion that post-compulsory education and training would be transformed '... by establishing a Standards Unit to identify and disseminate best practice' (DfES, 2002: 5). The Standards Unit, like so many other government agencies, has come and gone (with all its costly CDs, videos and curricular materials), but the policy of identifying and transferring 'best practice' continues to be pursued by the Conservative-led coalition, government departments and government agencies. So our strictures about, for instance, the terms 'good', 'best' and 'excellent' practice being used interchangeably, about the absence of any publicly agreed criteria for judging practice, and about the need to take into consideration the 'immense diversity and complexity of local contexts' (Coffield and Edward, 2009: 371) went unheeded. So far, so predictable.

I was therefore dismayed, but not surprised, to read in the consultation document to establish a Guild for the Learning and Skills sector (AOC, 2013) that the phrase 'best practice' is used six times, 'good practice' twice, 'effective practice' once, 'the gold standard' once and 'excellent practice' once. This does a disservice to the English language in that it suggests that the words best, good, effective, golden and excellent are all synonyms. The English language deserves to be used accurately and 'best' still means superior to 'excellent'; and there is often a chasm between 'good' and 'excellent'. All the football teams in the Premier Division are excellent, but only one is the best.

I attended one of the consultation meetings on the establishment of the FE Guild, which has since been renamed the Education and Training Foundation. I raised these objections, left the chair with a copy of our research article and followed up the discussions by sending him a summary of the main arguments against their espoused model of change. I emphasised the danger of issuing a statement on teaching, learning and assessment (TLA), which was unconnected to any underlying theory or research and asked what the Guild's response would be if the 'best practice' they advocated turned out to be ineffective when tried by tutors. The FE Guild intends to set itself up as 'the expert voice' in TLA (Guild Project Team, 2013a: 11), so it cannot continue to avoid the issue of what theory (or theories) of learning underpins its recommendations; nor can it continue to ignore research it finds inconvenient or challenging.

Four months later in April 2013, the FE Guild Project Team issued its Implementation Plan and, yes, you have guessed correctly, 'developing provider good practice' is one of the Guild's five main themes. This document uses 'good practice' nine times, 'best practice' twice and 'excellent practice' four times, sometimes on the same page without any awareness that their writing gives the impression of muddled thinking. It even includes the admission that many items in the Learning and Skills Improvement Service's self-styled Excellence Gateway '… are very rarely used and therefore of questionable value'[1] (Guild Project Team, 2013b: 21). So the members of the Guild Project Team themselves find evidence that tutors do not use the large, expensive repositories of 'good practice' in the Excellence Gateway; but that does not lead them to question the validity of these materials. Instead, their thinking appears to be: we must intensify our efforts to identify and disseminate what tutors neither use nor value, namely, our notions of what constitutes 'good practice' for others to use.

The inability to change one's mind when confronted with disconfirming evidence appears to be pretty well entrenched at the highest echelons of the FE and Skills sector, and so it is by no means confined to classroom teachers.[2] But the problem is universal. The attraction of familiar old ideas, even when they have been repeatedly discredited by research, acts as a sharp brake on progress, partly because we all tend to fight vigorously to continue thinking and behaving in the way we have always thought and behaved; and partly because when we get into positions of power, we can react by rejecting new ideas as if we were being threatened by a socially embarrassing disease.

When the economist John Maynard Keynes remarked: 'When the facts change, I change my mind. What do you do?', he was challenging the typical stance of so many senior politicians and civil servants who, if they were to respond honestly, would reply to his question as follows: 'We are only interested in evidence which supports what we already think or the policies we are determined to push through, irrespective of the research record'.[3] I have used this episode to make the general point that fundamental change is so easy to recommend for others, but unpleasantly challenging when we are the ones being called upon to drop ideas or practices which have long been part of our intellectual furniture or repertoire. We all need to be more tolerant of what is involved when we invite others to enact deep and lasting reform or even what appear to us to be rather obvious, effective and practical innovations.

The rest of this chapter will present a fuller critique of 'best practice', suggest the alternative of Joint Practice Development, propose a shift from Continual Professional Development to Professional Learning and end by discussing trust and how to regenerate it when it has broken down.

Why is 'best practice' such a bad idea?

For me, the central weakness in the strategy of identifying and disseminating 'best practice' is the psychological resistance it builds up within those at the receiving end, because they are being told implicitly, if not explicitly, that their current practice is, in comparison, poor or inadequate. If their practice is satisfactory, good or outstanding, why are they expected to adopt someone else's 'best practice'? And the recipients of 'best practice' almost certainly think their own practice is pretty effective, otherwise why would they be using it?

I first began to doubt the efficiency of the strategy when I watched with student teachers a video of an 'outstanding' teacher working with a small group of highly motivated, well-dressed and impeccably behaved pupils in a sun-lit classroom, equipped with every modern resource and technological aid. The implicit message being transmitted to my students was: you can easily replicate the success of Miss Newly Qualified Teacher (NQT) of the year in your run-down school serving a slum estate with 30 teenagers, a few of whom have English as their mother tongue, some of whom are war refugees and all of whom would rather be in paid employment. In such circumstances, 'best practice' begins to sound like a con-trick played by the unimaginative on the unsuspecting, particularly if the students are left to work out for themselves how to transfer the 'best practice' of the video to their own classrooms. The 'best' can quickly become the enemy of the 'perfectly good enough' in challenging circumstances. The video, which was presented as an example of 'best practice', did not discuss *why* the NQT's practice was considered to be exemplary and it only served to scare the average student teacher into self-doubt, insecurity and inaction.

My opposition to 'best practice' deepened as I reflected on a number of questions which are never posed, never mind answered, by the advocates of the strategy. Who, for instance, says that X is 'best practice'? On what grounds? Based on what criteria? Have the criteria been publicly debated and agreed before anyone's practice is examined? Have all the most important criteria been included; for example, effectiveness, value for money, other possible options, varieties of context, consistency and quality? Would another observer looking at the same class choose this teaching episode or strategy as 'best practice'? And if not, neither evaluation can claim to be valid. Does the 'best practice' which has been selected capture the full 'complexity, ambiguity and problematic nature of teaching' (Anderson and Krathwohl, 2001: 110)? What warrant comes with 'best practice' and is it qualified in any way?

How applicable is the 'best practice' in terms of impact? For instance, is it equally effective with all age groups and all subject areas? What I am objecting to is the consistent and causal connection being made between 'best practice' and better outcomes – in all classrooms, in all weathers.

Finally, what is the quality of the evidence advanced to support it? Is it backed, for instance, by a number of meta-analyses of methodologically sound primary studies, reporting consistently high, positive effects in standardised tests? Or which is far more common, is the 'best practice' which is being nationally advocated nothing more than the views of one ex-Principal who has been impressed by some teaching seen in a short visit to one class? This battery of questions deserves to be answered fully before any teacher is put under pressure to adopt what some manager has labelled 'best practice'.

I have saved what some commentators[4] regard as the most devastating critique of all to the last, namely, the notion that one 'best practice' can be applied in all contexts is an impossibility; and that it is naïve in the extreme to expect any such panacea. Those familiar with the theory of situated learning[5] will be aware that the idea of a simple, optimum solution, regardless of context, to intractable problems of the kind teachers have to face every day, is a dangerous delusion. Teachers quickly see through all-purpose, easy-to-implement and sure-fire, student-proof recipes. In classrooms, they have to constantly make quick professional judgements, which have immediate effects on diverse groups of individual learners with highly specific needs, interests and attitudes, who come from different backgrounds with widely varying respect for education and the full range of opportunities and obstacles in their local labour markets. The strategy of transferring 'best practice' fails because it treats very differing contexts as if they were all identical. If there are still any proponents of 'best practice' out there, perhaps they could tell us what theoretical justification it has?

There is an alternative: Joint practice development (JPD)

To expose the weaknesses in a major government strategy for reform is, I think, a useful, if not always welcomed, public service, but to be in a position to recommend a replacement is far more constructive. It is possible to avoid the difficulties involved in using the adjectives 'good', 'effective' and 'best' by talking instead of devising mechanisms for professionals to jointly (J) share their practice (P) in order to develop (D) it. Tutors, for example, for Construction, Child Care or Chemistry, come together in the teams they teach in to discuss their experiences of teaching their subject to a particular standard and for a particular board (Edexcel or Assessment and Qualifications Alliance, AQA). In an atmosphere of mutual trust and joint exploration far removed from the isolation of their classrooms, they explain their successes and their struggles in teaching their subject in order to learn from each other; and they then move on to observing and evaluating each other's classroom practice, in an atmosphere which encourages the creativity of both partners. This model completely avoids the psychological disadvantages built into the 'best practice' model, where one teacher (with implicitly poor practice) is put into the embarrassing position of having to accept instruction from another with apparently superior practice, who may well be equally embarrassed at having been identified as the carrier of 'best practice'; and their joint embarrassment is likely to inhibit rather than encourage learning.

I first came across the term 'JPD' in a research report written for the then Department for Education and Skills in 2005 by Michael Fielding and his colleagues (Fielding *et al.*, 2005). Theirs was an in-depth, qualitative research project involving classroom observations and interviews with over 120 practitioners who had been trying to transfer 'good practice' in a variety of secondary schools. Their main findings can be summarised as follows: they prefer the term 'JPD' to 'transfer of good practice', because the latter 'marginalises the importance of developing a new way of working that fits the different context of the partner teacher' (2005: 1). Second, trusting relationships are fundamental to JPD, which also requires significant investment of time, resources and commitment from teachers, principals and government.

Third, both partners in the exchange need to play the role of observer and observed, of being the originator and receiver of practical advice; and both roles are accorded equal status. This equality in the relationships between teachers in the JPD model compares very favourably with the superior-inferior status of the two tutors in the 'best practice' approach, which goes a long way to explain why the former is proving to be far more effective. Fourth, we need to 'build on systems which put teachers in touch with each other and leave space for professionals' skilled judgements rather than imposing orthodoxies' (ibid: 5).

One question leaped to my mind when I first read this report in 2007. Policy-makers are rightly on the lookout for means of 'scaling up' successful approaches from pilot projects to the national systems. Why, if this strategy had proved to be so successful had it not been 'rolled out' across the system? Two ideas occurred to me. First, JPD is expensive – it takes considerable time to develop relationships which are so trusting that the partners begin to discuss their weaknesses as well as their strengths. JPD also involves 'observation and evaluation of teachers' practice in classrooms which is far more challenging to participants than just exchanging information which for most teachers is the standard form of Continuing Professional Development (CPD) they receive' (Sebba et al., 2012: 5). Moreover, if teachers are put in touch with colleagues from neighbouring colleges to extend JPD, then there are obvious costs for transport and in covering for teacher absences to attend JPD sessions. Whether such collaboration should then develop into partnerships, alliances or chains is a proposal which needs evidence rather than the automatic assumption that such partnerships create a self-improving system.

My second idea is admittedly more cynical, but perhaps also more accurate, because governments can always find sufficient money to do whatever they are determined to do. JPD also involves a loss of control from the centre; no matter the political complexion of the administration in power, education ministers have exercised their power to tell teachers what to teach and how to teach it. JPD, in contrast, restores trust in the professional judgement of teachers; it encourages collaboration rather than competition; and it respects the professionalism of all those involved rather than believing that there is a large, hard core of inefficient teachers who must be gotten rid of.

From JPD to professional learning

What has happened to JPD in the nine years since Fielding and his colleagues published their research in 2005? Whenever it has been used in the post-compulsory sector, tutors have responded very positively to it. Andy Boon and Toni Fazaeli, reviewing the evidence collected by the Institute for Learning over a four year period, conclude that 'nearly all teachers carry out about double the number of hours of Continuing Professional Development required each year' (2014: 39). Now just because teachers have spent a large number of hours studying a topic does not necessarily indicate that they have learned anything new, nor that they have changed their practice as a consequence of the hours invested. On the other hand, Fazaeli and Boon report that 'teachers value sharing critical reflection, testing practice and learning from each other, both within and outside of their place of employment' (ibid). Before reading any further, I invite the reader to try the activity in Box 12.1.

Box 12.1   The Give and Take of Joint Practice Development (JPD)

Suppose you are in charge of introducing JPD into your college or organisation or you are a tutor interested in taking part. What questions would you set for the participants to ensure that everyone came to the discussion with something to teach and left with something they had learned?

Question 1:

Question 2:

Source: See Hargreaves (2012), for more information.

For David Hargreaves, JPD is the first and central building block in his model of a mature, self-improving school system. In setting up groups of teachers for JPD, he suggests that they be invited to answer two questions, which I have adapted here: what could I offer a colleague who teaches the same subject as I do? What would I like to gain from that colleague? What we are witnessing here is nothing less than the emergence of a new model of professional development which is:

> ... less about attending conferences and courses and more about school-based, peer-to-peer activities in which development is fused with routine practice. Professional development becomes a continuous, pervasive process that builds craft knowledge, rather than an occasional activity that is sharply distinguished in time and space from routine classroom work
>
> (Hargreaves, 2012: 8)

I would also like to follow Helen Timperley's lead (2011) in suggesting that we make a shift in our thinking from professional *development* to professional *learning*, because the former phrase has become devalued by its association with mere participation in CPD courses. My own definition of professional learning is an amalgam of a number that have been suggested and reads as follows: *it is a collaborative process of improving practice in the light of experience, research and reflection in order to become more effective and efficient in order to enhance outcomes for students.* Such professional learning is not a task for classroom teachers alone, but should be in evidence at all levels in the education 'system'. Fat chance.

Helen Timperley's work is important because she shows in detail how teachers create new professional knowledge through interaction with their colleagues; and when tutors access expert knowledge, the sequence is not one of theory being turned into practice, but theory and practice being built together. In her words: 'Professional learning is not a process of learning new things and then learning how to implement them. Implementation is part of how something is learned and more deeply understood' (2011: 60). The opposite approach is exemplified by those coaches who say: 'I told you how to do it. Why didn't you just do it?'

I have seen JPD used most effectively in a course run jointly by the Learning and Skills Improvement Service and Sunderland University for research development fellows (RDFs). Participants, who are drawn from all sections within the learning and skills sector, complete a small-scale piece of research of practical relevance to their job. For four years, I have watched these RDFs learn from each other's practice in an atmosphere of mutual respect and trust; they also collaborate closely to improve the quality of each other's project. In the most successful cases, the JPD approach has been picked up by colleagues who are not attending the RDF course and begins to permeate the college, adult learning centre or private training provider to which the RDF returns with the aim of slowly changing the learning culture of the parent organisation as a result. (See Gregson *et al.,* 2013, who argue that one of the great strengths of JPD is that it does not dismiss the merits of the RDFs' current practice, but seeks to enhance it by having it discussed openly with supportive colleagues.)

One interesting variant of JPD goes by the name of Lesson Study (LS), which has been practiced across Japan since the 1870s, but only recently introduced into this country. Briefly, LS brings together a group of teachers who want to work collaboratively at improving a lesson on a particular aspect of the curriculum – say, a topic that the teachers find difficult to teach or that students find difficult to understand. The teachers together plan a Research Lesson (RL), one of them teaches it while the others observe, and then they all discuss the strengths and weaknesses of the RL while making sure to involve the pupils as learning partners in improving it. A second RL is then jointly planned and about three 'case pupils' who represent, say, high, middle or low attainment groups are chosen for the teachers to observe. The second RL is then taught and discussed, again involving the views of the pupils; and the whole sequence is repeated a third (or even a fourth) time until all the participants (tutors and students) are satisfied with the lesson.

The claims being made for LS are that its focus on learning rather than on teaching provides a safe environment for teachers to learn from each other and their pupils, to experiment with different approaches and to suggest hypotheses about why their pupils learn (or do not learn), which are then tested. The different perspectives which the teachers bring to LS '*slow down* swiftly flowing, complex classroom activity in RLs, allowing teachers *to see more* of what happens in greater detail than they can alone and from several viewpoints' (Dudley, 2013: 118, original emphasis). I am fond of Michael Eraut's description of good teaching as like riding a bike skilfully through heavy traffic without wearing a safety helmet, but LS moves the discussion away from lone practice to a collaborative focus on the specifics of how students learn – or not – in crowded classrooms.

The advocates of LS, and there are now over 2,000 teachers in England who have been trained to use it, also claim that the planning, rehearsal and discussion of RLs help teachers to internalise new practices. In addition, explaining LS to others helps teachers to incorporate those new practices into their standard repertoire in ways that are likely to be lasting. Those who remain to be convinced point to the disruption caused by the staff cover and to the extra resources needed to release a group of teachers repeatedly to plan and improve RLs. Despite these disadvantages, LS is being seriously studied and developed as a technique in primary and secondary schools and the time has surely come for it to be tried out in the post-compulsory sector.

Sometimes a concept can be more fully grasped if its opposite is described and, for me, the antithesis of the JPD model is *The Apprentice* programme on BBC television, which each year assembles, in my opinion, a group of arrogant, self-promoting and untrustworthy young executives who stab each other in the back in the ruthless pursuit of winning at all costs. The potential damage of such a programme is that it implicitly suggests that you have to be an aggressively unpleasant self-seeker in order to succeed in British industry. This brings me to the final topic to be discussed in this chapter – the necessity of trust between colleagues and between staff and students.

Trust

Effective JPD depends crucially on developing trust and the educational literature is replete with reference to its importance. For Helen Timperley, trust is forged through daily social interactions and she defines it as:

> ... a genuine sense of listening to others, personal regard shown by a willingness of people to extend themselves beyond what is formally required, and beliefs that colleagues have the knowledge, skills and/or technical capacity to deliver on intentions and promises
>
> (2011: 108)

Trust also emerges as a key element in research into good leadership in universities, where it 'gives people the security to be open, honest and critical in discussing strategy development, and creative, experimental and risk-taking in their interpretation and implementation' (McNay, 2012: 8). Trust can also be very quickly destroyed as, for example, when a football manager publicly berates his players for making mistakes.

For David Hargreaves, school leaders have the potentially discomfiting task of not only modelling trust in their relationships within their institution but also of monitoring the levels of trust the staff have in the senior leadership team and in one another, as well as the amount of trust students have in the staff. He encloses in an annex forms for auditing different dimensions of trust, which could easily be adapted for the FE and Skills sector (Hargreaves, 2012). See Box 12.2 for an activity about the dimensions of trust and how they could be audited.)

How does the concept of trust play out in that sector? I agree with Denis Gleeson's assessment that over the years successive governments have created a culture of mistrust, where fear (rather than trust) has become the predominant driving force for change: 'Though FE colleges are officially independent of central government's control, the sector operates within a context of licensed autonomy, with professionals treated as trusted servants rather than as empowered professionals' (2014: 23). Increasingly, they are now treated as mistrusted servants. Similarly, Ofsted has evolved into a punitive arm of government and has lost the trust of the teaching profession.

It was only, however, when I was reading Richard Sennett's book on the rituals, pleasures and politics of cooperation that I began to understand more

---

Box 12.2   Developing and Auditing Trust

What do you think are the main dimensions of trust? Can you list the ones you think are the most important?

1.
2.
3.
4.
5.

See Box 12.3 at the end of the chapter to see a list of possible dimensions.
    Suppose now that you wanted to audit how much trust, say, the staff have in the Senior Management Team (SMT). Can you think of a number of statements to exemplify the dimensions you have listed above and then produce a proforma where staff could agree or disagree with the item? For example:

1 Communications in this college are good because the SMT actively listens to complaints from staff and responds appropriately.

   Agree strongly ☐ Agree ☐ Disagree ☐ Disagree strongly ☐

Source: See Hargreaves (2012) for audits of trust in SMT by staff, by staff in one another and by students in staff.

---

fully why it has become so difficult for so many staff in the sector to make the leap of faith in their leaders which trust requires. He describes how before the crisis of 2008 in banks and investment houses, trust by the front-line financial specialists in their superiors was eroded by invidious comparison, because the latter were considered to be technically incompetent by the former: 'the top don't know what's going on every day in the firm; they lack hands-on knowledge' (2012: 171).

    What I think has happened in a goodly number of FE colleges is that, as the SMT has steadily withdrawn from teaching since incorporation in the early 1990s, while at the same time proclaiming it to be the core business of the organisation, classroom teachers have steadily lost respect for their leaders as educators, as opposed to financial managers, who in some cases become objects of ridicule from whom it then becomes impossible to learn. The result, according to Sennett, is a growing belief in 'an inverse relationship between competence and hierarchy, a bitter reversal which dissolves trust in those above' (ibid: 172). Good teachers who see teaching as a craft, who wish to continue improving just for the sake of it, tend not to be pleased but become embittered by such an outcome.

The culture of mistrust in colleges is a replication of the relationship between government and the institutional leaders in the sector, with the latter treated as assets to be controlled, 'sweated' and micro-managed by ministers in the interests of greater economic efficiency. A current example is the aggressive and inappropriate language of the Skills Minister, Matthew Hancock, who has, I understand, never been in charge of anything in his short life but who writes of holding 'principals' feet to the fire on behalf of students' (2013: 4). The end apparently justifies the means. What also complicates the picture in education is the co-existence of two models which are in direct conflict – a professional model where all staff, teachers and managers wish to be treated as members of the same profession; and a management model where SMTs run the organisation and unions protect the interests of their members.

Mike Bottery, in addition to describing no less than seven different forms of trust, makes some useful suggestions about how trust between policy-makers and professionals could be regenerated through a benign spiral (2003). A number of his suggestions could equally well be used by SMTs to remedy any breakdown in trust within an FE college; and with these proposals, I shall end this chapter.

Governments and SMTs could, for instance, publicly and repeatedly acknowledge what a difficult job teaching is; they could reduce workloads that have become too heavy and stressful; they could lighten the administrative demands on teachers by cutting their incessant requests for data and so increase the time they could devote to TLA; they could trust the integrity of educators by allowing them greater freedom over pedagogy and curriculum; they could stop grading lesson observations and institute instead a policy of JPD; they could introduce intelligent rather than punitive accountability, which replaces one-off, unrepresentative visits with more longitudinal evaluation of teachers' work. Above all, SMTs could return to teaching and discussing TLA with their colleagues from a basis of recent and relevant classroom experience.

Trust, however, is a two-way process and it may prove necessary for the teachers' unions and professional bodies to take the initiative in making proposals to management and government in order to get the benign spiral of trust started. Teaching staff could, for instance, demonstrate their commitment to raising the achievement of all students by offering 'wholehearted commitment to the provision of evidence of the monitoring of student progression, and of portfolio evidence of student improvement' (Bottery, 2003: 258). Tutors could also commit themselves to becoming a fully research-informed profession; and one aspect of that commitment would be a move to a new model of professional learning based on JPD rather than wasting their time trying to identify and transfer 'best practice'. (See Box 12.3 for a list of possible dimensions of trust.)

Box 12.3   Dimensions of Trust

1 Talking straight
2 Demonstrating concern
3 Creating transparency
4 Righting wrongs
5 Showing loyalty
6 Participating in professional learning with colleagues
7 Consulting before deciding
8 Confronting reality
9 Clarifying goals and expectations
10 Practising accountability
11 Active listening
12 Keeping commitments
13 Extending trust to all employees
14 Belief that colleagues can keep promises
15 Personal regard for all staff and students
16 Accepting and using principled dissent
17 Coping with risk and uncertainty
18 Relying on the integrity of fellow professionals
19 Modelling trusting relationships with staff
20 Creating and enhancing a learning culture in the college

Source: Adapted and extended from Hargreaves (2012: 14).

Notes

1 I shall not pursue further the logical non-sequitur of this statement which suggests that ideas are of dubious worth if they are rarely used because that would rule out philosophy, Christianity and thinking itself.
2 The strategy of first identifying and then disseminating 'best practice' is alive and well, despite all its attendant problems, in all the main texts being produced by and for the sector; to take just one more example, the report from the Commission on Adult Vocational Teaching and Learning (CAVTL, 2013) within 34 pages uses 'best practice' six times, 'good practice' twice and 'effective', 'innovative', 'sophisticated', 'sustained' and 'leading edge' practice once each. I suspect that all these terms are being used loosely to mean the same thing. If not, I think we should be told what the differences are.
3 A good example is Michael Gove's determination to introduce Free Schools to England, all the while claiming that Swedish evidence supported his insistence when in fact that evidence showed that Free Schools lowered standards.
4 See, for example, James and Biesta (2007).
5 Situated learning, as proposed by Jean Lave and Etienne Wenger, two American anthropologists, shifts 'the analytic focus from the individual as learner to learning as participation in the social world, and from the concept of cognitive process to

the more-encompassing view of social practice' (1991: 43). In my words, their theory explains how newcomers slowly learn the knowledge, skills and dispositions of experts by being drawn in from the periphery to the centre of their activities. Please do not be put off by the intimidating title of their book – *Situated Learning: Legitimate peripheral participation* – it is an insightful and novel demonstration of the quintessentially social character of learning. They studied the cognitive apprenticeships of novices who changed their identities as they slowly became midwives, tailors, quartermasters, butchers and nondrinking alcoholics. As Lave and Wenger argue, if you want to take a fresh look at authentic learning, the last place you would study is an educational institution, because so many of them have been turned into exam factories (see Coffield and Williamson, 2012).

References

Anderson, L.W. and Krathwohl, D.R. (eds) (2001) *A Taxonomy for Learning, Teaching and Assessing: A Revision of Bloom's Taxonomy of Educational Objectives.* New York: Longman, Abridged Edition.

Association of Colleges (AOC) (2013) *Consultation to Establish a Guild for the Learning and Skills Sector.* London: AOC.

Blair, T. (2013) Labour must search for answers and not merely aspire to be a repository for people's anger. *New Statesman*, 12–25 April.

Boon, A. and Fazaeli, T. (2014) Professional bodies and continuing professional development: A case study. In Crowley, S. (ed) *Challenging Professional Learning.* London: Routledge, 31–53.

Bottery, M. (2003) The management and the mismanagement of trust. *Educational Management, Administration and Leadership*, 31(3), 245–261.

Coffield, F.(ed) (2014) *Beyond Bulimic Learning: Improving Teaching in Further Education.* London: Institute of Education Press.

Coffield, F. and Edward, S. (2009) Rolling out 'Good', 'Best' and 'Excellent' practice. What next? Perfect practice? *British Educational Research Journal*, 35(3), 371–390.

Coffield, F. and Williamson, B. (2012) *From Exam Factories to Communities of Discovery: the Democratic Route.* London: Institute of Education.

Commission on Adult Vocational Teaching and Learning (CAVTL) (2013) *It's About Work … Excellent Adult Vocational Teaching and Learning.* Coventry: LSIS.

Department for Education and Skills (DfES (2002) *Success for All: Reforming Further Education and Training: Our Vision for the Future.* London: DfES.

Dudley, P. (2013) Teacher learning in lesson study. *Teaching and Teacher Education*, 34, 107–121.

Fielding, M., Bragg, S., Craig, J., Cunningham, I., Eraut, M., Gillinson, S., Horne, M., Robinson, C. and Thorp, J. (2005) *Factors Influencing the Transfer of Good Practice.* Research Brief No RB615. London: DfES.

Gleeson, D. (2014) Professional identity, trading places: On becoming an FE professional. In S. Crowley (ed) *Challenging Professional Learning.* London: Routledge, 20–30.

Gregson, M., Nixon, L., Spedding, T. and Kearney, S. (2013) *Unlocking Improvement in Teaching and Learning: a leader's Guide to Joint Practice Development in the FE System.* London: LSIS.

Guild Project Team (2013a) *Consultation to Establish a Guild for the Learning and Skills Sector.* London: AOC/NIACE/AELP.

Guild Project Team (2013b) *FE Guild Implementation Plan: Summary Version.* London: AOC/NIACE/AELP

Hancock, M. (2013) A sector in charge of its own destiny. In I. Nash (ed) *Twenty Years of College Independence*. www.feweek.co.uk. Accessed 24 April 2013.

Hargreaves, D. (2012) *A Self-improving School System: Towards Maturity*. Nottingham: National College for School Leadership.

James, D. and Biesta, G. (2007) *Improving Learning Cultures in Further Education*. Abingdon, Oxon: Routledge.

Lave, J. and Wenger, E. (1991) *Situated Learning: Legitimate Peripheral Participation*. Cambridge: Cambridge University Press.

McNay, I. (2012) Leading strategic change in higher education – closing the implementation gap. *Leadership and Governance in Higher Education*, 4, 46–69.

Sebba, J., Kent, P. and Tregenza, J. (2012) *Joint Practice Development: What Does the Evidence Suggest are Effective Approaches?* Nottingham: National College for School Leadership.

Sennett, R. (2012) *Together: The Rituals, Pleasures and Politics of Cooperation*. London: Allen Lane.

Timperley, H. (2011) *Realizing the Power of Professional Learning*. Maidenhead: Open University Press/McGraw-Hill Education.

Chapter 13

Running ever faster down the wrong road

An alternative future for education and skills

Policy is not the bandage. It's the wound. I adapted that remark of Dennis Potter's to summarise my growing disenchantment with the proliferation of policy. Drawing on my own research, this (much reduced) inaugural lecture at the Institute of Education, London University, in December 2006 (and published by the Institute) concluded that, despite some significant investment and successes, the new, more intensive model of reform of the public services was doing more harm than good.

In 2007, I gave a talk at Cambridge to a group of principals of FE colleges. The conference was opened by Boris Johnson, then Shadow Minister for Business, Innovation and Skills. He arrived late, burst on to the platform like a Spanish bull racing into the ring, and began talking. He entertained the audience with his comparison between academic subjects and breakfast cereals. Some Mickey Mouse subjects, he suggested, like Media or Business Studies, were soft, easy to digest, but bad for you like Coco Pops or Frosties. Others, like Latin and Greek, which he'd studied at Oxford, were hard, took years to master, but improved your mind and body, like Granola or Bran Flakes. At this point, he suddenly addressed the audience directly: 'Sorry, whom I talking to? You see, I was picked up this morning by Central Office and driven here so I haven't had the time to find out'. A voice rang out: 'We're principals of FE colleges'. Johnson replied: 'FE? What's that? No, don't tell me. I know. You used to be called Secondary Moderns'.

Introduction

I would like to begin with a confession. When it comes to inaugurals, I am a serial offender, having delivered one at Durham (Coffield, 1982) and Newcastle Universities (Coffield, 1999). I also wish to begin with a promise to myself, to my family and to this audience: this is my third and last. Three strikes and out. I have found the cure; it is called retirement. I would like to consider this as both an inaugural and a valedictory lecture. *'Ave atque vale'.* Hello and goodbye.

DOI: 10.4324/9781003476146-17

I would also like to begin with another promise and a health warning. I promise that the next hour will pass without mention of 'transformational visions', 'stakeholders', 'step changes', or 'strategic purchasing functions', except when I quote disapprovingly from official sources. The phrase 'strategic purchasing function' simply means a shopping list, but government departments need to imagine they are involved in a much grander enterprise. We tend to ridicule these phrases when we first hear them, but within a few months, we are using them. In this way, these pretentious inanities vitiate our language, our thinking and our culture. The case I present tonight will be made in clear English, which is one of our most potent weapons in the battle of ideas.

Let me present a brief overview of my argument. My case is that the government's programme of reform in public services, despite significant investments and successes, is now doing more harm than good. It needs to be fundamentally redesigned and later I will briefly outline a few proposals for a different system. But first, we must stop running faster down the wrong road. The destination is inappropriate, the curriculum outdated, the policing too heavy and the determination to put the foot down even harder on the accelerator is a symptom of a dangerous machismo, best left to *Top Gear* presenters.

In one lecture, it is not possible to deal with all the reforms which have been introduced into the public services since the 1980s. I cannot even deal with the reforms of the education service as a whole, but instead will confine myself to the post-compulsory sector, hereafter known as the Learning and Skills Sector (LSS), with the exception of higher education (HE). The same fault lines run through the reform agenda of the government whether they affect the primary, secondary, higher education or post-compulsory sectors (or the health service or the probation service, for that matter).

Now the health warning for those of you who have never been inside the LSS before. It is a vast and complex world which is restructured so frequently that it has become a full-time job just to read about the latest twists of policy, never mind respond to them. This will be a brief excursion into a turbulent, insecure but desperately important world; a world which remains invisible to most politicians, academics and commentators because, with very few exceptions, neither they nor their children have ever passed through it.

Background

England does not have an educational system, but instead three badly coordinated sectors – schools, post-compulsory education and HE. The mental image suggested by these structural arrangements is of three well-intentioned but dyspraxic and myopic elephants, who are constantly bumping into each other and standing on each other's feet instead of interweaving smoothly in one elegant dance.

The post-compulsory sector has been aptly termed 'the neglected middle child between universities and schools' by Sir Andrew Foster (2005: 58). That neglect has, however, begun to be addressed since 1997 by the keen interest taken by the New Labour government. My first task is to show how the weaknesses in the present arrangements now outweigh their strengths; the second job is to suggest ways in which this internally fragmented *sector* could be turned into a well-integrated *system* with the capacity to learn.

The data for both sections of this paper – the critique and the alternative – are drawn from the research project, entitled *The Impact of Policy on Learning and Inclusion in the New Learning and Skills Sector*, which is part of the Teaching and Learning Research Programme, funded by the Economic and Social Research Council.[1] What follows draws on the work of a team of eight staff, but only the present author should be held responsible for the views expressed here.[2]

From the very beginning, we set ourselves the task of outlining the main characteristics of effective, equitable and inclusive local learning *systems*; and at the end, I shall offer a preliminary response, which I hope will be improved through public debate. I shall begin by briefly reviewing existing strengths.

Charting the impact of government policy on practice has not been, however, a simple matter of recording linear, evolutionary, coherent or cumulative progress. Rather, the processes of change have been complex, uneven, dynamic, ambiguous, hotly contested and often contradictory. Policies have not only evolved or been radically altered as Secretaries of State and senior civil servants have come and gone, but some policies were abandoned, while others were from the start internally inconsistent or flatly contradicted existing policies.

The writings of John Clarke and Janet Newman (Clarke and Newman, 1997; Newman, 2000, 2001, 2005) make clear that no one dominant model is being imposed from above – the picture is far more complicated than that. For example, Newman has produced a framework which represents four different models of governance and government policy draws on all four.[3] Change, therefore, as enacted by New Labour, is a multidimensional, dynamic and conflictual process; top-down control and an obsession with targets have also intensified since 1999, taking England much further in the wrong direction than either Scotland or Wales.

I have also used the work of Jan Kooiman (2003) on the diversity, complexity and dynamics within governance. The work of these theorists cautions against presenting the two parts of this lecture as 'a stereotyped and demonised past' giving way to 'a visionary and idealised future' (Clarke and Newman, 1997: 49). We must build on the strengths of the sector as well as facing up to where it is going wrong and responding appropriately.

Unprecedented government intervention

The New Labour government has taken post-16 education more seriously than any previous administration by allocating substantial funding, establishing new structures and agencies and creating the first-ever national strategy for skills. The scale of the increased funding can be judged from the grant to the Learning and Skills Council (LSC), which will more than double from £5.5 billion in its first year of operation in 2001–02 to £11.4 billion in 2007–08 (Johnson, 2006, Annex B). Investment in FE colleges has increased by 48% in real terms since 1997 (DfES, 2006a: 14); but investment in schools by 65%.

Moreover, a torrent of new policy has flooded out from the DfES, including a programme of reform for further education and training, called *Success for All* (DfES, 2002); a *Five Year Strategy for Children and Learners* (DfES, 2004, which was updated in October this year [DfES, 2006b]); and a White Paper on *Skills: Getting on in business, getting on at work* (DfES, 2005b). A Skills Alliance of government departments and key organisations, representing employers and unions, has been formed to oversee this strategy. A new planning and funding body, the LSC, was established in 2001 (see Coffield *et al.*, 2005; Hodgson *et al.*, 2005); a new network of Sector Skills Councils began to be formed in 2003 to identify the current and future skill needs of employers; and in 2005, a new Quality Improvement Agency (QIA) was formed to 'drive up' quality throughout the sector.

In addition, the government commissioned two far-ranging reviews. First, a review of the future role of further education colleges was conducted by Sir Andrew Foster (2005), and at the same time, Lord Leitch (2005) was commissioned by the Chancellor, Gordon Brown, to review future skill needs. Both reports were heavily drawn upon in the White Paper on FE, which ushered in a whole new set of policies, agencies and initiatives, because FE is considered by senior ministers as 'not achieving its full potential as the powerhouse of a high skills economy' (DfES, 2006a: 1). And a Further Education and Training Bill is currently making its way through Parliament.

So the depth, breadth and pace of change coursing through the sector and the unprecedented level of government activity are apparent in:

- a set of new strategies
- new stretching targets
- a constant stream of initiatives
- new curricula and qualifications
- new partnerships between schools and FE colleges
- new types of institution, e.g. City Academies, Skills Academies and vocational, specialist schools
- and a new model of public service reform, of which more later (PMSU, 2006).

It may seem churlish to criticise what some may see as creative dynamism and others as frenetic hyperactivity, but the very scale and cost of the enterprise prompt serious questions such as:

- Have the new investments and policies resulted in a well-integrated, equitable and inclusive learning system? Are the reforms creating the 'radical and enduring change', envisioned by David Blunkett (2000: 1)?
- Are the reforms creating a healthy, innovative and self-confident sector? Is it headed in the right direction?
- Have the main problems facing the sector been acknowledged and are they being tackled?

Current strengths

David Raffe warned against the danger of seeing English post-16 education and training as 'not only distinctive, but distinctively pathological ... [where] reform proposals have been dominated by a deficit model' (2002: 11). He suggested an alternative approach which begins by identifying the strengths of the sector and then building on them. He offered the following positive features: institutional flexibility and responsiveness; a tradition of local innovation and second chances; a tradition of pastoral care, and of learning in and through employment with high levels of early career mobility; and young people with a strong sense of agency. I agree with David, and our project suggests further strengths: a deep commitment from tutors to students which is at the core of their professionalism; very high levels of satisfaction among students; meeting the needs of those students who have performed poorly at GCSE and whom no other organisation is keen to teach; the vast range of provision from below Level 1 to Level 5 and for students aged 14 to 99; a steady supply of most of the country's intermediate skills; and the role of adult and community education in strengthening social cohesion. The interim report of the Leitch review of skills in the United Kingdom suggested one further strength: 'a strong record of improvement over the past decade' (2005: 1). It went, however, to warn that 'Even if the Government's current ambitious targets were met' by 2020, 'the UK will continue to be an 'average performer' – positioned at best, in the middle of the OECD ranking' (Leitch, 2005: 10). In short, these very real strengths and improvements have to be set against a set of long-standing, structural, political, theoretical and operational weaknesses.

Current weaknesses

Our research project simultaneously looks down into the sector from the perspectives of senior officials at national and regional levels; and it looks up into the sector from the perspectives of 'front-line' managers, tutors and learners in our 24 learning sites. This scrutiny suggests seven glaring deficiencies:

A badly coordinated sector, headed in the wrong direction

The White Paper on FE of March 2006 accepted the main recommendation of the Foster Report (2005) and established a new mission for the sector: its 'key strategic role ... is to help people gain the skills and qualifications for employability' (DfES, 2006a: 21). It also argued that the sector should be 'reconfigured' around this mission and claimed that 'this strong focus on economic impact does not come at the expense of social inclusion and equality of opportunity – the two reinforce one another' (DfES, 2006a: 29). Since the publication of the White Paper, however, the main mission for FE is slowly becoming the sole mission, with colleges up and down the country closing courses not linking to it.

Serious and inequitable as that is, a greater error lies in the choice of employability as the core mission, for it is an empty, unsatisfying concept which will sell our people short. For some, such as Jacky Brine, drawing on the work of Ulrich Beck, employability means 'a state of constant becoming', a readiness to be trained and re-trained for whatever types of employment are available, which leaves learners searching for individual solutions to systemic problems (Brine, 2006: 652). In the language of C. Wright Mills, employability turns the public issue of the dearth of good jobs into the private trouble of constant retraining.

Basil Bernstein preferred to criticise what he called the 'jejune concept of trainability', which for him does not create an individual, psychological condition, but a new social identity arising out of a new social order, based on short-term capitalism (Bernstein, 1996: 67). And Richard Sennett has shown how the principle of 'no long term ... corrodes trust, loyalty and mutual commitment' (1998: 24). Employability, then, cannot be the core mission for this crucial sector, because it militates against students understanding or criticising power relations in college or at work or forming a strong vocational identity. The sector needs a different future which gives equal weight to social justice and economic prosperity; and why not, for once, in that order?

Furthermore, within the post-compulsory sector, relations between the key partners are either dysfunctional or disorganised or both. Our earlier reports on the LSC (*Coffield et al.,* 2005; Hodgson *et al.,* 2005) showed how the DfES micromanaged the LSC, which in turn controlled the regional and local LSCs, which then attempted to micromanage the FE colleges and training providers in their locality. After considering the relations between the DfES and LSC, Foster recommended that their roles should be refined so as 'to lighten the impact of centralised control and monitoring, and to minimise duplication and undue central demands' (2005: 62–3).

Co-ordination between the maintained school sector and the LSS is also poor, as can be seen from what the policy-makers themselves call 'the scandal of our high drop-out rate at 16' (DfES, 2004: 71). The OECD has for years been emphasising the extent of that scandal in its annual reports, where it compares internationally the participation rate of 17-year-olds in education or training. The latest report shows that the United Kingdom record is worse than that of 19 other countries (OECD, 2006). Part of the problem is that the best resourced routes, which also happen to be the most clearly signposted, are for those students who find learning easiest, while the poorly resourced routes, which are the most complicated to follow, are for those who find learning difficult.

The official rhetoric talks of 'seamless progression' but every year almost 300,000 fall out of the system at age 16. Part of the explanation is the accountability regime for secondary schools, which pushes teachers to concentrate their efforts on those students who can reach the government-imposed target of five good GCSEs to the detriment of those who cannot. In their effort to push up the 'key marginals' (Hyman, 2005) from D to C grades, teachers, in order to protect themselves, ignore those who are unlikely to reach this level and many then leave school damaged as learners. This is a structural problem of the first importance, which is landed on FE colleges and employers.

The measure of five good passes perpetuates the historic division in English education between O-level sheep and CSE goats, between educating learners and training followers (see Edwards, 1997); it also intensifies the polarisation of performance between highly successful and poorly achieving schools, with 56% cent of 16-year-olds gaining five good GCSEs, which means that 44% still do not (DfES, 2005c: 14). Five good grades at GCSE have come to be regarded as the measure of success expected of all pupils, but, as Peter Mortimore has pointed out, the GCSE 'is not an examination that has been designed for everyone to pass' (2006: 39). We need different measures of school effectiveness and we need to stop the damage done each year to the bottom 45% of each age cohort, who learn that they have failed to reach the minimal standard necessary for employability – and employability is becoming the sole mission of FE.

The priority for policy should be the design of lifelong progression routes which carry students over transitions and on to the completion of courses: participation is no longer sufficient. The Foundation Learning Tier is an important innovation, but, at present, Level 1 and Level 2 students who have left school cannot continue with courses of general education but must choose between the 5,000+ vocational qualifications in the National Qualifications Framework (Foster, 2005: 71); and the information, advice and guidance available to them is 'out of date, fragmented and ill informed' (2005: 39).

Current policy also tends to concentrate on the learning of young people, but the final report of the Leitch review of skills points out that 'Today, over 70 per cent of our 2020 workforce have already completed their compulsory education' (Leitch, 2006: 1). The further education of adults, employed and unemployed, is the larger and more pressing task.

Further problems are created by the sheer diversity and complexity of the LSS. What is missing is the diversity in values, goals, interests and power.

By 'complexity' I mean more than that the sector is difficult to understand or change; I mean it is composed of a number of interrelated sub-systems, each of which is more or less organised or disorganised.

Earlier this year, that landscape was 'rationalised', both by the government creating a single agency (QIA) for quality improvement and by organisations such as the LSC creating new Local Partnerships and Economic Development Teams. However, the result could hardly be described as a slimmed-down sector; in fact, the landscape has become even more crowded as new agencies come into being. Is it any wonder that Ewart Keep (2006) has called state control of this sector 'playing with the biggest train set in the world'? In March 2005, the White Paper on Skills acknowledged that 'there has been concern about the complexity of the organisational landscape', but argued 'To some extent, that complexity is inevitable in such a vast system' (DfES, 2005b Part 2: 69). The landscape urgently needs to be simplified and I shall make some proposals in the final section.[4]

It is difficult to capture the third of Jan Kooiman's (2003) three central features of governance, i.e. not only diversity and complexity but dynamics – the innumerable interactions among the partners within the sector and the pressures for reform from government departments, which result in tensions both between and within organisations.

Three harmful assumptions

Educational policy continues to be based on three underlying and damaging assumptions: first, that 'our future depends on our skills' (Foster, 2005: 9); second, that in all matters concerning vocational education and the skills strategy it is appropriate 'to put employers in the driving seat' (DfES, 2004: 45); and third, that market competition is essential to make providers efficient and responsive. All three of these assumptions have been roundly criticised for almost 30 years (e.g. Karabel and Halsey, 1977; Coffield, 1999; Bartlett *et al.*, 2000; Ball *et al.*, 2000; Wolf, 2002), but they continue to appear in ministerial pronouncements as though they were eternal truths which only a fool would deny.

Politicians throughout the developed world have seized upon a debased version of human capital theory to legitimise their conversion of social and economic inequalities into educational problems. Witness Tony Blair who claimed: 'A country such as Britain in the 21st century will succeed or fail by how it develops its human capital' (2005). This dangerous oversimplification needs to be compared with the Treasury's more sophisticated argument, where skills are only one of the five drivers of productivity, along with investment in physical capital, science and innovation, competition and enterprise (HM Treasury, 2001). In short, we need to ditch 'the belief in a simple, direct relationship between the amount of education in a society and its future growth rate' (Wolf, 2002: 244). Policies based on such a belief raise expectations unreasonably of the likely effects of investment in education on either rectifying unjustifiable inequalities or stimulating economic growth.

One effect of this concentration on human capital is that education is expected to carry the lion's share of the burden of reform. The government's own figures show that only 'one fifth of the gap [in productivity] with France and Germany is a result of the United Kingdom's comparatively poor skills' (Leitch, 2005: 4). So we need to ask Lord Leitch: where are the plans to deal with the factors which are responsible for 80% of that gap? Investment, for example, 'as a proportion of Gross Domestic Product in the UK is, at 17 per cent, the lowest in the G7' (Leitch, 2005: 25). Moreover, the economic returns to investment in qualifications are declining, as more and more young people graduate and face competition from well-educated and professionally trained graduates from Poland, India and China.

As to the second assumption, the history of the repeated attempts by governments of different political complexions to give employers the leading role in developing new policy for the sector is one long story of spurned advances. The previous Secretary of State, Ruth Kelly, described their uneasy relationship thus: 'In the past, Government has let down employers when it has tried to guess what different sectors need. But equally, employers have been guilty of watching Government initiatives from the sidelines and expressing disappointment when they inevitably land wide of the mark' (2005). Leaving aside the admission that governmental initiatives 'inevitably' fail, I would argue that the behaviour of employers is better interpreted as a lack of interest in the roles which government continually proposes for them. Kelly, in her White Paper on 14- to 19-year-olds, underlined her determination 'to put employers in the driving seat, so that they will have a key role in determining what the 'lines of learning' should be and in deciding in detail what the Diplomas should contain' (DfES, 2005a: 45). Employers do not want this responsibility.

Should they, however, have been offered such a privileged position over both the vocational curriculum and the national strategy for skills? Such a commanding role may very well damage the government's attempt to form a new Skills Alliance, which in its own words is meant to be 'a new social partnership for skills' (DfES, 2003: 100). The relationship between government and employers needs to be rethought, with the government being prepared to take the leading role on behalf of the whole community. Instead of offering business and industrial leaders roles they do not want, the government needs to acknowledge the continuing failures caused by our deregulated labour market, and move away from the voluntary organisation of training by challenging those employers who do not train their own workers (see Coffield, 2004).

The third harmful assumption is that the introduction of market forces into public services will guarantee efficiency, responsiveness and greater choice for users; but the government's determination to create more diversity is a euphemism for introducing a new hierarchy among schools. Moreover, 'the key trope for all social policy is the private firm, which is presented as the model of effectiveness' (Ball, 2005). The final report of the Leitch review of skills refers to comparative research on management in the USA, United Kingdom, France and Germany, which showed 'UK firms to be the most poorly managed' (2006: 52).

What is so harmful about these propositions is that they are advanced without any empirical evidence to support them and often in the teeth of findings which flatly contradict them. What is being forgotten is that historically public services were provided to overcome injustices created by free markets and so considerations of equity should take precedence over economic factors such as efficiency. And yet, exactly the opposite happens in the latest publications on the pursuit of excellence from the LSC (2006a, 2006b) and the QIA (2006). As James C. Scott argues, 'in markets, money talks, not people' (1998: 8).

The proliferation of policy

Peter Hyman switched from writing speeches for Tony Blair in Number 10 to working in an inner-city school in London and witnessed in his former post 'the tyranny of momentum politics at first hand.... Constant ... activity to show a department was serious about change ... conspired to make the lives of frontline staff more frustrating and more difficult' (2005: 272). In order to prevent the media from running hostile stories, Number 10 felt it had to seize the headlines every day: 'Because we wanted to show momentum, departments and Number 10 were constantly looking for things to announce' (2005: 269). The inconsistencies, confusions and illogicalities in the Schools White Paper, Higher Standards, Better Schools for All (DfES, 2005c) suggest that it is a prime example of momentum and presidential politics, where policy-making has become over-centralised and confrontational (see Eagle, 2006).

Rather than awaiting the verdict of evaluations, the ministerial response to previous policy tends to be more policy; but the sheer volume of policy, and the tensions created by conflicts within policy now constitute one of the main barriers to progress. 'Between 1997 and the general election of 2005 there were eight Acts of Parliament on education issues' (House of Commons Education and Skills Committee, 2006: 6). To adapt a famous remark of Dennis Potter's: 'For me, policy is not the bandage. It's the wound'. The post-compulsory sector is currently saturated with policies which deflect resources and energies from the central tasks of teaching and learning. Government ministers do not need to be persuaded of this argument; it is their practice which needs to change. Witness Charles Clarke's admission: '[Education reform] depends on Ministers like me holding our nerve and being able to resist the lure of the next initiative in favour of a system that drives its own improvement more and more' (2004: 5). He did not resist; the flood of initiatives has continued unabated.

Over-regulation

Given the barrage of criticism that has been levelled at the heavy-handed regulatory regimes imposed by the government on the public services (e.g. Power, 1997; Newman, 2001; O'Neil, 2002; Ball, 2003), one might have hoped that lessons would have been learned and that the high point of excessive regulation would have passed by now. Certainly, the language of official texts has altered and some of the terminology of the leading critics has been incorporated into official rhetoric. For instance, the LSC's *Agenda for Change* asserted that 'rigorous, comprehensive *self-assessment* is at the heart of organisational development and an essential tool for managing change' (2005b: 6, original emphasis). Similarly, the White Paper on 14–19 Education and Skills argued that the new 'intelligent accountability framework ... should mobilise and motivate institutions' (2005: 81–2). The new wording is a tribute to the philosopher Onora O'Neil, who in her Reith lectures, argued that: 'If we want greater accountability without damaging professional performance we need intelligent accountability', which she defined as requiring 'more attention to good governance and fewer fantasies about total control. Good governance is possible only if institutions are allowed some margin for self-governance' (2002, Lecture 3, 5).

Whether these official protestations about a change of heart will be borne out in practice only time will tell, but already the signs are not good. The LSC's *Framework for Excellence* (2006b), for instance, proposes seven new 'key performance indicators', but each of these is divided into several constituent measures, making up a minimum of 27 new indicators in all. And yet the LSC believes the new regulatory framework will require 'the minimum of additional work' (ibid.: 11). It would be laughable if it were not so serious.

What we are witnessing is an accountability framework, whose measures become steadily more numerous and, at the same time, ever more stretching, robust, tough and challenging, being accommodated and normalised, as professionals develop ever more creative methods of coping. Ministers are likely to run out of adjectives to describe the intensifying rigour of their approach before professionals run out of ingenious methods of complying.

Governments throughout the western world currently employ policy 'instruments', which vary from being coercive to enabling, in their attempts to shape public services. These 'new technologies of power', as Newman (2005: 12) called them, are not, however, nearly as powerful as those who wield them desire. For example, the percentage of 16-year-olds in full-time learning (75.4%) has been stuck on a plateau for almost 10 years.

Moreover, policy 'drivers' suggest a model of change which is crudely mechanical rather than interactive and sensitive. The theory and the language which governments and policy-makers currently employ to describe the management of change in education are not suited to the task. For example, neither the curriculum nor targets can be 'delivered' as though they were the post or pizzas. 'Levers', 'drivers' and 'steering mechanisms' suggest that control can be exercised mechanically over fixed objects by applying the appropriate 'tool': but talk of 'toolboxes' and 'tools for the job' suggests that policy can be 'implemented' as easily as pulling the right levers. Both the language and the model of change are inappropriate and need to be replaced.

The current fashion for over-regulation has one further, and hopefully fatal, weakness: the very countries whose higher productivity we are seeking to emulate achieve 'a high level of quality and standing without the heavy central control and complex accountability arrangements operating in our FE system' (Foster, 2005: 97). The English sector was compared by Sir Andrew Foster and his advisory group with its equivalent in the United States, Denmark, Australia, the Netherlands and Ontario and the key difference was the lack of trust in professionals by English politicians and policy-makers.

Lack of democratic accountability

Over many decades, and under both Conservative and Labour administrations, the powers of local government have been gradually whittled away.[5] The upshot is what Geoff Mulgan has called the great irony of English local government: 'it's neither very local, nor much like government' (2006: 10).

The same period has also seen an explosion in the number of local partnerships involving the public, private and voluntary sectors, e.g. local strategic partnerships and local learning partnerships, whose decisions are not subject to local political accountability. The current shape of local governance can be summarised as *central command and local delivery*.

The rhetoric of government now favours 'double devolution', whereby power is to be passed down apparently not only from the centre to local government but also from cities and counties to neighbourhoods and communities. Its predominant practice since 1997, however, has been just as remorselessly to increase central control because of a basic distrust of local government, which is considered to be 'incompetent and parochial, mediocre and stagnant' (Mulgan, 2006: 8). The recent White Paper on Local Government admits that there are currently 600 separate elements in the performance management of local government by central government, and that '80% of reporting [is] focused on meeting top-down requirements' (Department for Communities and Local Government (DCLG), 2006: 117). The foreword by the Prime Minister contains no hint of an apology for such self-indulgent and intemperate centralism but has the gall to claim he now wants 'to see local authorities rising to the challenge of leading their areas' (DCLG, 2006: 3). Can the proposed reform of local government, however, break out of the dilemma whereby central government will not devolve power until local government becomes more accountable and competent; but local government claims it cannot become more accountable and competent without greater devolution?

In all these discussions, there is little discussion of accountability to the citizens who provide the money. In the LSS, for instance, the Chair and Chief Executive of the LSC, the members of its National Council, its Adult Learning Committee and its Young People's Learning Committee and the council members of the 47 local LSCs are all appointed by the Secretary of State. The same is true of the Sector Skills Development Agency, which is not so much a voice of the employers as an agent of the DfES. Hence, Skelcher (1998) talked of 'the Appointed State', where governance is based on appointed rather than elected bodies. In the financial year 2004–05, the LSC devoted only 1.29% of its huge budget to the Local Initiatives Fund (LSC, 2005a).

The contradiction in policy is at its most acute in this area, as the White Paper promises 'to deliver a step change in promoting [local] cohesion' (DCLG, 2006: 12), while the Prime Minister's Strategy Unit imposes City Academies on town halls. In one of our research areas, the main players in 14–19 education formed a successful learning partnership centred on a shared, educational value, namely, a commitment to raise the attainment of *all* young people in the area and not just that of a minority. That common stance brought them into direct conflict with national educational policy, as advanced by Number 10, which insisted on the establishment of a City Academy and threatened to withdraw funds for the renovation of school buildings if its wishes were not complied with. The cohesion of local communities is weakened by the government, which then introduces new measures to rectify the problems it has caused.

If 'double devolution' is to become more than a fashionable slogan, it will need to be defined as the devolution of substantial power and resources and perhaps even the right to raise local taxes. When FE Colleges are given discretionary control of, say, 20% of their core budget, we shall know the government is serious about localism (see NIACE, 2005: 4).

'Upskilling and reskilling the workforce'

The language and the thinking behind this phrase are ugly and come from government publications where parents, students or employers are placed 'in the driving seat' and given the key role in reform. By implication, those who are permanently parked in the back seat are professionals. The image of the ideal practitioner in the LSS conveyed by the official texts is of a technician who is regularly upgraded in order to implement without question the latest government initiative, who 'personalises' the learning of all his or her students, while simultaneously responding to the ever-changing, short-term needs of local employers. The White Paper on 14–19 summed up this attitude in a chilling phrase: 'We will ensure that the workforce can implement what they are asked to do' (DfES, 2005a: 25). The government's aim is a workforce which passively receives the training thought appropriate for it rather than a profession of experts capable of self-improvement. The teaching profession is being re-formed, as Geoff Whitty argued, with teachers being restricted to 'craft skills rather than professional understanding' (1997: 304). The aim appears to be initiatives which are 'professional proof', i.e. immune from teachers' innovation, incompetence or subversion.

The Prime Minister's Strategy Unit has also published a new model of public sector reform which consists of four elements, each of which is intended to exert pressure for change:[6]

- top-down performance management, e.g. targets, standards, inspection;
- market incentives, e.g. competition and contestability;
- users shaping the sector from below, e.g. so-called 'choice and voice';
- increasing the capacity of organisations and the capability of 'the workforce'

This model will bear down hard upon the staff, who will have to contend with pressures coming at them from above, below and from both sides. And yet their experiences, concerns and innovative ideas are conspicuously absent from the model, which is a closed system. It claims to have embedded incentives for continuous improvement and innovation, but instead treats the workforce as another lever to be pulled. In short, professionals in the LSS are neither equal nor full partners in reform, they are the *target* of reform.

What is missing from this approach are two ingredients of success. First, Seymour Sarason (1990) explained the predictable failure of all educational reform as follows: tutors cannot create and sustain the conditions for their students to become lifelong learners, if those conditions do not exist for the tutors. Those conditions currently do not exist in the sector. Just look at the libraries in FE colleges compared with those in HE; they are living proof of generations of underfunding.

Second, there is no systematic feedback loop (or set of loops) whereby managers and tutors can report back to policy-makers on the strengths and weaknesses of the reforms.[7] Traffic in educational policy remains strictly one way.[8] Tutors, managers and LSC staff need to be involved at all stages in the development, enactment, evaluation and re-design of policy, but the separation of policy and 'delivery' has made it far more difficult to involve in policy-making the very people who know most about the struggle to make sense of the constant through-put of new policies and initiatives.

Towards a learning system?

A new settlement

First, we need nothing less than a new settlement between the government, officials, employers, researchers and professionals. Sir Andrew Foster was right to argue that, as the architect of education, 'DfES should provide a coherent and managed framework spanning schools, FE and HE' (2005: 7). Certainly, we should learn to work across the sectors, and we also need 'a new, open and trust-based relationship between LSC and DfES' (2005: 80), but something more fundamental must come first.

We need a change in the culture of government at the highest level, because those who demand continuous change of others are exactly those in most need of changing their own practices. There are, in other words, demands for reform that we should make *of* the government as well as receiving demands *from* it. The first requisite of a learning system is a government which shows itself capable of learning, of having at times the confidence to be uncertain or to admit it was wrong, and which acts as a role model for all the organisations, professionals and students within the system. Instead, since 1979, we have had governments untroubled by doubt, counterargument or research, who feel passionately about each and every one of their projects, however ill-considered, and who ignore or ridicule constructive criticism rather than learning from it.

The rapidity with which ministers and civil servants are reshuffled also adversely affects all government departments and not just education, as Chris Mullen MP has pointed out.[9] There have been, for example, seven Ministers for Lifelong Learning since 1997[10]; and in the Cabinet reshuffle of April 2006, Douglas Alexander became the seventh Minister of Transport in nine years and John Reid took up his ninth post in nine years. Such constant movement disrupts working relationships, prevents the deep understanding of the challenges faced by particular ministries and promotes short-term thinking and action. We must also have a decisive break with momentum and presidential politics and the culture of constant interference and endless initiatives tied to ministerial careers. This government's tragic flaw has been to imagine that such a massive, diverse and dynamic sector could be micro-managed from 10 Downing Street.

Some amalgamation also needs to take place between the regional LSCs, the RDAs and the Regional Skills Partnerships to strengthen and streamline regional governance. At the local level, the local strategic partnerships should absorb both the LSC partnership teams and the local learning partnerships. And the proliferation of new bodies needs to stop.

The politicians of all parties also need a new story to tell. An increasingly sophisticated electorate deserves better than insulting rhetoric to the effect that education on its own can create economic prosperity and social justice. Instead, we want to hear how education will become part of a coordinated strategy of social, economic and fiscal policies to tackle deep-rooted inequalities.

Social partnership

The main difference between post-16 education in England and the rest of Europe is that we lack the close involvement of all the social partners (government, employers, trade unions, voluntary and community organisations and locally elected representatives) in a forum where consensus is formed on, for instance, the skills, qualifications and training needed to respond to changes in the labour market. Business and education need to work more closely together than ever before, but in a relationship where the private sector is prepared to learn from the public sector as well as vice versa.

Local learning systems

A new geography of power is slowly being constructed. Since 1997, measures supporting both devolution and centralisation have been pursued in government policy. Within the LSC, responsibilities and funding have been transferred from the 47 local offices to nine regional offices, and at the same time, the LSC is being reorganised into 148 local partnership teams. So what we are witnessing is a complex redistribution of power and resources between different levels of governance rather than a simple transfer to or from the centre. In the words of Stephen Ball, 'Arguably what we are now seeing is more localism *and* more centralisation' (2005: 218, original emphasis). I would add: *and* more regionalisation,[11] despite the overwhelming rejection of a directly elected Regional Assembly by voters in the North East.[12] The critical fact here, however, is that neither the LSC nor the RDAs have a democratic mandate to bring about any change. A further problem concerns the drawing of boundaries in ways which make full use of local knowledge, while at the same time identifying areas with sufficient power and resources to effect change.

This is not the place to discuss the detailed reforms needed in the power relationships between central, regional and local governments. Instead, I shall suggest the following minimal conditions as necessary for effective, equitable and inclusive local learning systems:

- We need to acknowledge the primacy of local knowledge and informal relationships. There is no substitute for fine-grained knowledge of local areas and institutions (their history and traditions, geography, culture and performance) and of local labour markets (e.g. levels of skill and productivity). National policy should be shaped to fit local needs, values and aspirations.[13]
- In order to re-introduce cohesion and trust, the relationship between all the social and economic partners should be one of *cooperation*, with each partner having clearly defined roles and responsibilities and a formal duty to cooperate. One democratically accountable organisation, the Local Authority, should be given the power and responsibility to form local plans, as agreed by all the main players, and by local MPs and councillors, to whom the LSC and RDAs should also be accountable on a regular basis. Local authorities will require the active participation of citizens in decision-making and policy-making (see Lowndes et al., 2006).

- Governance and accountability should be organised nationally and re-gionally to ensure a fair distribution of resources in order to reduce unjus-tifiable inequalities.
- The central principle of local partnerships should be a commitment to rais-ing the education and training level of all people in the area and not that of a minority: and the planning and funding of all provision should be based on this principle. Providers within an area should be held jointly responsible for local levels of participation and achievement (see Stanton and Fletcher, 2006).
- Funding should be longer-term (a minimum of three years), stable and flex-ible, with greater local discretion to stimulate innovation.
- This sector, for all the massive injection of extra funds since 1997, remains seriously underfunded. Sufficient, additional funds are needed to break the inverse law of education, whereby those most in need of high-quality education are least likely to get it. Funding, for example, on Levels 1 and 2, students should rise to equal that spent on higher education students. The existing pattern of funding shows that some children, young people and adults matter far more than others. We are currently providing sec-ond-class funding for working-class people in institutions which have been under-resourced for generations.

Staff as full, equal partners with a different mission

It is all very well for Sir Andrew Foster to claim that the sector needs 'a pur-poseful, skilled, professional and inspiring workforce' (2005: 10), but he was silent about the gap which exists between the funding of staff and students in FE colleges and schools (Fletcher and Owen, 2005). The FE White Paper proposes to narrow but not to close this funding gap: 'When resources allow, further steps will be taken' (DfES, 2006a: 68). This is a serious political mis-judgement which undermines the government offer of a 'new relationship' with the colleges: this genuine grievance will fester until 'comparable learn-ing is funded at a comparable rate' (ibid.). It will also make it more difficult for the sector to attract new staff.[14] If the current Secretary of State is looking for a quick way of winning over the staff in FE colleges, he should persuade the Treasury to close this gap now.

The most significant finding in our data, in all three types of settings, is that the relationship between the tutor and students is the heart and soul of the job. If improving teaching and learning were to be acknowledged as the core business, then let me suggest what should result. For example, senior management (apart from financial directors, obviously) in schools and col-leges should teach, in order to demonstrate its over-riding importance. They are, after all, educational leaders first and business leaders second. Moreover, improving teaching and learning is a collective responsibility which requires an institutional response (see Grubb, 1999). One way to improve the quality of teaching and learning would be to give tutors an entitlement to sabbatical leave, reduce the number of their teaching hours per week to, say, 21 and involve them instead in quality circles, peer observations and discussions on the latest research into pedagogy. Written policies on teaching and learning need to go way beyond administrative details and offer an explicit model of learning and of change; and be able to show how both are used to make students, tutors, the senior management team and the institution itself better at learning in a person-centred learning community (see Fielding, 2006). A useful set of 'principles of procedure for improving learning' in FE has also been produced by Hodkinson *et al.* (2006).

Although I have argued for staff in the sector to be made full and equal partners in the formation, enactment, evaluation and re-design of policy, I do not idealise them all as heroic, stressed, underpaid and long-suffering reformers. There are a small number of public-service workers who need to be reminded that they are supposed to be offering the public a service. We do not need, however, a formidable battery of regulatory measures to deal with this minor problem. In over 40 years of work in education, I cannot recall a government that engaged the goodwill and creativity of the teaching profession.

Final comments

This government has taken the sector more seriously than any previous ad-ministration. It has allocated substantial new funding; it has established new structures, agencies and initiatives. Their approach has also chalked up some substantial achievements which deserve to be celebrated, e.g. more than 1.25 million people have improved their basic literacy, numeracy and lan-guage skills. The diligence, inventiveness and commitment of ministers can-not be faulted; it is their judgement, their culture and their failure to act on the main problems which I am questioning here.

After nine years of constant reform,[15] the sector is still inchoate, over-cen-tralised, democratically unaccountable, unequal, woefully under-researched and without robust data for decision-making.[16] The skills strategy is also based on some ill-founded assumptions that need to be re-thought and replaced. As the impatience of ministers has grown with what they see as the slow rate of progress, so their interventions have become more frequent, more hector-ing and more controlling. This repeated cycle of unrealistic expectations and short-term punitive interventions is a recipe for long-term failure.

The challenges of creating radical and enduring reform have been seriously underestimated by government; the language of 'transformation' is inappro-priate for a long, slow process which may take more than a decade to com-plete; the battery of mechanisms selected to 'deliver' such change has proved too mechanical; and the climate of fear which permeates the sector must give way to a climate of mutual trust.

Can this disorganised, troubled but pivotal sector still be turned into a learning system? That would require politicians and policy-makers to change some of their fundamental beliefs and practices and to think and talk differently; institutions to reorder their priorities in favour of pedagogy; and professionals to be given the space and resources to improve their existing expertise. The chances are very slim, but it could be done.

Notes

1   The researchers wish to acknowledge with gratitude the funding of this project by the ESRC (reference number RES-139-25-0105).
2   The research team consisted of Sheila Edward, Ian Finlay, Maggie Gregson, Ann Hodgson, Ken Spours, Richard Steer, Louise Wilson and Jo Lakey.
3   Newman's framework places the four types of governance on two dimensions. The vertical axis represents the degree to which power is centralised or decentralised, while the horizontal axis depicts the orientation towards continuity or change. The resulting four quadrants produce four models of governance – the hierarchical model, the rational goal model, the open systems model and the self-governance model. Current government policy for the sector is not concentrated in any one or two of the quadrants but is scattered throughout all four. For instance, the standardisation of teaching materials by the Standards Unit is firmly within the hierarchical model, but its regional networks of subject coaches belong to the self-governance model because the coaches are meant to be agents of self-improvement; the focus on targets, goals and performance indicators is a good example of the rational goal model; the devolution of responsibility for achieving outcomes to the 'frontline' is characteristic of the open systems model; while the long-term investment in staff training and the proposed move to self-regulation are part and parcel of the self-governance model.
4   The Leitch Report also included a chart of the major organisations in the sector which contains 45 entries and still has to add the caution that 'some institutions have been omitted' (2005: 114).
5   'Their ability to raise revenue [was] cut from 60 per cent to 25 per cent, some £30 billion of services transferred to unelected quangos, and its other services micromanaged from the centre' (Guardian Leader, 16 December, 2005).
6   I have just started a new project to appraise critically the evidential basis of this model of reform. I wish to acknowledge the financial support of the Director and the Dean of Research within the Institute of Education.
7   Kooiman, for example, has argued that there has been a general shift among governments away from 'one way traffic' to 'two way traffic', where 'aspects, qualities, problems and opportunities of both the governing system and the system to be governed are taken into consideration', (quoted by Newman, 2001: 15).
8   In 1999, the Cabinet Office issued a report on Modernising Government which stipulated that 'Government should regard policy making as a continuous learning process, not a series of one-off initiatives..... Feedback from those who implement and deliver policies and services is essential'. Quoted by Newman (2001: 63). Ministers know what they should do, but the culture of momentum politics and the need to make their mark quickly both militate against them accepting such advice.
9   'We have had six Asylum and Immigration Ministers so far, seven Europe Ministers, nine Ministers with responsibility for entry clearance, of whom I was also one, and the Department of Health has been more or less cleaned out twice in the past 18 months or so. I know that decisions on such matters are for people

far above my pay grade, but I gently wonder whether that is the most efficient use of resources and officials' time and whether we get the best out of people by reshuffling the pack with such terrifying rapidity'. Chris Mullin, speech in House of Commons, Foreign Affairs and Defence, 18 May 2005.

10 Dr Kim Howells, George Mudie, Malcolm Wicks, John Healey, Margaret Hodge, Alan Johnston and Bill Rammell.

11 The proposed re-organisation of 43 police authorities in England and Wales into 12 regional forces is part of the same pattern, but at the same time the Police and Justice Bill (2006) increases the power of the Home Secretary to intervene in poorly performing divisions.

12 In November, 2004 78% of voters in the North East, on a turnout of 48%, rejected a directly elected Regional Assembly.

13 For example, Sunderland Council has developed a distinctive model where three academies will work in partnership with all other schools and the FE College.

14 Forty per cent of the current employees are over 50 and only 20% are under 35 (Hunter, 2005).

15 The interim report of the Leitch review of skills summarised the position as follows: 'In 2005, most agencies responsible for identifying or delivering skills are less than ten years old and still finding their feet as stand along institutions or as part of emerging partnerships at national, regional and local levels' (2005: 151).

16 In 2006–07, the LSC had a budget of £10.5 billion and the research budget of the Learning and Skills Research Centre was £1 million, i.e. 0.009%.

References

Ball, S.J. (2003) The teacher's soul and the terrors of performativity. *Journal of Education Policy*, 18(2), 215–28.

Ball, S.J. (2005) Radical policies, progressive modernisation and deepening democracy: The academies programme in action. *Forum*, 47(2 & 3), 215–22.

Ball, S.J., Maguire, M. and Macrae, S. (2000) *Choice, Pathways and Transitions Post-16*. London: Routledge Falmer.

Bartlett, W., Rees, T. and Watts, A.G. (2000) *Adult Guidance Services and the Learning Society*. Bristol: Policy Press.

Bernstein, B. (1996) *Pedagogy, Symbolic Control and Identity: Theory, Research, Critique*. London: Taylor & Francis.

Blair, T. (2005) We must never concede the politics of aspiration for all. *Guardian*, 18 November.

Blunkett, D. (2000) *Remit Letter to Learning and Skills Council*. London: DfES.

Brine, J. (2006) Lifelong learning and the knowledge economy: Those that know and those that do not – The discourse of the European union. *British Educational Research Journal*, 32(5), October, 649–65.

Clarke, C. (2004) Foreword. In *DfES five year strategy for children and learners: Putting people at the heart of public services*. London: The Stationery Office, Cm 6272, 3–5.

Clarke, J. and Newman, J. (1997) *The Managerial State*. London: Sage.

Coffield, F. (1982) *Cycles of Deprivation*. Durham: University of Durham.

Coffield, F. (1999) *Breaking the Consensus: Lifelong Learning as Social Control*. Newcastle: University of Newcastle.

Coffield, F. (2004) Alternative routes out of the low skills equilibrium: A rejoinder to Lloyd and Payne. *Journal of Education Policy*, 19(6), November, 733–40.

Coffield, F., Steer, R., Hodgson, A., Spours, K., Edward, S. and Finlay, I. (2005) A new learning and skills landscape? The central role of the learning and skills Council. *Journal of Education Policy*, 20(5), 631–56.

Department for Communities and Local Government (2006) *Strong and Prosperous Communities: The Local Government White Paper*. London: The Stationery Office, Cm 6939-I and II.

DfES (2005a) *14–19 Education and Skills*. London: The Stationery Office, Cm 6476.

DfES (2002) *Success for All: Reforming Further Education and Training: Our Vision for the Future*. London: DfES, November.

DfES (2003) *21st Century Skills: Realising Our Potential*. London: Stationery Office, Cm 5810.

DfES (2004) *Five Year Strategy for Children and Learners: Putting People at the Heart of Public Services*. London: The Stationery Office, Cm 6272.

DfES (2005b) *Skills: Getting on in Business, Getting on at Work*. London: The Stationery Office. Cm 6483-11.

DfES (2005c) *Higher Standards, Better Schools for All: More Choice for Parents and Pupils*. London: The Stationery Office, Cm 6677.

DfES (2006a) *Further Education: Raising Skills, Improving Life Chances*. London: The Stationery Office, Cm 6768.

DfES (2006b) *The Five Year Strategy for Children and Learners: Maintaining the Excellent Progress*. Sherwood Park, Annesley, Notts: DfES Publications.

Eagle, A. (2006) Make up your mind on education. *Guardian*, 15 March.

Edwards, T. (1997) Educating leaders and training followers. In A.D. Edwards, T. Edwards, R. Haywood, F. Hardman, N. Meagher, C. Fitzgibbons (eds) *Separate but Equal? A Levels and GNVQs*. London: Routledge, 8–28.

Edwards, T. (2001) Educational performance, markets and the state: Present and future prospects. In R. Phillips and J. Furlong (eds) *Education, Reform and the State: Twenty-five Years of Politics, Policy and Practice*. London: RoutledgeFalmer, 239–53.

Fielding, M. (2006) Leadership, personalization and high performance schooling: Naming the new totalitarianism. *School Leadership and Management*, 26(4), September, 347–69.

Fletcher, M. and Owen, G. (2005) *The Funding Gap: Funding in Schools and Colleges for Full-time Students Aged 16–18*. London: LSDA.

Foster, A. (2005) *Realising the Potential: A Review of the Future Role of Further Education Colleges*. London: DfES.

Grubb, W.N. (1999) *Honored but Invisible: An Inside Look at Teaching in Community Colleges*. New York: Routledge.

HM Treasury (2001) *Pre Budget Report: Building a Stronger, Fairer Britain in an Uncertain World*. London: The Stationery Office, Cm 5318.

Hodgson, A. et al. (forthcoming) Learners in the English learning and skills sector: The implications of half-right policy assumptions. *Oxford Review of Education*, 33(3), 315–330.

Hodgson, A., Spours, K., Coffield, F., Steer, R., Finlay, I., Edward, S. and Gregson, M. (2005) *A New Learning and Skills Landscape? The LSC within the Learning and Skills Sector*. London: Institute of Education.

Hodkinson, P., Biesta, G. and James, D. (2006) Principles of procedure for improving learning. Online: www.ex.ac.uk/sell/tlc/publications.htm

House of Commons Education and Skills Committee (2006) *The Schools White Paper: Higher Standards, Better Schools for All*. First Report of Session 2005–06, Volume 1, HC 633-1, London: The Stationery Office.

Hunter, D. (2005) Boosting skills begins with the teachers. *Times Educational Supplement*, FE *Focus*, 16 December.

Hyman, P. (2005) *1 Out of 10: From Downing Street Vision to Classroom Reality*. London: Vintage.

Johnson, A. (2006) *LSC Grant Letter: 2007:08*. London: DfES.

Karabel, J. and Halsey, A.H. (Eds.) (1977) *Power and Ideology in Education*. New York: Oxford University Press.

Keep, E. (2006) State control of the English education and training system – Playing with the biggest trainset in the world. *Journal of Vocational Education and Training*, 58(1), 47–64.

Kelly, R. (2005) Ministerial foreword. *National Skills Academies: Prospectus 2005/6; An Innovative Approach to Meeting employers' Needs for Training*. London: DfES.

Kooiman, J. (2003) *Governing as Governance*. London: Sage.

Leitch, S. (2005) *Skills in the UK: The long-term challenge. Interim Report*. London: HM Treasury.

Leitch, S. (2006) *Prosperity for all in the global economy – World class skills*. Final Report, London: Stationery Office.

Lowndes, V., Pratchett, L. and Stoker, G. (2006) *Locality Matters: Making Participation Count in Local Politics*. London: IPPR.

LSC (2005a) *A Clear Direction, Annual Report and Accounts, 2004–05*. Coventry: LSC.

LSC (2005b) *Learning and Skills – The Agenda for Change*. Coventry: LSC.

LSC (2006a) *New Measures of Success, Letter to Providers*. Coventry: LSC, 6 January.

LSC (2006b) *Framework for Excellence: A Comprehensive Assessment Performance Framework for the Further Education System*. Coventry: LSC.

Mortimore, P. (2006) *Which Way Forward: An Education System for the 21st Century*. London: NUT.

Mulgan, G. (2006) Central reservations. *Society Guardian*, 1 March, 10.

Newman, J. (2000) Beyond the new public management? Modernising public services. In J. Clarke, S. Gewirtz and E. McLaughlin (eds), *New Managerialism, New Welfare?* London: Sage/Open University, 45–61.

Newman, J. (2001) *Modernising Governance: New Labour, Policy and Society*. London: Sage.

Newman, J. (Ed.) ((2005) *Remaking Governance: Peoples, Politics and the Public Sphere*. Bristol: Policy Press.

NIACE (2005) *Eight in Ten: Adult Learners in Further Education*. Leicester: NIACE.

O'Neil, O. (2002) *Reith Lectures*. London: BBC.

OECD (2006) *Education at a Glance: OECD Indicators 2006*. Paris: OECD.

Power, M. (1997) *The Audit Society: Rituals of Verification*. Oxford: Oxford University Press.

QIA (2006) *Pursuing Excellence: An Outline Improvement Strategy for Consultation*. Coventry: QIA.

Sarason, S. (1990) *The Predictable Failure of Educational Reform: Can We Change Course Before It's Too Late?* San Francisco: Jossey-Bass.

Scott, J.C. (1998) *Seeing Like a State: How Certain Schemes to Improve the Human Condition Have Failed*. New Haven: Yale University Press.

Sennett, R. (1998) *The Corrosion of Character: The Personal Consequences of Work in the New Capitalism*. New York: W. W. Norton.

Skelcher, C. (1998) *The Appointed State*. Buckingham: Open University Press.

Stanton, G. and Fletcher, M. (2006) 14–19 institutional arrangements in England – research perspective on collaboration, competition and patterns of post-16 provision. Nuffield Review of 14–19 Education and Training, Working Paper 38. Online: www.nuffield14–19review.org.uk

Whitty, G. (1997) Marketization, the state and the re-formation of the teaching profession. In A.H. Halsey, H. Lauder, P. Brown, and A.S. Wells (eds) *Education: Culture, Economy, Society*. Oxford: Oxford University Press, 299–319.

Wolf, A. (2002) *Does Education Matter? Myths about Education and Economic Growth*. London: Penguin.

Part 5

Improving education systems

Chapter 14

Government policy is no longer the solution

We have come to a pretty pass when a government department publicly admits that practitioners are being distracted from 'delivery' by the sheer scale of change imposed by ministers. This article was published in the magazine of the University and College Union for October 2008, and detailed the avalanche of policy pouring down upon the education system. One outcome has been a huge drop in the number of adults taking courses. The problem that remains is that clever and committed ministers are so convinced that they are acting in the public good that they cannot comprehend that the task of enacting policies is far more difficult than forming them.

Many of those who have held senior posts in education seem not to have reflected on their job so, on retirement, they have little to say. C. Wright Mills urged academics to use their life experiences in their intellectual work, 'continually to examine and interpret it' (1970:216).

James Wright, the VC of Newcastle University, was the kind of leader for whom the phrase 'a gentleman and a scholar' was invented. Despite the onerous duties of being in charge of a large civic university, he taught students, set and marked their exams. When he returned to the Senior Common Room after retiring to receive a gift from his colleagues, he made an eloquent speech which I wish I had recorded. I do remember him saying that his first discovery on retirement was that Sundays were no longer followed by Mondays.

His deputy, Andrew Hamnett, left Newcastle to become Principal of Strathclyde University. Previously, his main task had been coping with the demands of heads of department, seeking to maximise their slice of the university's resources irrespective of the impact on others. He adopted the practice of Prince Metternicht, who, as Interior Minister of the Austrian Hungarian Empire, had imposed order on the many competing nationalities within it by 'keeping them in balanced and well-modulated discontent'.

Government policy is no longer the solution to our difficulties but our greatest problem. That's the conclusion that an increasing number of researchers, practitioners and senior managers within the education system are coming to. I came reluctantly to accept it by reflecting on the hyperactivity of ministers in every phase of education, although I shall concentrate on the

DOI: 10.4324/9781003476146-19

post-compulsory sector. It is little consolation to realise that what is happening to education is being replicated in all the public services.

The Early Years Foundation Stage, set up by the government, has established 69 'early learning goals' for the under-fives, which according to the experts are likely to confuse and demotivate the most disadvantaged children. Surely 6 or 9 would be enough for 4-year olds, but 69?

Gemma Moss (2007), a former colleague, has counted the number of documents sent by government agencies to all primary schools in England on the topic of literacy during the years 1996 and 2004. The total came to 459, which amounts to 51 per year or almost one a week for nine years.

In May 2008, the House of Commons Select Committee on Children, Schools and Families reported that it had 'received substantial evidence that teaching to the test, to an extent which narrows the curriculum and puts sustained learning at risk, is widespread' (p. 41) in English primary and secondary schools.

In the post-compulsory sector, the Learning and Skills Council, in its statement of priorities for the next 3 years, lists 7 priorities and 86 separate goals; and behind each of these goals lies a detailed strategy, each with its own performance indicators. For such an extensive and complicated sector, I could understand 16 or 18 goals, but 86?

The post-16 learning sector also suffers from a permanent revolution in structures which change name and remit every time ministers are reshuffled. Ministers have to make their mark in such a short time that little, if any, consideration is given to the staff working in these organisations, many of whom are made redundant at heavy cost to the taxpayer and at considerable emotional cost to them and their families. So, for instance, what was once the Further Education Unit (FEU) was merged with the Staff College to become the Further Education Development Unit (FEDA), which in turn was turned into the Learning and Skills Development Agency (LSDA), which was then divided into the Quality Improvement Agency (QIA) and the Learning and Skills Network (LSN); the QIA was then amalgamated with the Centre for Excellence in Leadership (CEL), to form a new group, now called the Learning and Skills Improvement Service (LSIS).

The gap between the rhetoric of policy and the reality of practice in this sector has also become a chasm. So, for example, the government is determined to create a 'demand-led system', where funding is supposed to follow the choices made by learners and employers, but the government has added two provisos. The learners must not demand too much (funding for English for Speakers of Other Languages (ESOL) courses was restricted in 2007 because too many immigrants and asylum seekers enrolled for them). Nor must they demand the 'wrong' type of course (skills for 'employability' take precedence over learning for personal development; and funding will only be forthcoming for those vocational qualifications approved by Sector Skills Councils). Moreover, FE colleges and private trainers have little control over the investment decisions that employers make or over industrial policy, both of which are very influential in shaping the amount and kind of training that employers demand.

John Denham, then Secretary of State for Innovation, Universities and Skills, in the preface to his department's Business Plan for 2008–09, claimed '...we have ambitious plans to go further and faster in the coming year'. His department will have to be very fleet of foot because the Business Plan consists of: 2 Public Service Agreements (PSAs, which are misnomers: they are targets which haven't been agreed either by the public or by the public services); 6 departmental strategic objectives; 70 key performance indicators; contributions to 28 cross-government PSAs; 3 new programmes; a blueprint for success which has 4 elements and 10 projects; 8 strategic messages; 18 'key policy deliverables' (targets are so passé, don't you think?) and 7 corporate risks.

I'll quote the fifth risk in full because it deserves to be savoured: 'Sector Instability and Reform Overload in FE – that the key delivery partners become distracted from delivering "business as usual" due to uncertainty over the future organisational shape of the sector, or as a result of the sheer scale of change' (p. 38). What confidence can we have in an organisation that has to admit publicly that its own behaviour poses one of the greatest threats to the sector which has been entrusted to it?

In adult education, there have been over the last 20 years 15 junior ministers and 15 different civil servants in charge, so is it any wonder that policy changes so fast? Meanwhile, the last two years have seen 1.4 million fewer adult learners in the FE sector because the government is concentrating funding on adults taking courses on 'economically valuable skills'.

What are we to make of these avalanches of policy pouring down on the system? We have a hyperactive government which thinks that schools, colleges and universities will be changed, and changed for ever along radical lines, only by intensifying the already frenetic pace of change.

The government since 1997 has certainly made significant, additional investments in all phases of education, but increasingly, some of their flagship policies have been roundly criticised by researchers and practitioners. For example, the unwarranted decision to impose synthetic phonics on all primary schools as the *only* way of teaching children to read; the damage done to local schools by the academy programme; and the withdrawal of funds from learners studying in HE for an equivalent or lower qualification which will result in fewer adult learners in HE. The response from ministers has been consistent: 'We know best and we shall not be deterred from imposing our ideas on you'.

What kind of person persists in a course of action that has been roundly criticised by all those who know about the topic? In rare cases, an unacknowledged genius is proved right and the critics wrong. Or a cold-hearted authoritarian has to be bundled in tears into an official car and driven away before she does any more harm. There is, however, a more common type who is still more dangerous: the well-intentioned amateur who is so convinced he is acting in the public good that he cannot comprehend that he is doing harm.

This is no way to run a country. This is no way to transform a system. Ministers have understood the urgent need for change without appreciating the concomitant need for continuity. The proposed new structures are more likely to result in yet another failure to create an equitable post-compulsory system than to produce 'world-class skills'. The permanent revolution imposed on public services by ministers is a symptom of a deep malaise in our political system because governments with an overall majority are literally out of control.

References

Department for Innovation, Universities and Skills (2008) *Business Plan for 2008-09*. London: Department for Innovation, Universities and Skills.

Mills, C. Wright (1970) *The Sociological Imagination*. Harmondsworth, Middlesex: Penguin Books.

Moss, G. (2007) Understanding the limits of top-down management. In Coffield, F., Steer, R., Allen, R., Vignoles, A., Moss, G. and Vincent, C. (eds) *Public Sector Reform: Principles for Improving the Education System*. London: Institute of Education, 19–33.

Chapter 15

Why the McKinsey reports will not improve school systems

Re-reading this article has suggested that the status of Michael Barber's policy of 'deliverology' is no greater than that of Ken Dodd's 'tickleology'. First published in the *Journal of Education Policy* (2012, 27(2) 131–149), this paper made so many criticisms of the two McKinsey reports that they cannot be used as a blueprint for improvement. Others such as Robin Alexander have pointed out even more weaknesses (see Alexander, 2022: 327–331). Yet politicians and policy-makers ignored these discomfiting findings and plumped for only one factor out of a highly complex set of interacting relations. McKinsey and Company produced two highly influential reports on how to improve school systems. The first McKinsey report *How the world's best-performing school systems come out on top* has since its publication in 2007 been used to justify change in educational policy and practice in England and many other countries. The second *How the world's most improved school systems keep getting better*, released in late 2010, is a more substantial tome which is likely to have an even greater impact. This article subjects both reports to a close examination and finds them deficient in ten respects.

*At Durham, I became friends with Mark Leaf, a lecturer in American Literature, who had once, but only once, been asked to give a talk to the first-year students. He took for his theme Erving Goffman's notion of total institutions. I was a fan of Goffman's work, having read the dedication to his book, **Relations in Public**, which reads as follows: DEDICATED TO THE MEMORY OF A.R. RADCLIFFE-BROWN WHOM ON HIS VISIT TO THE UNIVERSITY OF EDINBURGH IN 1950, I ALMOST MET.*

But back to Mark Leaf. He explained Goffman's idea of total institutions as places where large numbers of individuals are enclosed from the rest of society for large stretches of time and are subjected to strict rules and schedules which are rigidly enforced by staff. He claimed there were three such institutions in Durham ... the prison, the hospital and the university. He invited the students to work out which one they had been sent to.

DOI: 10.4324/9781003476146-20

Introduction

Since the publication in September 2007 of the first McKinsey report, its conclusions have quickly hardened into new articles of faith for politicians, policy-makers, educational agencies and many researchers and practitioners, both in this country and abroad. The claim made by the two authors, Michael Barber[1] and Mona Mourshed[2] (their study will from now on be referred to as the B and M report or the first McKinsey report[3]) is that they have identified the three factors behind 'world-class' school systems:

> getting more talented people to become teachers, developing these teach- ers into better instructors, and ensuring that these instructors deliver con- sistently for every child in the system.
> (Barber and Mourshed, 2007)

In the above quotation, teachers have become 'instructors', although this could be explained as the use of the standard term for a teacher in North America. The report has been received as though it will 'transform' the perfor- mance of schools anywhere, irrespective of their culture or socio-economic status.

A Google search (on 31 January 2011), for instance, produced 2,250 refer- ences to the first McKinsey report; and the entries include articles and reports from government agencies and researchers across the globe. The study has also been translated into French and Spanish and overwhelmingly, its reception has been favourable, being described, e.g., as 'a unique tool to bring about improvements in schooling', by Schleicher (2007), Head of the Education Directorate at the OECD.

The second report has had far less time to garner plaudits, but Professor Fullan, Special Adviser on Education to the Premier of Ontario, ends his fore- word as follows:

> This is no ordinary report ... It will, by its clarity and compelling insights, catapult the field of whole system reform forward in dramatic ways.
> (Fullan, 2010: 11)

The three themes identified by the first report constitute a serious over- simplification, but the two authors then claim that 'the main driver ... is the quality of the teachers' (op cit: 12). So their explanation of a highly complex set of relations is reduced to only one factor, which has been seized upon by even well-seasoned researchers:

> Evidence is accumulating from around the world that the single most significant means of improving the performance of national educational systems is through excellent teaching.
> (e.g. Pollard, 2010: 1)

Such a reaction is understandable given the derision which has been poured over the teaching profession for decades by politicians and the media (see Ball, 1990). But unaccustomed praise must not blunt criticism. After all, did not Ausubel (1968, vi) argue: 'The most important single factor influencing learning is what the learner already knows?' Moreover, it is a standard finding of educational research that, of the two main factors which influence test scores – the quality of the teaching and the quality of the student intake – the second is far more powerful. For example:

> 77% of the between school differences in student performance in the United Kingdom is explained by differences in socio-economic background. Among OECD countries, only Luxembourg has a higher figure (OECD/average 55%).
>
> (OECD 2010b: 1)

In other words, the superior performance of 'good' schools is explained, first by the high quality of their student intake, and then by a host of other factors, including the quality of teaching. The argument should be about complexity and multiple causation, not about the overwhelming significance of one factor.

In the first White Paper on schools, entitled *The Importance of Teaching*, issued by the Tory-led coalition government in England in November 2010, the second B and M report is quoted approvingly seven times in the first 20 pages; and the Prime Minister and Deputy Prime Minister in their joint foreword to the report make use of one of its summary statements: 'The first, and most important, lesson is that no education system can be better than the quality of its teachers' (DfE, 2010: 3). The belated importance now being accorded to teachers is welcome, but the success of an education system depends on far more than one central factor.

The attention paid to the first McKinsey report can partly be explained by the anxiety displayed by politicians of developed and developing countries to compete successfully in the global knowledge economy. When they are told authoritatively that this can be done most effectively, not by reforming the quality of goods and services, but by making three (or perhaps only one) changes to their schooling system, then the prominence of the report's conclusions in policy documents becomes easier to understand. Politicians are also understandably galvanised by the relative poor performance of their education system, as measured, e.g. by the surveys undertaken by the programme for international student assessment (PISA), run by OECD. The United Kingdom government responded to the latest international comparison by commenting:

> ... we are falling behind international competitors ... we fell from 4th in the world in science in 2000 to 16th in 2009, from 7th to 25th in literacy, and from 8th to 27th in maths.
>
> (Cabinet Office 2011: 1.7)

The USA did little better, performing below the average in maths, ranked 25th out of 34 countries (OECD 2010a).

Politicians continue to draw a simple causal connection between investment in education and increased economic growth: for instance, Hayes (2011: 1), the Minister of State for Further Education in England, argued recently: 'Higher skills bring higher productivity'. The research evidence, however, was well summarised by Wolf (2002: xii) almost 10 years ago: 'The simple one-way relationship which so entrances our politicians and commentators – education spending in, economic growth out – simply doesn't exist'. Yet the Department for Education in November 2010 sought to bolster its argument in favour of the relationship as follows: As President Obama has said: 'the countries that out-teach us today will out-compete us tomorrow' (DfE 2010: 4).[4] The main purpose of education is here reduced to improving the competitiveness of industry. A more comprehensive approach would be to argue that countries benefit economically from expanding education at all levels, but that the cultural, democratic and social goals of education are every bit as important.[5] Grubb and Lazerson in discussing 'the education gospel' in the United States call upon public figures, politicians and commissions

> to moderate their rhetoric, difficult as that might be in the era of the sound bite. Simple claims for education should be replaced with a deeper understanding of what education and training can accomplish, and which goals require other social and economic policies as well.
>
> (Grubb and Lazerson, 2004: 263)

The second McKinsey report, written by Mourshed, Chijioke and Barber, (hereafter called the MCB report or the second McKinsey report) provides, at more than three times the length of its predecessor, a much more considered explanation of continuous success. It had its American launch in December 2010 with the supportive participation of the US Secretary of Education, Arne Duncan. MCB claims to have identified formerly unrecognised patterns of intervention among the 20 school systems they studied by means of 200 interviews with education leaders during visits to these systems, and by collecting data on nearly 575 interventions tried by those systems. They chose systems that had 'achieved significant, sustained and widespread gains in student outcomes on international and national assessments from 1980 onwards' (MCB, 2010: 17). 'Gains in student outcomes' is, however, shorthand for rises in test scores in only three subjects: reading, maths, and science. The chosen 20 were then divided into two sets: the first set of 'sustained improvers' included countries like Singapore and England, provinces like Ontario in Canada, and districts like Long Beach in California; the second set of seven 'promising starts' included countries like Chile and Ghana and provinces like Madhya Pradesh in India and Minas Gerais in Brazil.

The 20 systems were then placed into one of five performance stages – poor, fair, good, great[6] and excellent – according to their test scores on a number of international assessments (e.g. PISA, TIMSS, PIRLS, etc.[7]), which were converted onto a 'universal scale' (*op cit*: 130) with the following cut-off points: 'poor' equates with scores of less than 440; 'fair' with scores of 440–480; 'good' 480–520; 'great' 520–560 and 'excellent' more than 560, a score not achieved by any of the 20 systems studied. It was, however, reached by Finland, which was excluded, without explanation, from the study. So the only country in the world to achieve educational 'excellence' according to this methodology was omitted.

One of their main claims is that each of these performance stages 'is associated with a dominant cluster of interventions, irrespective of geography, culture or political system' (*op cit*: 24), and these clusters are briefly represented in Figure 15.1. In all four stages from poor to excellent, the reins of power remain firmly in the hands of the centre and the 'strategic leader', although the role of the centre and the leader changes from highly prescriptive direction

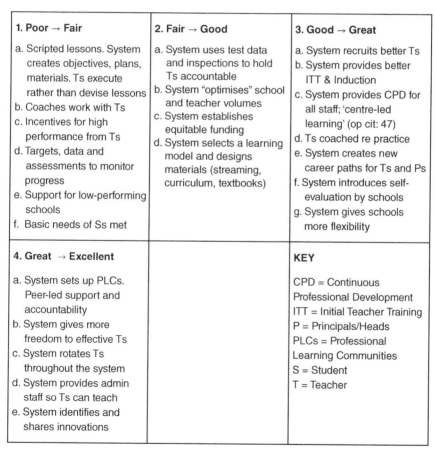

Figure 15.1 Five stages from poor to perfect.

Source: Based on Mourshed, Chijioke, and Barber (2010).

to granting more autonomy to those teachers and schools which the centre considers to have merited it. As school systems move across the continuum from poor to excellent, the centre also changes from 'prescribing adequacy' to 'unleashing greatness' (*op cit*: 52) by introducing such measures as school self-evaluation and professional learning communities.

Assessing the performance level of a school system (anything from 'poor to excellent') is the first of five strategies for improvement. The other four are: choosing the appropriate interventions for that stage; adapting those interventions to the particular contexts of the system (history, politics, culture, etc.); sustaining the improvements made; and 'igniting' the reforms, that is, how to get them started. See Figure 15.2 for an overview of these five strategies, which

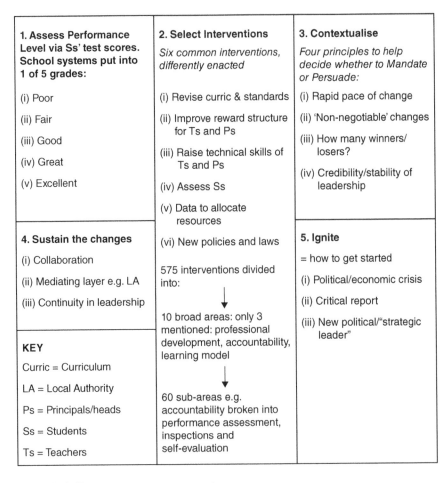

Figure 15.2 Five improvement strategies.

Source: Based on Mourshed, Chijioke, and Barber (2010).

consist of 21 factors in all. Within three years, the task of improving school systems has become decidedly more complicated with three factors being cited in the first report but 21 in the second; and yet, as this article will argue, it remains far more complex than even this more elaborate scheme allows for.

The structure of this article

Reports which have achieved such global influence within a short time deserve the closest scrutiny. Yet when they are so examined, the first fails for at least four reasons: it is methodologically flawed; selective; superficial; and its rhetoric on leadership runs ahead of the evidence. The second, although it corrects some of the faults of its predecessor and offers a more elaborate explanation of success, still possesses six faults: it has an impoverished view of teaching and learning; its evidential base is thin; its central arguments are implausible; its language is technocratic and authoritarian; it underplays the role of culture in education; and it omits any mention of democracy. These failings are listed in Figure 15.3.

The four deficiencies in the first report

Methodologically flawed

The B and M report contains two methodological weaknesses. First, it is in essence a comparative study of 25 school systems, but it does not compare like with like.

1	Methodologically flawed
2	Selective
3	Superficial
4	Emphasis on leadership unsupported by evidence
5	Impoverished view of teaching and learning
6	Thin evidence base
7	Implausible central arguments
8	Technocratic and authoritarian language
9	Role of culture underplayed
10	Democracy omitted

Figure 15.3 Ten weaknesses.

The English system (with 23,000 schools) is constantly being compared unfavourably with Alberta (4,000 schools), Singapore (351 schools) and Boston (150 schools). To deal just with the category of size, the challenges faced by a national system of over 20,000 schools are of a different order than those faced by a city with 150. Besides, the English system has different aims and values; what it wants from its schools is very different from what Singapore wants.

Other dimensions could be mentioned: there are, for instance, far more languages (over 100) spoken in primary schools in Tower Hamlets (a London borough) than in the whole of Finland (about five). Comparison, no matter how crude, has, however, become a means of governance: 'Comparison is used to provide evidence that legitimises political actions' (Ozga, 2009: 158). There is not sufficient acknowledgement of the complexities involved in attempting to derive lessons from another country (never mind 25), because of enormous differences in educational history, politics, socio-economic conditions, culture, and institutional structures.

Second, the manner in which B and M discuss the National Literacy Strategy in England does not meet two important criteria of research ethics. In the first place, Michael Barber does not declare a personal interest in his presentation of the statistics, which, it is claimed, show 'dramatic impact on student outcomes ... in just three years' (B and M, 2007: 27). During those years, he was Chief Adviser to the Secretary of State for Education on school standards in England. In short, he is defending his own record, and the trust of readers who do not know of his involvement is being abused. In the second place, he fails to include in his account any of the publicly available data, which flatly contradict his claim. A more independent judgement is called for.

Dylan Wiliam, an internationally acknowledged expert in assessment, has studied the attempts by successive English governments to raise student achievement and concluded that they 'produced only marginal improvements' (Wiliam, 2008). In more detail, the largest rise in test scores in literacy took place before the strategy was introduced in 1999. A modest improvement took place after the first year of the strategy, but the test scores flatlined in subsequent years. Much the same pattern can be discerned in the test scores for numeracy. But the most interesting data refer to the test scores in science, which performed best of all, but had *no national strategy*. What conclusion can be drawn? Teachers became highly skilled at preparing their students to take tests long before the national strategies in literacy and numeracy were introduced. These two interventions proved largely ineffective but were hugely expensive at a cost of £500 million. Both of these findings should have been included in the B and M report.

Members of the international education community deserve to be given the full rather than such a partisan account. When they are not so treated in good faith, they represent a highly contentious claim as an established research finding: see, e.g. Wei *et al.* (2009: 3).

Disablingly selective

In their preface, the authors state: 'We have chosen not to focus on pedagogy or curricula, however important these subjects might be in themselves' (*op cit*: 9). The McKinsey report claims to be an international benchmarking study of school improvement and yet it omitted to study what subjects the schools were teaching or how they were taught. But it is not only pedagogy and curricula which are absent. Their analysis lacks any discussion of: governance and policy; discrimination whether of class, race, religion or gender; parental influences on education; how culture and teaching come together as pedagogy; or the aims and purposes of education.

Superficial

One of the tacit assumptions in the report is that 'best practice' can be readily identified and disseminated throughout a school or a system. The notion of 'best practice' is referred to no less than seven times, so it is a central plank in their argument. Yet even a casual acquaintance with the extensive literature on transfer would have alerted the authors to this enduring problem, which has puzzled researchers since William James's experiments in the 1890s and which continues to do so (e.g. Grose and Birney, 1963; McKeough *et al.*, 1995; Eraut, 2002).

There are two classes of difficulty – one concerning the identification of 'best practice' and the second with its dissemination. It is not possible to say that a particular practice is 'good', 'best' or 'excellent' in all settings, on all occasions and with all students. The criteria or norms by which these judgements are made are rarely explicitly stated. How can one 'best practice' cope with the immense diversity of local contexts and individual needs? The terms used, 'good', 'best' and 'excellent practice', are also ambiguous, flabby and used interchangeably (see Coffield and Edward (2009) for more on this theme).

The notion of one 'best practice' also betrays a misunderstanding of the situated nature of learning. As James and Biesta (2007: 37) argue:

> Because of the relational complexity of learning and of the differing positions and dispositions of learners [and, I would add, of teachers], there is no approach that can ever guarantee universal learning success.

Instead, B and M make the extraordinary claim that 'best practices ... work irrespective of the culture in which they are applied' (*op cit*: 2), but they offer no evidence to support it.

Disseminating 'best practice', usually by means of cascade training, is also fraught with difficulties. The approach may appear to be intuitively sensible, it is a cheap way to seek to influence large numbers of teachers, and it operates in the main with existing staff. Evidence for its effectiveness is, however, very hard to come by. The outcomes tend to be described as inconsistent (e.g. Adult Learning Inspectorate, 2007), which is a euphemistic way of saying patchy or difficult to discern. The conclusion of most empirical studies can be expressed as follows: what begins as a cascade at the centre becomes a trickle in the classroom (e.g. Hayes, 2000). Its critical weakness, however, is that teachers at the receiving end are passive in relation to the content and process of the 'best practice'; but they tend to exert their professional independence by appearing to comply, while adapting, ignoring or rejecting top- down reforms (see Coffield *et al.*, 2008). Instead, teachers who 'own' the innovation, who are both the originators and recipients of 'good practice', tend to learn from other teachers in equal partnerships, based on mutual trust (see Fielding *et al.* (2005) for a fuller explanation). Galbraith (1992: 27) memorably captured the similar difficulty with the trickle-down theory of wealth: 'If the horse is fed amply with oats, some will pass through to the road for the sparrows'. In more prosaic language, if you are concerned about the welfare of sparrows, feed them directly.

The rhetoric on leadership runs ahead of the evidence

B and M claims 'The evidence suggests that strong school leadership is particularly important in producing improvement' (*op cit*: 30). The main source for this statement is a study by the National Centre for School Leadership (NCSL) in England, which in 2006 produced *Seven Strong Claims about Successful Leadership* (Leithwood *et al.*, 2006). The NCSL is an interested party in any discussion on the effectiveness of leadership, as it has to justify its existence to the government which funds it.[8] The NCSL report presents, however, far less compelling evidence than its title would suggest. It concludes, e.g. that 'research on school leadership has generated few robust claims' (Leithwood *et al.*, 2006: 15). It also admits that 'leadership explains only 5–7% of the difference in pupil learning and achievement across schools' (*op cit*: 4). Certainly, 5–7% will affect a substantial number of students, but it would be preferable to work with the factors which explain the other 93–95%, even when the amount of variance covered by measurement error is discounted.

Unlike B and M, Hartley (2007, 2009) has reviewed the extensive literature on leadership and concluded:

> attempts to show a direct causal relationship between leaders' behaviour (be it distributed or otherwise) and pupils' achievement have yielded little that is definitive ... the policy is ahead of the evidence.
>
> (2007: 204)

The style of leadership favoured by the first McKinsey report, which describes principals as 'drivers of improvement in instruction', appears to be of the strong, hierarchical type, where aspiring heads 'shadow top private sector executives' (*op cit:* 31). The claim appears to be that there are context-independent qualities of leadership, which enable captains of industry to run FE colleges successfully; or equip heads of outstanding schools in the leafy suburbs to repeat their success in the inner city. B and M are in danger of resurrecting the myth of the hero-leader or hero-innovator:

> the idea that you can produce, by training, a knight in shining armour who, loins girded with new technology and beliefs, will assault his organisational fortress and institute changes both in himself and others at a stroke. Such a view is ingenuous. The fact of the matter is that organisations such as schools and hospitals will, like dragons, eat hero-innovators for breakfast.
>
> (Georgiades and Phillimore, 1975: 315)

The six deficiencies in the second report

Before introducing these weaknesses, a brief comparison between the two McKinsey reports is called for. The second report is a considerable improvement on the first and accords a much enhanced role to collaboration, which becomes 'the main mechanism for improving teaching practice and making teachers accountable to each other' (*op cit:* 4). Fullan's latest work is well integrated into the argument: 'Collective capacity generates the emotional commitment and the technical expertise that no amount of individual capacity working alone can come close to matching' (quoted by Mourshed *et al.*, 2010: 84). Fullan, however, then introduces the notion of 'collaborative competition' as a force for change, where educators are expected to 'outdo themselves and each other' (*op cit:* 138). This is a clever-sounding oxymoron dreamed up by a policy adviser to chivvy teachers.

The MCB report also has the virtue of asking two vital questions: 'How does a school system with poor performance become good? And how does one with good performance become excellent?' (*op cit:* 2). This time their answers are more intricate and include the claim that:

> six interventions occur equally at every performance stage for all systems … building the instructional skills of teachers and management skills of principals, assessing students, improving data systems, facilitating improvement through the introduction of policy documents and education laws, revising standards and curriculum, and ensuring an appropriate reward and remuneration structure for teachers and principals.
>
> (*op cit:* 3)

This statement is clearly a major advance on the earlier argument that the quality of teaching is the single most significant factor, but where is the

evidence for the claim that 'six interventions occur equally at every performance stage for all systems?' The second selection of factors remains an oversimplification of the complexities involved; and it represents a continuation
of command and control from the centre despite repeated talk of decentralisation; and it suffers from a fatal omission. The six deficiencies in MCB will
now be described.

Impoverished view of teaching and learning

Despite references to a 'system's pedagogy' (op cit: 99), the MCB report
contains neither an explicit view of teaching and learning nor a vision of
education. Their implicit model can, however, be pieced together from the
metaphors they employ. For instance, they discuss 'the transmission of effective teaching strategies' (op cit: 48); 'the best delivery methods' (op cit: 50)
and 'once a teacher had adopted the right approach (op cit: 88). These remarks suggest that the authors adhere to the acquisition model of learning,
where the minds of learners are viewed as containers to be filled with knowledge, but they give no indication that there are other competing models such
as participation (Lave and Wenger, 1994), construction (Evans et al., 2006)
and becoming (Biesta et al., 2011). The acquisition metaphor characterises
the growth of knowledge in students as a step-by-step process of gaining facts,
skills and understanding – the equivalent of steadily walking upstairs. It frequently is so, but every so often the breakthroughs students make in their
thinking are more like the leaps salmon make in foaming rivers. We need
more than one metaphor as Sfard (1998) has argued.

  Moreover, the belief in one right approach to teaching needs to be rejected.
The authors also approve of a shift in 'emphasis on what teachers teach to
one on what students learn' (op cit: 89). This has in recent years become a
policy cliché used by technocrats who are far removed from the classroom.
The alternative is to treat teaching and learning as part of a single process, as
the two sides of the same coin, where teachers and students are partners in
learning, who work together in harmony and who are both involved at different times in teaching and learning. The second report, in claiming that teachers 'deliver' facts and skills to students, betrays an impoverished conception
of teaching and learning. The later change in emphasis to students' learning
is welcome, but it continues to treat teaching and learning as two separate
processes.

A thin evidence base

MCB do not locate their findings within the relevant literatures; there is no
bibliography, only nine incomplete references to other books and articles and
only two to policy documents. There is no mention of the large, critical bodies
of research on cascade training (e.g. Wedell, 2005), on the transfer of training

(e.g. Tuomi-Gröhn and Engeström, 2003), on the psychology and sociology of teaching and learning (e.g. Bernstein, 1996; Wenger, 1998; Daniels, 2001; Hart *et al.*, 2004; Illeris, 2007; James and Biesta, 2007; Rudduck and McIntyre, 2007; Ball, 2008; Coffield, 2010[9]). The authors also approve of management exercising control by means of continuous flows of performance data: witness their supportive description of Aspire, a set of American charter schools in California: 'At the heart of Aspire's implicit values is a rigorous attention to data-driven improvement. The system has an almost religious commitment to empirically (*sic*) analysis of what works in practice and then applying it' (*op cit:* 87). There is nothing wrong in asking the perfectly reasonable question: what works? The problem is that the answer is invariably complex. MCB also seem unaware of the highly critical literature on the 'what works' approach. Gert Biesta, to give but one example,[10] has criticised:

> the whole discussion about evidence-based practice [being] focused on technical questions – questions about 'what works' – while forgetting the need for critical inquiry into normative and political questions about what is educationally desirable. From the point of view of democracy, an exclusive emphasis on 'what works' will simply not do.
>
> (2007: 21–22)

According to Ozga (2009: 149), the Department of Education in England claims to be moving towards self-regulation through self-evaluation, thus giving the appearance of deregulation, 'but the centre retains control through its management and use of data, and local government remains peripheral'. Management by means of data has, according to Ozga, become a powerful instrument of policy and 'governing through data is leaner, simpler and less heavy and mechanical in its use of power [than command and control], but it is still insistent and demanding' (*op cit:* 159). This is not to denigrate the importance of data – better a gramme of evidence than a kilo of supposition – but to question control being increasingly exercised through relentless demands for data.

The authors' handling of statistical terms is also potentially misleading. On pages 26, 34, 52, 60 and 135, the report talks of a 'strong' or 'striking' correlation or it refers simply to 'a correlation'. But the report uses the term 'correlation' as if it means a direct causal relationship between the 'tightness of central control' and the stage of improvement of a school system (*op cit:* 34), when the term strictly means no more than an association.

Implausible central arguments

Why are the interventions located at particular stages in the 'improvement journey' from poor to excellent? For instance, the strategy (of releasing teachers from administrative burdens by providing administrative staff) is allocated to the final stage of moving from great to excellent and as such is apparently part of a 'unique intervention cluster' (*op cit*: 36). Does this mean that teachers, considered to be working in systems described as poor, fair or good, should not be released from such burdens? If they were to be so released, would their journey from poor to fair, or fair to good, or good to great not be all the shorter and less stressful? No explanation is offered as to why this intervention should be used only at the final stage. All teachers, at whatever stage their school system is in, need to be freed from as much administration as possible so that they can concentrate on the learning needs of their students. Moreover, teachers are burdened with these administrative tasks because of the demands for data made by management and the state.

Criticisms could also be made about the positioning of other interventions. For instance, the detailed prescription of teaching objectives, plans and materials by the centre for a 'poor' system is highly likely to drive any self-respecting teacher out of the profession; and the more talented the teachers, the less likely they will put up with being told what to do. According to MCB, teachers should wait until their system is declared 'great', at which point the centre accords them 'pedagogical rights' to choose how they will teach (*op cit*: 36).

A further concern. What evidence is there that the schools within any of these systems all deserve the same grade at the same time? The authors produce none. Is it not more likely that the larger the school system, the more schools will be spread out along the continuum from 'poor' to 'excellent'? Given the growing polarisation of educational outcomes in countries like England, it would not be surprising to find concentrations of 'excellent' and of 'poor' schools within the same system, and even pockets of 'excellently' and 'poorly' performing students within the same school.[11]

What should have been central to the arguments in the two McKinsey reports is a considered response to the central finding of educational researchers that 'pupil prior attainment and background explain the vast majority of variation in school outcomes' (Gorard, 2009: 761). If these 'global' policy analysts were to respond to that consistent finding, which they seem not to know about, their recommendations would be very different.

Technocratic and authoritarian language

Educators have a choice about the language they use and their choice is very likely to reveal their thinking and their values. The second McKinsey report is cast in technocratic jargon:

> This correlation between system performance and the degree of central control over the school system has parallels to lean operations. A given production system must combine inputs and process in order to produce

output. When input quality is low, the production system must have tight processes in order to deliver a quality output.

(op cit: 60)

A page later, the authors are quick to point out 'Our intent here is not to imply that school systems are manufacturing processes' (*op cit:* 61), but the comparison has been made. The report at this point discusses head teachers, teachers and students as if they were industrial inputs to be processed in order to ensure an improvement in quality, where quality is defined as an increase in test scores in a limited set of subjects. Education professionals are here being treated as human capital, as assets or 'human resources' to be managed, used or discarded as policy-makers dictate. So an Armenian intervention is praised for: 'the optimization of teachers, from 65,000 to 40,000' (*op cit:* 44); this euphemism refers to the sacking of 15,000 teachers.

Their third chapter also contains a detailed comparison between an educational system and a personal computer, where collaboration between teachers becomes 'the user interface'; the mediating layer (such as a local authority) between the centre and the schools becomes 'the operating system'; and leadership becomes 'the central processing unit' (*op cit:* 83–99). At no point do the authors consider that their comparison of a dynamic educational system, composed of human beings, with an inanimate object is inappropriate and insensitive.

An authoritarian streak also runs through this second report. The three authors argue that '.. sustaining change requires altering the very fabric of the system – changing not just the way teachers' (*sic*) teach and the content of what they teach but how they think about teaching' (*op cit:* 83). But who can be trusted with deciding what changes should be made not just to the curriculum and pedagogy, but to teachers' thinking? The report is not clear, but it is highly likely that it will be the same people who 'monitor compliance' (*op cit:* 92); who 'manage any resistance to change' (*op cit:* 93); and who decide which changes are 'non-negotiable' (*op cit:* 71). The second report contains no discussion of how these all-powerful 'strategic leaders' are appointed or how they are democratically accountable.

MCB also approve of the way in which Madhya Pradesh in India produced 'significant quality improvement' by:

using a highly standardised teaching model designed to improve teaching and learning … Every classroom lesson now had a newly prescribed lesson plan, teaching materials, student worksheets, and a set of teaching techniques based on activity-based learning. As one system leader described: 'Everyone has to teach the same curriculum at the same time in the same way'.

(Mourshed *et al.*, 2010: 55)

The resulting modest rise in test scores on reading cannot be considered 'a significant quality improvement', when it is obtained by such overly prescriptive methods. The MCB report does not record the number of students who passed the test but were put off reading for good, but it notes that in Western Cape in South Africa the improvement strategy 'mandated 30 min a day for pleasure reading' (op cit: 40). A new category is being introduced into education: compulsory 'pleasure reading'.[12]

The role of culture underplayed

MCB devote one of their four central chapters to 'contextualising', which they define as 'the influence of history, culture, values, system, structure, politics, etc.' (op cit: 71). Yet in their very next paragraph, the context is reduced to only three aspects:

1 professional development requirements,
2 language of instruction, and
3 student achievement targets (ibid)

In this manner, they avoid any exploration of the history, culture, values and politics of the 20 systems they are comparing. Instead, the claim is made that: 'each performance stage is associated with a dominant cluster of interventions, irrespective of geography, culture or political system' (op cit: 24). But how is it possible to understand the content and process of education in any country without knowing in detail how they have been shaped by its history, geography, local culture and politics? Alexander (2009: 7) has criticised studies like the first McKinsey report where culture 'is reduced to one factor among many, something which is external to school life rather than that which actually creates it and gives it meaning'.

The omission of democracy[13]

The only mention of democracy in the second report's 139 pages comes when the authors are discussing the introduction, by countries previously under the control of the Soviet Union, of 'fresh topics such as civics and democracy' (op cit: 105); that is, as an additional curriculum subject to be 'transmitted' to students. The authors also claim that 'stakeholder engagement serves to depoliticise education' (op cit: 111). That remark merits criticism on two grounds. First, it is not possible to 'depoliticise' education, because at least from the time of Plato's Republic, education has been seen as perhaps the most important function of the 'polis' or community; through education, a society decides what kind of young people it wants and who are to fulfil the different roles in society. Plato was also of the view that those who put themselves forward as philosopher kings or 'strategic leaders' are precisely the people who should be prevented from taking such powerful positions (see Cornford, 1961).

Second, to engage 'stakeholders', or preferably partners, is not to 'depoliticise' education, but instead to engage in the very practice of democracy, whereby we learn from each other how best to educate each new generation. No mention is made of the important role that teachers' unions should play in reform; this is a surprising omission given that Sir Michael Barber was once an official of England's biggest teachers' union, the NUT.

MCB also provide a model of system improvement. Although their model rightly 'requires intergration (*sic*) and coordination across every level' (*op cit*: 92), control is retained by the centre, which stipulates the type of accountability and the decision-making power for each level within the system. 'The middle layer' monitors compliance; school leaders 'drive' improvement 'consistent with direction from the middle/center', and teachers 'deliver' instruction (*ibid*). The beneficiaries of all this hierarchical endeavour – the students – have, however, disappeared from the diagram. The beneficiaries of all this hierarchical endeavour – the students – have, however, disappeared and there are no feedback mechanisms whereby the centre could learn from the experiences and creative ideas of professionals at the other levels. As such, it is a hierarchical, anti-democratic model.

Final comments

This article has examined the explicit claims and implicit assumptions in the two reports and found them wanting. The first report, which was warmly welcomed by many governments, researchers and practitioners across the world as a blueprint for school and system improvement, has been tested to see if its main conclusions stand up to examination. Four serious weaknesses have been described, each of which lowers the credibility of the report. Taken together, they so damage its credibility that it cannot be used to justify the narrow set of policies and practices it advocates. The second report, although much improved in detail and in some of its perspectives, is also fundamentally flawed; nor has it responded to the explicit criticisms made of the first report by Alexander (2009), Schratz (2008) or Braun (2008); and so it cannot serve as a master plan either.

These reports are the work of 'global' policy analysts, remote from both the complexities of classrooms and from the discomfiting findings of researchers, which pose such difficulties for politicians in search of quick 'transformations' of school systems before the next election (see Edwards, 2000). They espouse a high-performance model of schooling, which is characterised by relentless pressure, competition, line managers, customer services, data for performance management, accountability and value for money; and professional autonomy for teachers only when granted by the centre. The interventions they favour are more likely to create exam factories than communities of learning. Their notion of teaching and learning is also narrowly conceived and technocratic. Their model of a school system is highly prescriptive, top-down and mechanistic. Teachers are reduced to the status of technicians, of agents of the state who 'deliver' the ideas of others; and who, even during the journey from great to excellent, can be 'rotated' (MCB: 51) throughout the system at the behest of the all-powerful centre.

Many of the strategies advocated by Mourshed *et al.* (2010) are already in place in schools in the United States and England. The testimony of Ravitch (2010), assistant secretary of education in the administration of President George H.W. Bush from 1991 to 1993, is therefore relevant. She has become disillusioned with these strategies which she once considered promising; now she considers that the repeated testing of basic skills is undermining education: 'Eighth grade students improved not at all on the federal test of reading even though they had been tested annually by their states in 2003–2007'.

MCB have moved considerably from their first report, which advocated a toolkit which contained essentially one tool – improve the quality of teaching – to a second study which asks some of the right questions and recommends 5 strategies and 21 factors, some of which are welcome; and yet their model remains unsophisticated, impracticable and undemocratic. Unsophisticated because the complexities inherent in comparative education, in the psychology of teaching and learning and in the sociology of education policy have been ignored. Impracticable because it deals with too narrow a range of factors, and fails to discuss, never mind tackle unjustifiable inequalities. Undemocratic because the interventions are chosen by unaccountable 'strategy leaders' without any consultation with those who must enact them. As such, their recommendations are educationally and socially dysfunctional and therefore should not be part of school reform in a democracy. There are other options which merit as much, if not more, debate and support than these dystopian McKinsey reports, but these options need to be explained at length elsewhere (see Coffield and Williamson, 2011).

Notes

1 Sir Michael Barber was formerly a teacher, an official of the National Union of Teachers and professor of education at the Universities of Keele and London. He is currently an Expert Partner in McKinsey and head of its 'Global Education Practice' (*sic*). He was Chief Adviser on Delivery to the British Prime Minister, Tony Blair. His latest co-authored book is called *Deliverology 101: A Field Guide for Educational Leaders*.

2 Dr Mona Mourshed is also a partner in McKinsey and leads their education practice, covering the Middle East, Asia and Latin America.

3 McKinsey and Co is an international management consulting firm.

4 The US Department of Education is currently running a $4 billion competition called *The Race to the Top*, where states submit bids outlining their plans for comprehensive education reform; specifically, states need to show how they will

improve education in science, technology, engineering and maths, 'driven by an economic imperative' (Robelen 2010, 6).

5 I suspect that Braun (2008, 317) is right when he argues that the interest of policy-makers 'in education stems largely from an appreciation of the role of human capital development in economic growth'.

6 To be 'great' apparently is not as good as being 'excellent'.

7 These acronyms refer to international assessments of student attainment in tests. PISA, programme for international student assessment; TIMMS, trends in international maths and science study; and PIRLS, progress in international reading literacy study.

8 The Tory-led coalition government in England decided in 2010 to seriously reduce funding for the NCSL as part of its austerity measures.

9 I have deliberately given only a few key references to these substantial research literatures to avoid including long lines of names and dates, so those given should be taken as gateways to rich fields of knowledge.

10 Again, I have restricted myself to one reference in the text, but interested readers could also consult Phil Hodkinson's (2008) valedictory lecture at Leeds University on the same theme. The authors of the McKinsey reports need to acknowledge that such criticisms of their ideas exist and they also need to respond to them. One of the criteria that Michaels et al. (2008) have proposed for educational debate is accountability to the learning community: reports should 'attend seriously to and build on the ideas of others'. This criterion will need to be addressed if there is to be a third McKinsey report on school systems.

11 The PISA results for 2009 usefully discuss 'resilient students', that is, those who come from the bottom quarter of the socially most disadvantaged students, but who perform among the top quarter of students internationally. In the United King-dom, '24% of disadvantaged students can be considered resilient' and 31% is the OECD average (OECD 2010b, 7).

12 The three authors are committed to improving the quality of learning but seem to have no concern for the English language. At times, their prose is clumsy: 'school systems' performance journeys' (op cit: 123); and 'incremental frontline-led im-provement' (op cit: 60). At other times, they introduce ugly neologisms: 'architect-ing tomorrow's leadership' (op cit: 27); and 'schools ... not only outperform ... but also "out-improve"' (op cit: 132).

13 Another surprising omission concerns the relative absence of comment in either report on information technology. This prompts me to ask: how many classrooms did the three authors observe?

References

Adult Learning Inspectorate (2007) *The National Teaching and Learning Change Pro-gramme: A Review of Teaching and Learning Frameworks*. Coventry: Adult Learning Inspectorate.

Alexander, R. (2009) World class schools – noble aspiration or globalized hokum? BAICE Presidential Address, September 16, Oxford.

Alexander, R. (2022) *Education in spite of Policy*. London: Routledge.

Ausubel, D.P. (1968) *Educational Psychology: A Cognitive View*. New York: Holt, Rinehard and Winston.

Ball, S.J. (1990) *Politics and Policy Making in Education*. London: Routledge.

Ball, S.J. (2008) *The Education Debate*. Bristol: Policy Press.

Barber, M. and Mourshed, M. (2007) *How the World's Best-performing School Systems Come Out on Top*. London: McKinsey and Company.

Bernstein, B. (1996) *Pedagogy, Symbolic Control and Identity: Theory, Research, Critique*. London: Taylor and Francis.

Biesta, G. (2007) Why 'what works' won't work: Evidence-based practice and the democratic deficit in educational research. *Educational Theory*, 57(1), 1–22.

Biesta, G., Field, J., Hodkinson, P., MacLeod, F. and Goodson, I. (2011) *Improving Learning through the Lifecourse: Learning Lives*. Abingdon: Routledge.

Braun, H. (2008) Review of McKinsey report: How the world's best performing school systems come out on top. *Journal of Educational Change*, 9, 317–20.

Cabinet Office (2011) *Open Public Services*, Cm 8145. http://www,cabinetoffice.gov.uk (accessed July 18, 2011).

Coffield, F. (2010) *Yes, but What's Semmelweis Got to Do With My Professional Development as a Teacher?* London: Learning and Skills Network.

Coffield, F. and Edward, S. (2009) Rolling out 'good', 'best' and 'excellent' practice. What next? Perfect practice? *British Educational Research Journal*, 35(3), 371–90.

Coffield, F. and Williamson, B. (2011) *From Exam Factories to Communities of Discovery*. London: IOE.

Coffield, F., Edward, S., Finlay, I., Hodgson, A., Spours, K. and Steer, R. (2008) *Improving Learning, Skills and Inclusion: The Impact of Policy on Post-Compulsory Education*. London: Routledge.

Cornford, F. (1961) *The Republic of Plato*. London: Oxford University Press.

Daniels, H. (2001) *Vygotsky and Pedagogy*. London: Routledge Falmer.

Department for Education (2010) *The Importance of Teaching: The Schools White Paper*, Cm. 7980. London: DfE.

Edwards, T. (2000) All the evidence shows': Reasonable expectations of educational research. *Oxford Review of Education*, 26(3/4), 299–311.

Eraut, M. (2002) The interaction between qualifications and work-based learning. In K. Evans, P. Hodkinson and L. Unwin (eds) *Working to Learn: Transforming Learning in the Workplace*.. London: Kogan, 63–78.

Evans, K., Hodkinson, P., Rainbird, H. and Unwin, L. (2006) *Improving Workplace Learning*. London: Routledge.

Fielding, M., Bragg, S., Craig, J., Cunningham, I., Eraut, M., Gillinson, S., Horne, M., Robinson, C. and Thorp, J. (2005) *Factors Influencing the Transfer of Good Practice*. London: DfES, Research Brief No RB615.

Fullan, M. (2010) Foreword to M. Mourshed, C. Chijioke and M. Barber (2010) *How the World's Most Improved School Systems Keep Getting Better*. London: McKinsey and Company.

Galbraith, J.K. (1992) *The Culture of Contentment*. London: Sinclair-Stevenson.

Georgiades, N.J. and Phillimore, L. (1975) The myth of the hero-innovator and alternative strategies for organizational change. In C. Kiernan and F. Woodford (eds) *Behaviour Modification for the Severely Retarded*. Amsterdam: Association Scientific, 313–9.

Gorard, S. (2009) Serious doubts about school effectiveness. *British Educational Research Journal*, 36(5), 745–66.

Grose, R.F. and Birney, R.C. (1963) *Transfer of Learning: An Enduring Problem in Psychology*. Princetown: Van Nostrand.

Grubb, W.N. and Lazerson, M. (2004) *The Education Gospel: The Economic Power of Schooling*. Cambridge: Harvard University Press.

Hart, S., Dixon, A., Drummond, M.J. and McIntyre, D. (2004) *Learning without Limits*. Maidenhead: Open University Press.

Hartley, D. (2007) The emergence of distributed leadership in education: Why now? *British Journal of Educational Studies*, 55(2), 202–14.

Hartley, D. (2009) The management of education: From distributed leadership to collaborative community. *Journal of Educational Administration and History*, 2, 1–15.

Hayes, D. (2000) Cascade training and teachers' professional development. *ELT Journal*, 54(2), 135–45.

Hayes, J. (2011) Vision for Further Education. Department for Business, Innovation and Skills, 15 June, Speech at Warwickshire College, Rugby, 1–5. Accessed July 18, 2011.

Hodkinson, P. (2008) What works does not work! Researching lifelong learning in the culture of audit. *Valedictory Lecture*, 23 June, University of Leeds: School of Continuing Education.

Illeris, K. (2007) *How We Learn: Learning and Non-learning in School and Beyond*. London: Routledge.

James, D. and Biesta, G. (2007) *Improving Learning Cultures in Further Education*. Abingdon: Routledge.

Lave, J. and Wenger, E. (1994) *Situated Learning: Legitimate Peripheral Participation*. Cambridge: University Press.

Leithwood, K., Day, C., Summons, P., Harris, A. and Hopkins, D. (2006) *Seven Strong Claims About Successful Leadership*. Nottingham: National College for School Leadership.

McKeough, A., Lupart, J. and Marini, A. (1995) *Teaching for Transfer: Fostering Generalisation in Learning*. Mahwah: L. Erlbaum.

Michaels, S., O'Connor, C. and Resnick, L.B. (2008) Deliberative discourse; Idealized and realized: Accountable talk in the classroom and civil life. *Studies in Philosophy and Education*, 27(4), 283–97.

Mourshed, M., Chijioke, C. and Barber, M. (2010) *How the World's Most Improved School Systems Keep Getting Better*. London: McKinsey and Company.

OECD (2010a) *What Students Know and Can Do: Student Performance in Reading, Mathematics and Science*. Vol. 1 of PISA 2009 Results. Paris: OECD.

OECD (2010b) *Viewing the United Kingdom school system through the prism of PISA*, http://www.oecd.org/dataoecd/33/8/46624007.pdf (accessed March 28, 2011).

Ozga, J. (2009) Governing education through data in England: From regulation to self-evaluation. *Journal of Education Policy*, 24(2), 149–62.

Pollard, A. (2010) *The importance of teacher expertise*. http://cloudworks.ac.uk/cloud/view/3539 (accessed February 2, 2011).

Ravitch, D. (2010) Why I changed my mind about school reform. *Wall Street Journal*, March 9.

Robelen, E.W. (2010) STEM plans embedded in winning proposals for the race to the top. *Education Week*, September 15,6.

Rudduck, J. and McIntyre, D. (2007) *Improving Learning through Consulting Pupils*. Abingdon: Routledge.

Schleicher, A. (2007) Foreword to Barber, M. and Mourshed, M. (2007) *How the World's Best-performing School Systems Come Out on Top*. London: McKinsey Company.

Schratz, M. (2008) Review of McKinsey report. *Journal of Educational Change*, 9, 321–4.

Sfard, A. (1998) On two metaphors for learning and the dangers of choosing just one. *Educational Researcher*, 27(2), 4–13.

Tuomi-Gröhn and Engeström, Y. (2003) *Between School and Work: New Perspectives on Transfer and Boundary-Crossing*. Oxford: Elsevier Science.

Wedell, M. (2005) Cascading training down on to the classroom: The need for parallel planning. *International Journal of Educational Development*, 25, 637–51.

Wei, R.C., Andree, A. and Darling-Hammond, L. (2009) How nations invest in teachers. *Educational Leadership*, 66(5), 28–33.

Wenger, E. (1998) *Communities of Practice. Learning, Meaning and Identity*. Cambridge: Cambridge University Press.

Wiliam, D. (2008) The education reform act 20 years on. http://www.dylanwiliam.net (accessed February 25, 2011).

Wolf, A. (2002) *Does Education Matter? Myths about Education and Economic Growth*. London: Penguin Books.

Chapter 16

From exam factories to communities of discovery

The democratic route

Over the last 40 years, the language of the market (line manager, inputs and outputs) has pushed out the language of education (trust, collaboration). Power within education could be redistributed by building Communities of Discovery, i.e. learners and educators working together with democratic practices and values to address the main threats to our collective well-being and to the planet. What follows is the first chapter of the book I wrote with Bill Williamson in 2011 with the above title.

Durham University has been imaginative in its choice of Chancellor, appointing luminaries from the world of the Arts. The post of Chancellor is largely ceremonial, with a well-known figurehead who, for example, chairs graduation ceremonies.

Dame Margot Fonteyn, the famous prima ballerina, stood up in Durham Cathedral, no more than five feet tall, but with a commanding presence and crystal-clear voice declared: 'I didn't go to a university but I realise its significance in the modern world. To the staff of this university I say: Open your doors and let the people in'.

Later, Sir Peter Ustinov as Chancellor saved the university's face at a ceremony in Durham Castle to confer higher degrees. That year, a Nigerian doctor was the first female from her country to be awarded a prestigious Doctorate of Medicine. As she climbed up onto the platform, her family, dressed in traditional costumes, began ululating. The Vice Chancellor of the time, jumped to his feet and commanded: 'Stop that! Stop that noise!' Sir Peter brushed him aside, strode to the front of the stage and ululated louder than any of the Nigerians present.

Sir Thomas Allen, the operatic baritone, born in Sunderland, was another inspired choice. He told of appearing in an opera with Luciano Pavarotti and Placido Domingo. At a break in rehearsals, the three maestros went for lunch together, over which Sir Thomas asked Luciano if he had ever considered directing or conducting, as he and Placido had done. 'What?' exclaimed Luciano, 'With a voice like mine?'

DOI: 10.4324/9781003476146-21

Introduction

> That's the trouble with words. You never know whose mouth they were in last.
>
> (Dennis Potter)[1]

A book on the power of democracy to transform education must be written in democratic language, accessible to all. So we begin with a promise: we shall not use any jargon, we shall present our arguments in clear English, and if we occasionally use a technical term, we will explain it in a note. As we are not writing primarily for our academic colleagues, we will not pepper our text with references to the academic literature; however, we do need to acknowledge our considerable debts to other writers and thinkers by mentioning them in the text, with fuller details in notes at the end of each chapter and a full bibliography at the end of the book.

We have written this book for the benefit of educators working in a wide variety of settings – in schools, colleges and universities, in work-based learning and within communities – and for all those who despair that the current educational policies of the three main political parties in England (and similar ones elsewhere) are set to continue. We reject their policies because the summit of their ambition is to reform, yet again and in different ways, the present 'system'. That 'system', however, is deeply undemocratic, inequitable, inefficient and inadequate to address our present problems and future threats.

To use an analogy from the transport industry, it is as if all our policies in education are like the efforts of road hauliers to make their old-fashioned juggernauts travel faster on modern, overcrowded motorways. They can make as many marginal adjustments to fuel injectors, transmissions and exhaust systems as they like, but they remain trapped within the logic of a transport system that is essentially absurd. Improvements in the design of juggernauts only amplify congestion and increase environmental damage. Such marginal improvements in the technology of the juggernaut highlight the absurdity of vehicles invented in the early 20th century struggling to cope on 21st century motorways. Similarly, in education, the response of politicians and policymakers to any difficulty has always been to build an extension to the 'system' (e.g. pupil referral units were created to deal with disruptive behaviour) rather than to deal with the underlying causes of the difficulty. In this way, a grotesque educational juggernaut has been pieced together and added to over the years and is now a shuddering pantechnicon, some parts of which are nevertheless capable of excellent performance.

Despite many different viewpoints, the main political parties and the ever-increasing number of think-tanks, advisers, education journalists, teachers' unions, employers' associations, worried parents and pressure groups that frame the key debates on education have this one aim in common: they want change within current, taken-for-granted assumptions about the purposes of education. They want to keep making changes so that our 'system' catches up with, and then overtakes, those judged the best in the world. They all appear to accept the simplistic belief that a 'world class' education system will automatically improve the competitiveness of our economy and so ensure that prosperity keeps on growing, at least for those in secure employment.

There is, however, to push the transport metaphor harder, thick fog ahead on the motorway along which this juggernaut is trundling, but it is now being forced to increase speed without a clear view of the dangers in front of it. The many drivers on board are all pulling different levers to improve its performance, with only a vague notion of where it is headed: a society of aspiration and opportunity. This is a laudable ambition until the fog lifts and suddenly there is a pile-up ahead, and no one knows what has caused it or how to remove it or how to stop the juggernaut in time. We need to act before the old juggernaut crashes into the back of the queue of cars ahead.

Reclaiming the language of education

We also need to care more about the effects of language on our educational thinking and practices. We should abandon such arrogant phrases as 'future proofed' (have we learned nothing from the financial crisis of 2008?); 'seamless progression', especially when the 'system' loses thousands of learners at transition points; and 'UK plc', the phrase from 'managementspeak' which reduces the diversity, richness and vitality of British society to the narrow concerns of a public limited company. Politicians of all parties also talk about 'raising standards', but by this term, they mean nothing more than raising the test scores of students in a limited number of subjects. We need to return to more collegial forms of address; e.g. head of department rather than 'line manager', as there are no production lines in education, only ways of treating educators as if they were 'producers' of standard 'products'. Schools, colleges and universities have become 'providers of learning opportunities', and quality in education has come to mean conforming to government policy, as enforced by Ofsted, the inspection service.

We place so much importance on this point because in the last 30 years, the language of management and economics has virtually replaced the language of education. The process is insidious: at first hearing, such phrases as 'the bottom line', 'the business model' and 'more for less' are clearly limited and objectionable, but within a short time, so great is the power of money, that we catch ourselves using them without a qualm.

Junk language is as damaging to our minds as junk food is to our bodies; it corrupts our thinking but it also dehumanises our relationships. Performance management has turned students into customers, then into 'inputs and outputs' and finally into the contemptuous phrase 'bums on seats'. This phrase concentrates on one part of a student's anatomy – but not on the place where psychologists have located the seat of learning. For years now, managers have been unashamedly talking about 'bums on seats'; slick publishers produce books with patronising titles about how to get the 'buggers' to behave,[2] but educators should insist on respect for all their students.

For some years now, some educational institutions have, under pressure from the market, moved beyond mere advertising to market themselves as brands in order to develop their 'business'. They employ full-time brand managers with branding assistants (to wield the branding iron, no doubt), whose job it is to produce brand value and brand visual identity, brand guidelines and brand templates, a brand book and 'signoff protocols for externally facing literature'. (These are real examples taken from a university's marketing strategy.) A strategic marketing group is then established, with the 'mission' of training 'faculty champions', producing 'customer relationship management solutions' and conducting 'competitor analysis' in order 'to create a culturally impactful presence'. Such 'brand development' will apparently enhance corporate strategy by 'extending global reach' (this means attracting a few more foreign students who will pay top fees). Resources of money, time and energy are spent on branding and rebranding, resources which could have been used to prevent job losses, to train staff or to attend to the needs of students. Educational institutions are diminished rather than enhanced by their trite brand images.

We do not mean to imply that senior staff voluntarily choose to develop such marketing strategies. Rather, faced with the prospects of intensifying competition from academies and 'free schools' which may result in further cuts, closures or redundancies, managers feel compelled to adopt such market mechanisms as branding in order to seek advantage over competitors. In this way, they too are being dragged under the wheels of the juggernaut, which turns school against school, college against college and university against university.

We agree with Gert Biesta that 'the language of education has largely been replaced by a language of learning'.[3] Teaching, he argues, has been reduced to facilitating learning, education to the provision of learning opportunities, and adult education has come to mean nothing more than employability skills. 'Employability' is an ugly word for the ugly idea that learners should willingly accept the responsibility of constantly updating their skills in the hope that an employer will one day recognise their constant struggle to remain fit for employment by offering them a job, any job. So the term 'lifelong learning', which retains some liberating and democratic possibilities, is increasingly being used as an instrument of control. Politicians and employers insist that it is up to learners to keep themselves up to date and, if they are unemployed or made redundant, they have only themselves to blame because they have not learned enough. The trick being played here is simple but highly effective because the language of lifelong learning transfers responsibility away from ministers and employers to individuals.

We want to argue in reply that the focus of public attention should not be on individuals but on the structure of opportunities. The problems are not de-motivated young people or work-shy adults. The vast majority of people want to work as much as they ever did. The problems are the lack of decent jobs and the lack of progression and training in the low-paid jobs that do exist. In the UK in 2011, there are almost a million unemployed 16- to 25-year-olds. Chief executives in both the private and public sectors have seized the opportunity of free labour by exploiting young people who are desperate to work by offering unpaid internships, while paying themselves mega-salaries, bonuses and pensions.

At the same time, young people disengage from school in their hundreds of thousands, as they have been doing since 1944. For decades, they have been claiming that the curriculum is irrelevant to their needs, interests and fu-tures, but successive governments have turned a deaf ear to this inconvenient message. Once they have left school, the only choices open to these young people are the same as they were in the 1980s, when they described them as: 'shit jobs, govvie schemes or the dole'.[4]

Young people continue to disengage in significant numbers because they feel that the schooling on offer does not meet their needs. They are not wrong in this, and they are seriously disadvantaged by the assumption that too many are left to make, namely that prolonging their education is not in their long-term interests. There are complex cultural factors at work that explain the poverty of expectations of many working-class young people. Formal schooling of the kind that has been offered to them did not, and does not, offer them challenging or engaging options. Alison Wolf's rec-ommendation that those who fail to obtain a C grade in English or Maths should continue taking exams until they pass is likely to result in further disengagement.[5]

Since 1988, Conservative, New Labour and the Conservative-led coalition governments have claimed that we need a national curriculum to establish a basic entitlement for all students and so raise standards across the board. Let us accept these two claims at face value for the moment. Even so, shouldn't a national curriculum also be relevant to the present and future lives of those who have to study it? For years, John White, the English philosopher of edu-cation, has repeatedly stressed that, when we are designing or redesigning a national curriculum, it would be sensible to start by agreeing on its aims: 'This means working out first of all what the curriculum is meant to be for; and only after that deciding what vehicles are best to take us to our destina-tions'.[6] The hard task of deciding on the aims of education is being avoided by the coalition government as it has been by all its predecessors; and the clapped-out juggernaut of our educational 'system' is not up to the task of taking us where we need to go. We require, first and foremost, a genuinely open, public debate about the content and purposes of education and how it can renew our society.

We will use the term 'education' as the overarching idea within which the more limited term 'learning' is located. To us, education is the dynamic combination of such elements as:

- the transaction between the generations where historians or chemists or beauticians show students how to think and act like historians or chemists or beauticians by introducing them to the knowledge, skills and understandings of these disciplines;
- the means of creating the kind of society we want by opening minds, transforming lives and civilising society;
- a critical understanding of society by encouraging independent thinking and collective action;
- a commitment to improving the learning of all;
- a simultaneous matching of society to the needs of learners and learners to the needs of society;
- the preparation of all citizens as full, active members of a democratic society.

For the sake of variety, we will refer to both learners and students, but will talk about educators rather than teachers or tutors to emphasise both the broad, liberating remit of education and all the valuable learning that takes place outside schools and colleges. For us, the process of education is much more than an economic transaction, in which education is reduced to the status of a commodity that is 'delivered' by the 'providers' – the teachers – in order to meet the needs of the 'consumers' – the students – with these needs defined by the 'providers'. It is also much more than the dry, technical business of transmitting information to students, a process for which the pejorative term 'schooling' is more appropriate.

Some readers may ask: what is so wrong with treating our students as consumers or clients? If the customers are king, they may very well refuse the 'product' on offer. On the one hand, government policy papers argue that assessment should become more rigorous and, on the other, that students should be treated as customers. But how are tutors to tell these 'customers' that they will fail if they do not submit their assignments on time or if their work is not up to the required standard? The relationship between tutors and students must be such that the former can assess the work of the latter (and even fail some of their assignments) without that relationship breaking down. Teaching is not only complex intellectually but it draws on all our emotions – it is a subtle art to criticise students and still keep them motivated to improve.

Let us give a more specific example from post-compulsory learning and training. It is dispiriting to discover that after 11 years of compulsory school, the following are the highest demands that some young people make of the staff: the right to smoke anywhere in college, the need for sufficient parking places directly in front of the building where they have classes and the provision of nothing but burgers and chips in the college canteen. Is it our role as educators just to fulfil these desires? The analogy with businesses such as British Telecom or British Gas satisfying the needs of their customers is seductive but false, because it ignores the role of educators who at times have to stand up to students, coax them out of their 'comfort zones' and challenge them to try disconcerting ideas and new ways of looking at themselves. If we as educators are there simply to respond to the self-proclaimed needs of students, then what are we to do when students ask, as a few have done in the past, for coursework that does not involve them in any sustained work? Or students who have been tested and retested every year since they started school, and who want you to tell them the one book, or better still, the one article which will ensure them an A grade? Many students are attracted into education precisely because they do not know what their needs are. Our proposals cannot be dismissed as the fuzzy, soft outpourings of two white-haired lefties (well, we plead guilty to the latter charge), but as the rigorous and hard-headed reflections from two working lives within education, from our knowledge of the research literature and from shared reflections with other educators on practice.

There is, however, another language used to discuss education, which is just as alienating as that of management, and that is the language of much of the social sciences. We shall follow the charitable practice of the Roman Emperor, Marcus Aurelius, who, in his *Meditations*, never failed to record the names of those of whom he approved, but who drew a discreet veil of secrecy over those he thought had behaved badly. Who, for example, is likely to be inspired to take action by such terms as 'conscientisation' or 'legitimate peripheral participation' or 'transgressive holism' or 'prefigurative practice' or 'transcendental violence' or 'pedagogisation', which is difficult even to pronounce? The literature on education and lifelong learning is disfigured by such terms, but, more importantly, potential supporters are turned off. Our own particular pet hate is 'co-construction'. Can you imagine educators and students marching on Whitehall chanting the inflammatory words – 'What do we want? Co-construction! When do we want it? Now!' These clumsy terms are used to lend a spurious complexity to ideas that are essentially simple; for what does 'co-construction' mean but to build together?[7] Some of the worst damage is done to education, not by its enemies, but by its jargon-ridden friends.

Social scientists who use such ugly neologisms seem to have forgotten Karl Marx's famous insight: 'The philosophers have only interpreted the world differently; the point is to change it'.[8] We would caricature the outcome of the inelegant use of language by some social scientists as follows: 'If you describe the world in such off-putting terms, no-one will still be reading when you come to make recommendations about how to change it'.

What questions should we be asking?

The most important debate to have about education is this: how can we help more people to engage in creative forms of new learning that will enable them to overcome not only the deep-seated, cumulative obstacles of inequality faced by many, but also the collective threats now faced by us all?

In the short run, the spending constraints imposed by the coalition government on the public services to deal with the economic crisis created by the financial sector will further restrict the possibilities for change in education throughout the UK. Nevertheless, within those constraints, there are choices to be made. Those on offer at the moment by the coalition government on the right and New Labour on the left of political life in England, and the devolved administrations in Scotland and Wales, point to a future of acrimonious conflict, but conflict within the traditional terms of the debate. We must break out of this self-defeating consensus.

Nowhere is the cross-party consensus more clearly seen than in contemporary educational debates, where the parties seek to outdo one another in promoting educational excellence and opportunities, while their words speak of a view of society and of human possibility that is decidedly short term and instrumental. The politicians look superficially at a few aspects of a successful system such as Finland's and then draw naive, crude and misleading lessons for policy from the comparison. Tim Oates, chair of the expert panel set up by the Secretary of State for Education in England to review the curriculum, has persuasively argued that for a system to be regarded as coherent, at least 13 aspects (including content, assessment, inspection, the structure of institutions, funding, governance and selection) need to be 'aligned and reinforce one another'.[9] But for the last 30 years, ministers have tinkered with one aspect of the curriculum after another without considering the impact of, say, rigorous and repeated assessments on the motivation of students or the quality of their learning.

As we go to press, Tim Oates is quoted as saying that 'the curriculum has become narrowly instrumentalist'[10] and that climate change and other such topics may be dropped from the revised national curriculum. Instead, we should concentrate, as the Secretary of State for Education in England puts it, on providing 'a world class curriculum that will help teachers, parents and children know what children should learn at what age'.[11] While we, too, believe strongly in the centrality of knowledge of science and other academic disciplines, we also remember A.N. Whitehead's admonition that, 'A merely well-informed man is the most useless bore on God's earth'.[12] We must move beyond the false distinction of using *either* tradition ('the comfort of the ostrich'[13]) *or* the application of knowledge to social problems as the main argument in deciding what we should teach: we urgently need knowledge from the physical and social sciences and the humanities to help us address the threats we face and, in the process, we will create new knowledge. There is, however, a logical inconsistency in Tim Oates' insistence, on the one hand, that, 'Teachers do not need to be told how to do their jobs'[14] and, on the other hand, the curriculum review panel, which he chairs, prescribing the core scientific knowledge which all students should learn.

In this book, we will use not a new vocabulary but a different one because we wish to challenge the taken-for-granted language of the current debate. We urge people who work in or talk about education to stop using the language of the market and start using words and phrases like: 'democracy', 'trust', 'collaborative learning', 'the courage to take risks' and 'creative discontent with current economic and environmental conditions'. Such words have the power to challenge a debate that relies on terms like 'targets', 'high stakes testing', 'efficiency', 'learning outcomes' and 'world class' schools; and such bleak evocations of the power of language and the beauty of mathematics as in phrases like the 'literacy hour' and 'numeracy hour' to distinguish them, no doubt, from the illiterate and innumerate hours which precede and follow them.

This sterile language of performance management carries no criticism of the world being built around us; it is designed to control professionals, it ignores the threats we face and has an atrophied sense of human possibility. The use of the word 'aspiration' by all three parties is typical. Our politicians are agreed: education is about helping people to realise their aspirations. But our aspirations are shaped by our families and our class, and in our society, they are also highly commercialised. So it is not surprising that people are motivated to want what this society or their family or friends aim for them to achieve. The core aspiration is to become a financially successful, self-interested and dedicated consumer, not an engaged citizen in a democracy concerned with improving the well-being of all.

The language of democracy is not being spoken. The policies that would build wide, open-ended and free learning opportunities at all stages of life in order to give meaning to the term 'democratic education' are not even being considered. Instead, the dominant thrust in education debates is to improve the competitiveness of the British economy. Our concern is that other, equally important goals – the democratic, social and cultural purposes of education – are being quietly forgotten because in modern societies, economic arguments tend to trump all others.

There is also a worrying silence from our three political parties about the explosive growth of a highly skilled but low-wage workforce (in Asia and South America as well as in the West), which challenges the notion of any simple relationship between learning and earning. The conclusion of years of international comparisons by Phillip Brown, Hugh Lauder and David Ashton[15] is that the promise held out by governments to students – study hard, gain qualifications and you will land a good job with a comfortable lifestyle – has been broken by the fierce, global competition for the dwindling supply of middle-class jobs.

Our view of democracy and communities of discovery

The market model has turned our schools and universities into exam factories and our further education colleges into skills factories. The level of discontent with this state of affairs is rising among students, parents and educators, but that discontent is at present unfocused and uncoordinated. We propose both an alternative future – communities of discovery – and the means of getting there – by realising the collective creativity of students and educators through democracy. We need to explain what we mean by these terms that are the heart and soul of our argument.

We define *democracy,* not just as a form of government, not just as the activity of voting in a secret ballot once every four years, not just as majority rule and the protection of the rights of the minority, but as *the most equitable and harmonious means of living, learning and working together.* A democratic education would encourage learners to form an image in their heads of the kind of society in which they want to live and how they can bring it into being.

We owe it to Amartya Sen and other writers to ensure that our thinking about democracy goes beyond European and American models; that it goes beyond balloting and majority rule to include public reasoning and 'the extent to which different voices from different sections of the people can actually be heard';[16] and the realisation that democratic institutions only work if people seize the opportunities to *practise* democracy within them.

This book is an unashamed polemic, an exercise in public reasoning and an attempt to change the direction in which educational reform is headed. In more detail, we want to change the terms of the debate within education from an obsession with standards and skills to embrace a much more fundamental concern: the need to strengthen democracy. To achieve this, we must redistribute power within education and we shall do this by building *communities of discovery.* By this term, we mean that within schools, colleges, universities, workplaces and civil society, *learners and educators must work together with democratic practices and values to discover new ways to address the main threats to our collective well-being and to the planet.*

The issue that lies behind all the discussion so far is power. In 'communities of discovery', power is openly, widely and more equally shared among the members of those communities, whose main task is to encourage all citizens to play an active part in their democracy.

The private sector grows fat in an age of austerity

What drives our argument is the sense that, if we carry on as we are doing, the future will be bleak. Austerity is no a short-term problem. The evidence from across the world points to an intensification of the competitive pressures of globalisation and, in the West, continued efforts to reduce public spending on welfare. But the pressure being exerted by all three political parties for permanent reform of public services is a powerful part of the governing consensus we wish to break. Of course all public services, including health and education, could and should be improved, but the excessive concern with reforming them is diverting attention from the more pressing need to reform the private sector in case taxpayers' money has once more to be poured into the banks to save the financial sector from collapse.

Let us try to summarise what the future of education is likely to be if we continue with current policies. The maintained sector will face: an insistence that more must be done with less, as cuts bite deeply into all the public services; more tutors will be sacked while ministers claim that front-line services are being supported; more diversity, choice and selection will be introduced to protect and intensify existing hierarchies among institutions; repeated, wasteful structural changes; new initiatives imposed on top of existing initiatives, none of which are evaluated; an ever-expanding list of new responsibilities for educators; pressure for ever higher test scores and different sets of qualifications which will masquerade as higher standards of education; one funding formula swiftly replaced by another; more privatisation and more public/private partnerships as public funds are transferred to the private sector; requirements for intensified competition and increased cooperation to run simultaneously; sharply widening gaps between the attainments of students from advantaged and disadvantaged homes; more intrusive surveillance of professionals and more rigorous inspections of institutions; more millions wasted on the inspection service, Ofsted, as it strives to prove we are getting value for money; and fear as the main driving force of change.

Despite enormous political pressure to change – largely to save money to cut the public debt – resistance to the latest round of imposed change will intensify. To return to the juggernaut analogy used earlier, marginal improvements to educational performance are proving ever harder to achieve. Cries from the business community that standards are falling will intensify, as will graduate unemployment and debt. Graduates are already taking jobs that do not require degree-level qualifications, when they can get jobs of any kind; and resentment will increase among non-graduates who face higher levels of unemployment because graduates are taking their jobs.

Such resentments will strengthen the electoral support of racist, right-wing parties which will encourage their supporters to believe that their disadvantages are a consequence of high levels of immigration. The elite universities will become even more socially exclusive and middle-class parents will desert the urban comprehensives for the quieter, more socially exclusive pastures of the private schools, faith schools and 'free' schools. In short, the elitist model of superior education for the privileged will be protected and reinforced.

At the time of writing, the government's White Paper on higher education, *Students at the Heart of the System*, has just been published with its commitment 'to opening up the higher education market, including to Further Education colleges and alternative providers'.[17] Its contents confirm our suspicions.

Elite universities will be given additional places to be filled by students with the highest A-level qualifications, who come in the main from private schools. New types of providers will be allowed the title of 'university' to broaden out market-led opportunities for those less well qualified.

The first step is to stop and take stock, and to look ahead as far as we can and think about questions such as: Are the policies of the three main parties in England adequate responses to the problems we face? What are the problems for which our current arrangements for learning are the solution? Do they provide a basis for building the kind of society and global order we would wish to be part of in 30 years' time?

There are powerful forces at work in the modern world telling people how they should imagine their future lives. The worst excesses of the 20th century were perpetrated by men and women who knew what they wanted the future to be and imposed their will on their societies. The madmen have not gone away. We have a new lot. As before, too many people are trapped in circumstances that leave them unable to challenge the ideas of those seeking the power to define their future.

As we see it, the challenge for educators is threefold: first, our work should be informed by an alternative vision of the future for the learners we guide. Second, we should take an informed, critical view of our own practices and of the institutions within which we work and be willing, in concert with other like-minded professionals, to change both. Finally, we (though not exclusively) have a responsibility to build our work on an explicit and adequate diagnosis of the times we live in, and to that task we turn next.

Notes

1 A comment made by Dennis Potter in a TV interview shortly before he died.
2 There is a series of books with such titles as *Getting the Buggers to Behave* by Sue Cowley (2010).
3 Biesta (2005: 54).
4 A 'govvie scheme' is a government scheme to help young unemployed people and the 'dole' means unemployment benefit. The phrase was used by young people in the North East in a study by Frank Coffield, Carol Borrill and Sarah Marshall in 1986.
5 The Wolf (2011) Report on vocational education.
6 White (2010: 2).
7 Coffield (forthcoming).
8 Quoted by C Wright Mills (1963: 71).
9 Oates (2010: 13).
10 Oates, as quoted in Shepherd (2011)
11 Gove (2011).
12 Whitehead (1962: 1)
13 Young (1961: 73).
14 Oates (2011).
15 Brown, Lauder, and Ashton (2011).
16 Sen (2009: xiii).
17 DBIS (2011: 10).

References

Biesta, G. (2005) Against learning: Reclaiming a language for education in an age of learning. *Nordisk Pedagogik*, 25, 54–66.

Brown, P., Lauder, H. and Ashton, D. (2011) *The Global Auction: The Broken Promises of Education, Jobs and Incomes*. Oxford: Oxford University Press.

Coffield, F., Borrill, C. and Marshall, S. (1986) *Growing Up at the Margins: Young Adults in the North East*. Milton Keynes: Open University Books.

Coffield, F. and Williamson, B. (2011) *From Exam Factories to Communities of Discovery: The Democratic Route*. London: Institute of Education.

Cowley, S. (2010) *Getting the Buggers to Behave*. London: Continuum.

Department for Business, Innovation and Skills (2011) *Students at the Heart of the System*. Cm. 8122. London: TSO.

Gove, M. (2011) Department for Education Press Release, 20 January.

Mills, C.W. (1968) *The Marxists*. Harmondsworth: Penguin.

Oates, T. (2011) Letter in *The Guardian*, 17 June.

Oates, T. (2010) *Could Do Better: Using International Comparisons to Refine the National Curriculum in England*. Cambridge: Cambridge Assessment.

Sen, A. (2009) *The Idea of Justice*. London: Allen Lane/Penguin.

Shepherd, J. (2011) Climate change education should be excluded from curriculum says adviser. *The Guardian*, 12 June.

White, J. (2010) Much Improved: Should do even better. www.newvisionsforeducation.org.uk. Accessed 4 May 2010.

Whitehead, A.N. (1962) *The Aims of Education*. London: Ernest Benn.

Wolf, A. (2011) *Review of Vocational Education*. London: Department for Education.

Young, M. (1961) *The Rise of the Meritocracy: 1870-2033*. Harmondsworth: Penguin.

Chapter 17

Will the leopard change its spots?

A new model of inspection for Ofsted

A coroner ruled that a contributory factor to the tragic suicide of the primary school head, Ruth Perry, was the 'rude and intimidating' inspection of Ofsted. It has taken her death for a consensus to form that Ofsted's failings, although they have been exposed since 1993 by Carol Fitz-Gibbon and many others, including myself, have long been denied and ignored. The following extract forms part of Chapter 5 from the book with the above title, which describes a new model of inspection (Coffield, 2017). The leopard never had any intention to change its spots, but an incoming government will be looking for ideas. We still need inspectors as the cross-pollinators of challenging questions and novel practices.

Once on a train journey, I met a man who had been a fellow student at Glasgow University. I learned that he had become an HM Inspector of schools. His custom was to arrive early at the school to be inspected and walk around its catchment area to give himself a feel for the backgrounds the pupils came from. On one occasion, he arrived at the school gates to see a young man come out of the main entrance, pull his tie down and loosen the top button of his shirt. As he lit up a cigarette and took a deep drag, my friend asked him casually: 'Excuse me, but is this Parkdrive Comp?' 'Aye', came the reply. 'Do you teach here?' 'Yup'. 'What do you teach?' 'Bastards, mainly'. 'Let me introduce myself. I'm the lead inspector for the three day examination of your school'.

Inspection arrangements and procedures

In Guiseppe di Lampedusa's novel, *The Leopard*, the famous remark is made that matters will have to change if the status quo is to be preserved. Well, the old leopard of Sicily, the Prince of Lampedusa, may have wanted to preserve the *status quo*, but I do not. Before discussing what room for manoeuvre Ofsted has at its disposal, the scale of the proposed changes needs to be estimated by operationalising the nine components of the new model, detailed in Chapter 16. Instead of Ofsted's four-point grading scale of 'outstanding', 'good', 'requires improvement' and 'inadequate', the proforma in Table 17.1 invites inspectors to choose a point on a continuum from 'needs a little' to 'needs a lot' of support for each of the nine dimensions. The first dimension,

DOI: 10.4324/9781003476146-22

Table 17.1 Evaluation of TLA

DIMENSION TLA[3]	Choose a point on the continuum to indicate the amount of support needed	
Feedback	A little	A lot
Meta-cognition	A little	A lot
Peer tutoring	A little	A lot
What went well		Even better if
QUESTIONS	Chosen from the bank of questions to suit the age, specialism and stage of education reached by the students. Questions would clearly be different for pupils in the reception class in a primary school and for students of construction in an FE college.	
Specify support needed		

teaching, learning and assessment (TLA), is given as an example in Table 17.1 where its most effective aspects, according to research (Hattie, 2012; Hattie and Yates, 2014; Coe et al., 2014), are highlighted; and a similar procedure could be adopted for each of the nine dimensions, so that a new inspection report would consist of nine sheets, plus a covering commentary in clear English, free of jargon and accessible to all.

A caveat is needed here about turning the findings of research into simple recipes for schools. Tony Edwards makes the point well:

> ... research can only inform practice because it can never replace other knowledge which teachers bring to bear on practical problems; and that even the best research evidence is not available as fixed, universal relationships between methods and outcomes, but as local, context-sensitive patterns which have to be interpreted by practitioners within their particular working environments.
>
> (Edwards, 2000: 301)

The main advantage of this approach is that it does away with a single adjective – 'outstanding' or 'inadequate' – which can never sum up all the complexities of the extra-ordinary diversity within either colleges of further education or even within more homogeneous primary schools, for that matter. Complexity is responded to with complexity. The statistical absurdity and injustice of a single global assessment are done away with and league tables would no longer be able to be drawn up.

At an earlier stage, I thought to include an Evaluation Summary Form to present a quick overview of the performance of an institution on the nine components, but strong criticism from some of my friends persuaded me that this was a retrograde step, which would contradict my claim above that complexity should be respected. The complexities of TLA and the difficulties of leading and managing large, complex institutions should not be reduced to a superficial summary.

The range of this approach could be extended by substituting the main curriculum areas or departments within a college for the nine dimensions and again inviting inspectors to mark a point on the continuum between 'support' and 'strength' to register their evaluation. No calibration is made along any of the continua to prevent impressionistic judgements being turned into the spurious precision of numbers. The end result will be a more multifaceted and comprehensive summary of the strengths and weaknesses of an institution, together with specific details of the support it needs and where it should come from. Asking inspectors to specify both *What Went Well* and what could be done *Even Better If* is an attempt to pursue one of the main aims of Appreciative Inquiry, which rejects all deficit-based approaches and instead gives pride of place 'to everything that gives life to a system when it is most alive and at its exceptional best' (Cooperrider, 2012: 4). The focus of inspection will also switch from a preoccupation with leadership to an equal focus on classroom teaching and management.

Only when the proformas and the commentary have been completed will the inspectors have access to the institution's data and documents on test and exam results. This deals with the frequently voiced accusation that inspection teams arrive in schools to confirm the conclusions they have drawn from reading the data in advance. An experienced headteacher commented: their pre-judgements '... are virtually impossible to change. It almost makes the inspection itself irrelevant'.[1] This change in procedure would restore a balance between the present obsession with quantitative data and the neglect of a wide range of qualitative features of life in schools.

These arrangements will replace Ofsted's practice of making graded judgements on four areas: the effectiveness of leadership and management, which, needless to say, comes first; the quality of TLA; personal development, behaviour and welfare; and outcomes, that is, data on qualifications and progress. Inspectors then make a final judgement on overall effectiveness, having in the meantime evaluated the provision for the spiritual, moral, social and cultural development of students.[2] If a judgement of 'inadequate' is made on any one of these areas, then the overall judgement is also likely to be 'inadequate'. This new model offers a way out of this minefield or, to change the metaphor, Damocles had only one sword dangling over his head.

The inspection will be more accurate and effective if an inspector is attached to the institution before, during and after inspection, in order to assess benign and undesirable effects; work with it on agreeing and providing the support it needs; and be part of the team, working alongside inspectorial colleagues (with the specialist expertise the institution needs) and classroom teachers, to implement the recommendations. To show that nothing too radical is being suggested here, the following quotation is taken from the Further Education Funding Council's framework for inspection for 1993, produced after wide consultation within the FE sector, for the assessment of sixth form and FE colleges:

> Colleges will be invited to nominate a senior member of staff to act as the first point of contact with the inspectorate and to participate in the team inspection by joining team meetings, interpreting evidence and clarifying uncertainties.
>
> (FEFC, 1993: 8)

What was good enough for sixth-form and FE colleges in the 1990s should now be resurrected to become part of the inspection of all educational institutions: a link inspector and a college nominee. To ensure that inspectors and college staff are acting as equal partners, the principle of 50/50 contributions to the dialogue between them, used in peer reviews (Matthews and Headon, 2015), should be adopted. Another feature of the alternative model will be to have the inspection evaluated by both the institution which has been inspected and by the inspectors, using the same notions as discussed earlier in this chapter, such as: what went well; even better if; next time the questions should include. If these arrangements are followed, then the final report agreed upon between the institution and Ofsted would be published to ensure open accountability.

What abilities, experiences and knowledge will be required of inspectors to operate this alternative model? First, their deep and critical knowledge of the research and practice of TLA will have led them to espouse explicit theories of learning, which they will be in the habit of using to enhance their thinking and practice. They will also need recent and relevant teaching and management experience, including, for some, inspectors' vocational experience of the specialist areas they assess, and, for others, successful experience of teaching and managing in schools in the toughest areas. Inspectors should be restricted to observing and evaluating those subjects, areas or phases where they have experience and proven competence. A general training in the social sciences and, in particular, in the interpretation of statistics, finances and research evidence, and in the skills of evaluation will also be essential. The outcome should be the type of relationship the teaching profession had with HMI before Ofsted was established: open, genuine and productive dialogue with a cadre of respected and trusted colleagues, acting as the cross-pollinators of challenging questions and ideas, and novel practices and insights.

Ofsted will raise the status of the inspectorate in the eyes of the teaching profession, parents and society more generally by a public commitment to provide the following minimal information in every inspection:

- a justification of the size and representativeness of the sample chosen for evaluation
- a measure of the reliability or consistency of the judgements made
- an assessment of the validity or accuracy of the judgements
- an account after six months, say, of the benign and undesirable effects of inspection.

Readers may perhaps be reflecting that these new arrangements are as constricting and cumbersome as Ofsted's current processes. Table 17.2 presents the list of the 14 types of information required by Ofsted before inspection

Table 17.2 Information required by Ofsted before inspection

---

1   A summary of any school self-evaluation or equivalent
2   The current school improvement plan or equivalent, including any strategic planning that sets out the longer term vision for the school
3   School timetable, current staff list and times for the school day
4   Any information about pre-planned interruptions to normal school routines during the inspection
5   The single central record of the checks and vetting of all staff working with pupils
6   Records and analysis of exclusions, pupils taken off roll, incidents of poor behaviour and any use of internal isolation
7   Records and analysis of bullying, discriminatory and prejudicial behaviour, either directly or indirectly, including racist, sexist, disability and homophobic bullying, use of derogatory language and racist incidents
8   A list of referrals made to the designated person for safeguarding in the school and those that were subsequently referred to the local authority, along with brief details of the resolution
9   A list of all pupils who are open cases with children's services/social care and for whom there is a multi-agency plan
10 Up-to-date attendance analysis for all groups of pupils
11 Records of the evaluation of the quality of teaching, learning and assessment
12 Information about the school's performance management arrangements, including the most recent performance management outcomes and their relationship to salary progression, in an anonymised format
13 Documented evidence of the work of governors and their priorities, including any written scheme of delegation for an academy in a multi-academy trust
14 Any reports of external evaluation of the school, including any review of governance or use of the pupil premium funding

---

Source: Ofsted (2016: 15).

begins. I could have added the list of 20 different groups of learners that the 'inspectors will pay particular attention to' (Ofsted, 2015: 6); the list of 14 standards that inspectors must uphold in their work; the list of 10 expectations that Ofsted has of providers; the list of six indicators analysed by inspectors in risk assessment; the list of nine different sets of data to be analysed before inspection; the list of 13 tasks to be carried out by the lead inspector when the college is first contacted; and the list of seven activities inspectors have to carry out at the first meeting with senior management. So far, only the first 19 pages from a total of 73 of Ofsted's inspection handbook have been scrutinised for lists, but the point has, I trust, been made. Quantity acquires a quality all of its own. Demanding this amount of data from schools is shifting the burden of proof from the inspectors on to educators. Is it any wonder that a headteacher wrote to me to say: 'I do feel very strongly about the phenomenal waste of staff hours trying to second guess the vagaries and demands of Ofsted rather than spending this time providing a better education for the children in the classroom'.[4]

Another possible objection to the proposed changes is that they would overburden the present cohort of inspectors, to which there are three responses. First, we need to re-establish a more democratic structure of national and local inspection, where Ofsted inspectors work hand in glove with local authority (LA) advisers, who will know their local schools far better than any centrally based inspectors could ever do and who could monitor them more closely and less expensively. Inspection will also become more participatory by involving all the principal players in the school's community in peer reviews and formal inspections: not just students, teachers, governors and parents but local employers, local councillors and concerned citizens. These, after all, are the people who are left to pick up the pieces when a school or college is judged to be 'failing', so decisions that have serious consequences, for good or ill for a local community, should be taken by members of that community as part of the inspection team. Ofsted inspectors, with a much broader comprehension of standards across the country, will be well placed to counteract any parochial attitudes on the part of LEA advisers. Ted Wragg proposed that the latter 'should be available on secondment to HMI for 20 per cent of their time, one day a week on average, the other 80 per cent being for sustained and regular support, monitoring and advice for schools' (Wragg, 1997: 23). In this way, the skills of evaluation will be spread throughout the country.

Second, the multiple remits of Ofsted are unsustainable. Ofsted needs its responsibilities to be reduced or certain functions (e.g., evaluating probation services and education and training in prison), to be hived off to separate specialist organisations. The current overload is a recipe for patchy performance, if not outright failure. Ofsted should also stop using statutory test data to monitor standards over time. That task should be handed over to an independent body which would use the same secret tests repeatedly on 'samples of pupils of the same age at the same time of year. Testing samples rather than full populations makes the process efficient, and, compared with national testing, a much smaller operation. A secret test is needed because once the content of a test becomes known by teachers it is hard for them ... to keep the ideas in the assessment hidden' (Tymms, 2004: 478).

Third, instead of introducing the alternative model all at once, parts of it could be slowly brought in, step by step, over a number of years in a cumulative process of innovation. Early success and a favourable reception from educators will be assured, for instance, by Ofsted publicly accepting: the case for reform; the principles underpinning the new model as set out in Chapter 3; and the arrangements and procedures for inspection outlined at the beginning of this chapter, including access to quantitative data being delayed until the qualitative assessments have been completed. A start could be made by evaluating in the first year only the first three dimensions – TLA, professional learning and democracy – and in each of the two succeeding years, another three dimensions could be added to the inspection framework until all nine are being assessed simultaneously.

Let me summarise how I envisage the transformation could get under way. The heart of the proposed model consists of the five principles, the nine dimensions and the attendant questions. Ofsted could set the ball rolling by convening a meeting of all the main players (representatives of the teachers' unions and professional bodies, governors, parents and students) to find out how much support the main features of the model command. The move to consult and to enter into dialogue with the profession would in itself help to restore trustful, working relationships between inspectors and educators. Only when a new, agreed-upon set of principles, dimensions and questions has been settled would it be appropriate to operationalise it; and the specialists in Ofsted would be the best people to tackle that job. In this way, by a slow, careful process of evolution which incorporated the best ideas and arguments as it went along, inspection would become a powerful force for good.

The limitations of the proposed model are openly admitted. I am aware that no football manager's plan survives much longer than the first contact with the opposition. The model is not presented as a final blueprint or a detailed plan, but as the first outline of an alternative approach which is offered as a contribution to the debate on a vital public issue of significance to millions of students, hundreds of thousands of educators and ultimately to the future quality of education in England. It now needs to be peer-reviewed so that it can be modified, refined, made complete, and in the process gather support. A number of topics where I have no expertise – for instance, early years, work experience, apprenticeships, governance and safeguarding – have been omitted and will have to be added by others. If this book sparks off a public debate on Ofsted's principles, methods, effects and future, and gets the needed transformation started, then the effort will have been worth it.

Notes

1 Personal communication, 2017.
2 A primary school failed its inspection in part because it was said to satisfactorily promote its pupils social and moral but not their spiritual and cultural development. '... no evidence [was] presented to illustrate which observations convinced the inspectors of such finely differentiated effects' (Fitz-Gibbon and Stephenson, 1996: 11). The current inspection handbook lists four criteria for assessing spiritual, three for moral, three for social and five for cultural development. One criterion is quoted in full here to show how far Ofsted's reach now extends: 'The moral development of pupils is shown by their ability to recognise the difference between right and wrong and to readily apply this understanding in their own lives, recognise legal boundaries and, in so doing, respect the civil and criminal law of England' (Ofsted, 2016: 35). How many hours would be needed to assess this criterion fully and fairly? It is one of 15 such criteria in this sub-area.
3 The three strategies – feedback, meta-cognition and peer-tutoring – were chosen because research has demonstrated that they have the biggest impact. Research should similarly guide the choice of strategies to be evaluated in the other eight dimensions.
4 Personal communication, 2017.

References

Coe, R., Aloisi, C., Higgins, S. and Major, L.E. (2014) *What Makes Great Teaching? Review of the Underpinning Research*. Durham: CEM/Sutton Trust.

Coffield, F. (2017) *Will the Leopard Change Its Spots? A New Model of Inspection for Ofsted*. London: Institute of Education Press.

Cooperrider, D.L. (2012) What is appreciative inquiry? Online. www.davidcooperrider.com/ai-process (accessed 5 June 2017).

di Lampedusa, G. (1960) *The Leopard*. Trans. Colquhoun, A. London: Collins and Harvill Press.

Edwards, T. (2000) 'All the evidence shows ...': Reasonable expectations of educational research. *Oxford Review of Education*, 26(3–4), 299–311.

Further Education Funding Council (1993) *Assessing Achievement (Circular 93/28)*. London: Further Education Funding Council.

Fitz-Gibbon, C.T. and Stephenson, N.J. (1996) Inspecting Her Majesty's Inspectors: Should social science and social policy cohere? Paper presented at the European Conference on Educational Research, University of Seville, 25–28 September.

Hattie, J. (2012) *Visible Learning for Teachers: Maximizing Impact on Learning*. London: Routledge.

Hattie, J. and Yates, G.C.R. (2014) *Visible Learning and the Science of How We Learn*. London: Routledge.

Matthews, P. and Headon, M. (2015) *Multiple Gains: An Independent Evaluation of Challenge Partners' Peer Reviews of Schools*. London: Institute of Education Press.

Ofsted (2015) *The Common Inspection Framework: Education, Skills and Early Years*. Manchester: Ofsted. Online. www.gov.uk/government/publications/common-inspection-framework-education-skills-and-early-years-from-september-2015 (accessed 5 June 2017).

Ofsted (2016) *School Inspection Handbook*. Manchester: Ofsted. Online. www.gov.uk/government/uploads/system/uploads/attachment_data/file/553942/School_inspection_handbook-section_5.pdf (accessed 5 June 2017).

Tymms, P. (2004) Are standards rising in English primary schools? *British Educational Research Journal*, 30(4), 477–94.

Wragg, T. (1997) Inspection and school self-evaluation. In Duffy, M. (ed.) *A Better System of Inspection?* Hexham: Office for Standards in Inspection, 21–5.

Chapter 18

The music in the word 'education'

In this final extract (Coffield, 2008), I return to my roots in Glasgow to explain how my family used education to move from the precarious life of my paternal grandfather, punctuated as it was by long periods of unemployment as a steel worker, to the relative safety of the professions. What must be remembered are all those who have been left behind.

The last word goes to my mother, who in 1936 qualified as a primary school teacher and got her first job in a deprived part of Glasgow. She was given the reception class of five year olds and quickly learned that she had to establish some ground rules about going to the toilet. She explained that she needed to know how much time each child would take. If they wanted a 'pee', they were to say, 'Please, Miss, Number One'. If they needed a 'poo', they were to say: 'Please, Miss, Number Two'. She then asked the whole class: 'Is that clear? Are there any questions? One little boy put his hand up and asked: 'Please, Miss, what's the number for fart?'

I want to end on a personal, familial and social note. I come from an Irish Catholic family which emigrated to Scotland some time before the First World War in the search for work and in the hope of improving their lot and, more especially, that of their children. My father, James, was the first and only member of the family to go to university, Glasgow, in 1930, at a time when there were only university places for around 14,000 new entrants or 2% of his generation. He always said he would never have got through school and university if it had not been for the peace, space and books provided by the local public library. I went up (that's how I thought of it intellectually and morally) to the same university in 1960, when 93,000 or 5% of my age group entered higher education. In 2000, our daughter Emma, after an excellent foundation course in a local FE college, joined our *alma mater* and in that year, no less than 950,000 or 36.8% of her age cohort became university students. The increase from 2% to 5% to 36.8% represents nothing less than a transformation of British society.

Looking back over 100 years and three generations of my family, I can see three great social movements. First, every time the universities and FE colleges have prised open their doors a little, able students have come forward

DOI: 10.4324/9781003476146-23

in sufficient numbers to fill with success the places made available. Second, the Scottish education system in 1918 passed enlightened and inclusive legislation, which financed most of the building costs of separate schools for immigrants of an alien (and to many an unwelcome) faith. Third, education has been for my family, and for hundreds of thousands like it, the route into the professions, and to an honoured, secure and well-paid place in society. Our generation must not forget, however, that we are the beneficiaries of the long and often painful journey made by our parents and grandparents, who needed structural and financial help, as well as education, in order for us to move up in society.

All this is cause for celebration, gratitude and reflection; and so I warmly welcome the most recent advances, brought about by the substantially increased investment in education since 1997, as a result of which millions more have achieved qualifications or received training, some for the very first time. These desirable improvements are, however, accompanied by gross, rising, new and unjustifiable inequalities; in each generation, whole swathes of the community have been left behind and continue to be left behind in scabby estates, which should outrage our collective conscience.

Moreover, something vital to the whole enterprise is being forgotten. I learned from my father, as he learned from his, to hear the music, the excitement and the hope in the word 'education'. I also learned that it is the job of teachers to help other people's children to hear and respond to that music. We do it because teaching is a noble profession, which dedicates itself to the lot of those who have not had our advantages. We do it because we believe in social justice and, like our parents and grandparents, we want a better world for ourselves, our children and all children. That is the meaning of our lives as teachers.

References

Coffield, F. (2008) *Just Suppose Teaching and Learning Became the First Priority...* London: Learning and Skills Network.

Chapter 19

Final comments

Reform of the constitution

A central plank in the manifestos of the main political parties before a general election is usually devoted to reform of the public services, but what tends to be missing is what should come first. Politicians need to convince the electorate of their commitment to reform by reforming the institution in the United Kingdom that requires it most, namely, parliament itself. The public services are so dependent on a dysfunctional, undemocratic political system that there is little point in detailing what changes are needed in education until the malaise at the heart of our democracy is addressed.

The scale of the problem can be gauged from the remarks of Lord Judge, a former Lord Chief Justice:

> We have become habituated … to the steady, apparently unstoppable accumulation of power in No 10 Downing Street … while simultaneously the authority and weight of parliament itself, and the House of Commons in particular, have been diminishing… [He worried about powers] delegated to ministers to amend the law without a vote by MPs, thereby avoiding parliamentary scrutiny.[1]

This. he feared, could degenerate into a 'constitutional catastrophe'.

Concern over the superfluous powers exercised by the Prime Minister (PM) is nothing new. In 1980, Tony Benn was arguing that 'the present centralisation of power into the hands of one person has gone too far and amounts to a system of personal rule in the very heart of our parliamentary democracy'.[2]

Whether a written constitution is called for to limit the powers of the PM or whether the United Kingdom is better served by the flexibility of the current uncodified arrangements is a wicked issue. But the danger to our democracy is too great, in my opinion, when the PM can: decide on the levels of taxation and the date of the next general election, hire and fire ministers (even exonerate himself, or re-appoint those who have broken the ministerial code); and pack the House of Lords with cronies or financial backers. Education has suffered from prime ministerial power with ten secretaries of state for education

DOI: 10.4324/9781003476146-24

in 13 years; and when the innovative Tomlinson report was rejected in 2004.[3] It would have integrated vocational and academic pathways, bringing status to the former and breadth to the latter.

The blight that affects our parliamentary system extends well beyond the powers of the PM, as Chris Bryant has shown. He argues for a proportional electoral system to combat the 'winner takes all principle'; with coalitions being formed and candidates needing a minimum of 25% of votes to prevent extreme policies being enacted; and a single, independent body to regulate standards in parliament.[4] We need to reimagine the British state to end abuses and to devolve power and resources much closer to the people affected.

What the Conservative government's white paper, *Levelling Up the United Kingdom*,[5] and Gordon Brown's *Commission on the UK's future*[6] have in common is that they both see a connection between the overcentralisation in London and the escalating economic and regional inequalities caused by imbalances of power. Both parties propose to devolve skills policy to local government to help close 'the most profound divide on these islands … the huge disparity between the global mega-city of London with its south eastern hinterland and almost all other parts of the British Isles'.[7]

Will these pledges to revive local democracy in the most centralised state in Western Europe be fulfilled, no matter who wins the next general election? Without sweeping reforms, education cannot cope with the finding of the Joseph Rowntree Foundation that 'destitution has been increasing at an alarming rate since 2017 … approximately 3.8 million people experienced destitution in 2022, including around one million children'.[8] Destitution is defined as 'the most severe form of material hardship', lacking 'access to … the most basic physical needs' and 'extremely low or no income'.[9] Teachers cannot cope with deprivation on this scale if they are expected to educate children living in temporary accommodation, who sleep on floors for lack of beds or who come to school without being fed. Ending child poverty has to become a priority. Sure Start must be re-introduced.

Levelling up has failed but it has not been carried out in a way remotely comparable to that tried in Germany, which 'has spent almost two trillion euros over three decades in its attempt to level up the old East German Länder, and the job is not done'.[10] Regional government in this country has much to learn from the Federal Republic of Germany, made up of the *Bundestag*, equivalent to the House of Commons, and the *Bundesrat*, the Council of the 16 states. The primary duty of the second house is to protect the interests of the states, but it shares responsibility with the Bundestag for national policy, and has a right to propose, scrutinise and amend bills.[11] We could establish an equivalent by abolishing the House of Lords and electing a Senate of the Devolved Nations and Regions in its place. Political donations could also be capped at £10,000 and 'democracy vouchers' presented to every constituent to give to their preferred candidate.[12] If hypercentralisation is to be reversed, the powers and resources of regional and local government will have to be guaranteed in the new constitution. We will need to learn from some of the problems of the German constitution, for example, North Rhine Westphalia with 20 million inhabitants has the same political rights as Bremen with half a million.

As mentioned in Chapter 7, contempt for the Further Education (FE) sector is pervasive. Vince Cable, then Liberal Democrat minister for Business, Innovation and Skills, reported that the advice from his civil servants was: 'Why don't you just effectively kill of FE? Nobody will really notice'.[13]

Just as the government has increased its powers in education, the state has extended the powers of the police in a new Act of Parliament, which enables police chiefs to impose on protests a start and finish time, set noise limits and apply these rules to a demonstration of just one person.[14] Dissent is not to be tolerated.

A national disgrace

Turning to education, what must be addressed first is the biggest inequality in education, namely, the protracted underfunding of the 50% of 18–30-year olds who do not go to university. Sixty years ago, the Newsom Report, *Half Our Future*, warned that 'the country cannot afford this wastage, humanly or economically'.[15] That warning has been ignored. The figures provided by the independent Augar report show that more than six times is spent per head on university students than on those in FE. Addressing this huge disparity is, in the words of the report

> A matter of fairness … It is our core message … despite widespread acknowledgement that this sector is crucial to the country's economic success, nothing much has happened except for a steep, steady decline in funding.[16]

The Augar report was issued in May 2019, the government then took three years to respond, but it focused on the higher education sector. Yet the report's vision, of an inclusive post-18 system to integrate higher education and FE and which is accessible to all, must be realised. Major funding will be required to create their plan for a national network of high-quality FE colleges, providing technical and professional education within the reach of all.

The consequences of decades of underfunding, which deepened during austerity, are revealed in statistics from three different sources. First, 'almost 40 per cent of 25 year olds do not progress beyond GCSEs as their highest qualification'.[17] Second, 'in 2018/19 only around 20,000 people in the United Kingdom completed further education qualifications at or above level 4, compared with more than 430,000 people who completed their first university degree in the same year'.[18] Third, 'only 4 per cent of young people achieve a qualification at higher technical level by the age of 25 compared to the 33 per cent who get a degree or above'.[19]

The Augar report goes on to detail the multiple problems with apprenticeships. For example, they are overly regulated and bureaucratic, higher-level apprenticeships are only 10% of the total; and business studies dominate areas like construction where skills are desperately needed. Again, in Germany, the rights of apprentices are guaranteed by law and the content and objectives of the educational elements have to be agreed upon by the social partners.

The Augar panel also revealed a damaging continuity on the part of those employers, who are unwilling to train their workers, as explored in Chapter 6. I predicted in 2012 that the same, deep-seated problems would be found in ten years' time. Twenty years later, the Augar report talks of employers 'who did not seem to accept the need for apprentices to leave the job for training purposes'.[20] Other employers rebadged as apprenticeships graduate schemes for their already well-qualified employees and so diverted limited funds from those without any higher qualifications. To cap it all, the quality of many of the biggest providers was judged by Ofsted to be inadequate with some going out of business or being found guilty of fraud.

A government which is intent on re-energising social mobility must begin by reversing the deep cuts to FE colleges, to adult skills and lifelong learning more generally. The response from the government so far has failed to rise to the scale of the challenge. For instance, a key policy announced in the White Paper *Skills for Jobs* in 2021 was the Lifelong Loan Entitlement for those looking to 'upskill' or 'reskill'. But adults from disadvantaged backgrounds without any savings need grants for tuition and maintenance, not loans, which burden them with debt.

The same White Paper, which claimed to be a blueprint for the future, repeated three of the glaring failings in this area which Chapters 1, 6 and 7 in this book have criticised. First, it introduces new powers for the Secretary of State for Education 'to intervene quickly and decisively'.[21] Second, it places 'employers at the heart of defining local skills needs',[22] but that consigns disadvantaged areas to further disadvantage when such areas are known for low-level jobs with little demand for high-skilled workers. Third, the hands of FE staff are tied by inflexible control over their budgets; they need funding for three years rather than one to enable planning, stability and growth; and the financial freedom to adapt quickly to local economic conditions, which are going to shift constantly from now on. This would put a premium on local, situated knowledge and would place confidence in the experience and creativity of tutors who are currently demoralised.

In trying to recruit tutors, FE colleges are on the back foot because the pay gap with teachers in schools is £9,000 per year. Similarly, their students aged 16–18, including apprentices, need the re-introduction of the Educational Maintenance Allowance to prevent those dropping out for financial reasons.

To counter the decade-long downturn in investment by both government and business, what is called for is a bold initiative to make lifelong learning a statutory right of every adult. Artificial intelligence has made it impossible to anticipate what future skills will be required, so workers will need to be financially supported to learn new digital skills repeatedly. The cost could be shared between the worker, the employer and the state, with decisions transferred from the centre to regional and local offices.

A generation that profited from free tuition and maintenance grants has imposed huge debts on its successors. To redress that injustice, we need to abolish tuition fees and loans for undergraduates and their equivalents in FE. The fact that Scottish students do not pay fees shows that fees are a political choice.

Democracy and the young

Another major redistribution of power could be achieved by bringing back from government control into local democratic oversight the current chaotic range of secondary schools. That range includes – in steep, local hierarchies – comprehensive and grammar schools; academies and free schools; city technology, university technology and sixth-form colleges. One way to release them from relentless state pressures would be to follow the path devised by David Hargreaves 'towards a fundamentally different vision',[23] that of a self-improving school system. It would replace 'insulated individual schools with clusters of schools taking collective responsibility for the improvement of all their members by working collaboratively'.[24] Advances with this model have already been made even within the tight control exercised by the state, but so much more could be achieved if the schools were freer to innovate.

The threats to our democracy from within and without are now so pervasive that it requires the support of each new generation. But the young are turned off by policies which have put home ownership (and even renting) beyond the means of most of those without rich parents, or which through devices like the pension triple lock have favoured the old. Social mobility has not only stalled but is no higher than it was in the 1980s, with your place of birth and the wealth of your family being the key influences in determining your future.[25] Add to that a narrow, academic curriculum and a rigid exam system which fails half of each generation and the alienation of young people from politics is explicable.

The working-class adolescents we met in Chapter 4, although bright and articulate, could not be drawn on the subject of politics about which they confessed total ignorance. They failed to see any connection between national policies and their own unemployment. These entrenched attitudes will be hard to shift.

A start could, however, be made by lowering the voting age to 16 and involving young people in dialogue about topics that concern them. Why, for example, are they able to find only 'shit jobs' on the minimum wage, with no training or prospects and feeling exploited as a result? How are they to survive repeated periods of unemployment or zero-hour contracts? Why is the youth service not a statutory duty and always one of the first to be cut? If you seek proof of the inequities in education, contrast the libraries, sports and leisure facilities at your local university or private school with those at your local college, or if you still have one, your local youth club. More than 1,000 youth clubs have closed since 2010 because of savage cuts to local authorities.

What may already engage them is the prospect of the earth's system collapsing during their lifetime because of climate breakdown. At the time of going to press, scientists are recording that 2023 was the hottest year on record and that we as a nation are unprepared for extreme weather conditions, yet 700 oil and gas companies are continuing to invest billions in the search for new sources of fossil fuels and the Conservative government has 'announced 27 new North Sea oil and gas licences'.[26]

It may, however, not be a question of teachers trying to interest students in the climate crisis but of teachers being challenged by them to address the biggest threat to our collective well-being. It was after all a 15-year-old Swedish girl, Greta Thunberg, who went on strike outside parliament instead of attending school to advocate for climate justice. She is inspiring millions of pupils with her 'Fridays for Future' activism and these young people use social media to contact others across the world. Such moments of resistance may yet be turned into mass movements that make change irresistible.

The climate crisis will also test David Runciman's thesis that 'democracies are better at surviving crises than any alternative system because they can adapt'.[27] He warned, however, this crisis may be the one that we do not survive. Jordi Collet-Sabé and Stephen Ball are convinced that the schools are unequal to the challenge, creating 'the urgent need to think education without school'. Can our schools and colleges rise to the challenge and foster students adept at:

> Learning to ask questions rather than learning answers; practising ethics rather than studying them; politicising and troubling common issues rather than knowing and memorising them?[28]

Such abilities will not be advanced by the current curriculum and pedagogy, which, imposed as they are by the Department for Education, are unequal to the task.

Curriculum and pedagogy

As argued in Chapter 13, the national system of education belongs to all of us, but ministers hold a monopoly of power over it. For over 10 years, educational experts such as John White have been urging the establishment of a national commission on the curriculum. That idea needs to be extended to all phases of education. The commissioners would need to be independent of the government and drawn from teachers' unions and professional bodies, academic experts, employers, parents, students, governors and politicians, provided that the latter have no veto over the findings and proposals.

Politicians continue to do damage by, for example, suddenly announcing ill-considered change. For example, Rishi Sunak recently proposed to scrap A-levels in favour of a single 'Advanced British Standard' qualification to unite A-levels and T-levels, the latter being two-year post-GCSE qualifications that combine theory with an industrial placement. Two immediate problems. First, there is not, and never has been, a *British* education system as the devolved administrations have always had their own. Second, Ofsted had just issued a damning report on virtually every aspect of T-levels, which makes them a rocky foundation on which to build.[29] We can no longer do policy like this.

More power could be wrested from ministers by refusing to use the business studies language they employ to describe education. No one, not even a Secretary of State, can 'deliver' education as the post or pizzas are delivered.

In future, students will need to learn how to expose what I do not refrain from calling 'bullshit'. For the philosopher, Harry Frankfurt, the essence of bullshit is 'not that it is *false* but that it is *phony*'.[30] (Emphasis as in original.) Its proliferation has intensified in the 30 years since he wrote that essay. Currently, prize examples include 'future-proofing', but who correctly predicted the financial crash of 2008, the Russian invasion of Ukraine or Hamas's attack on the Israeli kibbutz? It is bad enough when politicians talk of 'turbo-charging this trail blazing policy', 'working night and day', 'leading the world' or 'we are all in this together', but it is galling to hear educationists tell students: 'You can become anything you want so long as you want it badly enough and are prepared to work hard'.

More equal power relations in education would also be introduced by adopting Robin Alexander's pedagogy based on dialogue 'that explicitly links spoken language with democratic education and engagement'.[31] He has over the years extended and refined his approach that:

> harnesses the power of talk to stimulate and extend students' thinking, learning knowing and understanding, and to enable them to discuss, reason and argue.[32]

Independent evaluation for the Education Endowment Foundation has also shown it to increase significantly students' motivation and learning outcomes.[33]

Communities of discovery

The notion that holds the previous ideas together is the one introduced in Chapter 16 – Communities of Discovery – which Bill Williamson and I defined as learners and educators working together with democratic policies and values to discover new ways to address the main threats to our collective well-being and that of the planet.

The best way to realise such communities is through a greater commitment to democracy in our educational institutions. During the World War II, the journalist Francis Williams argued that 'democracy is not only something to fight for, it is something to fight with'.[34] Making Ofsted a more humane organisation that supports rather than undermines teachers would help to loosen the strict hierarchies in schools where 'politicians have captured the head teachers and converted them into "deliverers" of government policies in general and of test and examination results in particular'.[35]

Communities of Discovery will not, however, free up the creativity of students and tutors without responding to the voices not just of the former but also of the latter. Much research has been conducted into student voice, especially by Michael Fielding, who described six ascending levels of participation – from, at the bottom, students being treated as a source of data through surveys of their views, to, at the top, students learning alongside teachers in a democratic institution.[36]

Inspired by his example, I produced 'a ladder of democracy' with increasing levels of participation by tutors in the life of their institution.[37] The lower level is where teachers' views are sought by means of a questionnaire, while at the highest level, the climate of the college becomes as conducive to the learning of tutors as it is to that of students, because 'the working conditions of teachers are the learning conditions of students'.[38] The practical significance of this approach is that tutors can check how democratic their institution is by their position on the ladder.

There are, however, limits to how democratic schools and colleges can become if the role of the state continues to draw ever more tightly those freedoms that teachers still possess. Education could be revitalised by teachers becoming powerful, democratic professionals, as I have argued elsewhere.[39]

The above proposals will be expensive and will go way beyond what could be paid for by current rates of taxation. We could introduce: a wealth tax for the rich; increased rates of tax to match those in France or Germany; a higher percentage of GDP spent on education; closing tax havens across the world; getting multinational companies to pay their fair share of tax; charging capital gains at the same rate as income tax; equalising the tax relief on pension contributions; and ending the tax advantages of private schools, which are anything but charities. Richard Murphy and Colin Hines suggest that linking our savings (Isas and pension funds) to 'new socially and environmentally necessary investment' would yield £100 billion a year.[40]

Coda

It has been a chastening experience to look back over my career of 50+ years and see such a divided, disorganised and dysfunctional 'system'. These feelings are not motivated by nostalgia for a non-existent golden age, but they are the result of a hard-headed assessment of the depredations visited on education. There is in fact not one 'system' but two: a well-funded, academic highway for the middle class and an impoverished, vocational path for the working class. We must urgently build a prestigious vocational route for the 50% of each generation who do not go to university. That route must be well-signposted, within their reach, worth walking and connected to the academic highway.

Reflecting on the criticisms in all the previous chapters has suggested the following indictment of government bungling in education over the last 50 years:

• The main purposes of education have been degraded to improving our economic competitiveness. The language of the market ('delivery', 'line manager') vitiates our thinking and constrains our understanding of the many roles education can play.
• The same naïve assumptions ('our future depends on our skills') continue to be trotted out decades after their inadequacies have been exposed. Politicians still talk of introducing 'what works' rather than what is educationally desirable. Complex problems must be responded to with complex policies. Instead, deep-seated economic problems are converted into ineffective, short-lived education projects aimed at individuals.
• Overblown rhetoric is employed ('we will eliminate failure') where humility would be more appropriate, given the catalogue of failures. The DfE too often shows itself impervious to constructive criticism and discomfiting evidence; and is untroubled by doubt or more successful approaches.
• Despite some measures of decentralisation, the culture of central command and local 'delivery' has led to ministerial hyperactivity, permanent restructuring, constant turbulence and relentless demands for data.
• The frenetic pace of change (policies are 'turbo-charged') has damaged the need of institutions for continuity and stability. The DfE's model of change is inappropriately mechanical (levers, drivers and toolboxes).
• Ill-considered policies are announced, consultation is a dishonest sham, and feedback mechanisms are omitted, so there is no learning from practitioners.
• Unaccountable power continues to be hoarded at the centre. It's one thing to wield excessive power, another to make such a mess of it. The powers of the over-mighty state must be pruned.
• Last but not least, students still receive an education according to their class rather than to their ability: funding per head for university students is many times that for those in the FE sector.

One could be forgiven for believing that FE stood for Further Employability rather than FE. By making employability the core mission of the FE sector, the public issue of structural changes in the economy is converted into the private trouble of employability and unemployment. Policy in this area has not moved forward since 2002 when I wrote the article that forms Chapter 12. What an irony that the organisation charged with improving the learning of the nation proves itself incapable of learning. It is the triumph of ideology over pragmatism. As I wrote in the Introduction, these problems have been with us for decades and are becoming more entrenched for being neglected.

Education is embedded in a discredited and undemocratic political culture which must be changed first. The unaccountable power of the state has to be curbed, especially that wielded by the PM, senior ministers and civil servants. Only a redistribution of power to the other key actors – local government, teachers' unions and professional bodies, parents, governors, teachers and students – will release their creativity. The task is daunting and will take years to accomplish, but a start must be made. Let us begin by facing up to the state we are in and deciding collectively to reverse the damage the state has done to education by reducing its power.

Notes

1 Lord Judge (2023: 6).
2 Tony Benn (1980: 1).
3 Tomlinson report (2004).
4 Chris Bryant (2023: 67). For further advantages of proportional representation see Ben Ansell (2023: 286–7).
5 HM Government White Paper (2022).
6 The Labour Party's Commission on the UK's future (2022).
7 Mawson (2020: 10).
8 Joseph Rowntree Foundation report (2023: 6 and 1).
9 Joseph Rowntree Foundation report (2023: 3).
10 Larry Elliott (2023: 29).
11 See Coffield (2020: 20–21).
12 Daniel Chandler (2023).
13 BBC News, 2014.
14 BBC News online (28 April, 2022: 2).
15 Newsom Report (1963: 3).
16 Augur report (2019: 5). The figures are £8+ billion spent on 1.2 million HE students versus £2.3 billion on 2.2 million FE students.
17 Augar report (2019: 9).
18 Institute for Government (2022: 7).
19 Department for Education (2021: 6).
20 Augar report (2019: 156).
21 Department for Education (2021: 12).
22 Department for Education (2021: 4).
23 David Hargreaves (2019: 11). I wish to acknowledge the huge impact of this book on my thinking.
24 David Hargreaves (2019: 172).
25 Institute of Fiscal Studies (2023).
26 G Monbiot (2023: 3).
27 David Runciman (2013: xv–xvi).

28 Jordi Collet-Sabé & Stephen J Ball (2023: 897, 899 and 904).
29 Ofsted (2023).
30 Harry G Frankfurt (1988: 128).
31 Robin Alexander (2022: 266).
32 Robin Alexander (2022: 196).
33 Robin Alexander (2018).
34 Francis Williams, quoted by Michael Fielding (2016: 129).
35 David Hargreaves (2019: 215).
36 Michael Fielding (2014).
37 Frank Coffield (2016: 76–98).
38 An Education Declaration to Rebuild America, 2018.
39 Frank Coffield (2016: 76–98).
40 Richard Murphy and Colin Hines (2023: 5).

References

Alexander, R.J. (2018) Developing dialogic teaching: Genesis, process, trial. *Research Papers in Education*, 33(5), 561–98.
Alexander, R.J. (2022) *Education in Spite of Policy*. London: Routledge.
Ansell, B. (2023) *Why Politics Fails*. London: Penguin Books.
Augar Report (2019) *Review of Post-18 Education and Funding*. London: Department for Education, CP 117.
Benn, T. (1980) The case for a constitutional premiership. *Parliamentary Affairs*, 33(1), 7–22.
Bryant, C. (2023) *Code of Conduct: Why We Need to Fix Parliament – and How to Do It*. London: Bloomsbury.
Chandler, D. (2023) Democracy vouchers could restore faith in British politics. *The Guardian,* Journal, 29 August, 1–2.
Coffield, F. (2016) Teachers as powerful, democratic professionals. In Higgins, S. and Coffield, F. (eds) *John Dewey: Democracy and Education: A British Tribute*. London: UCL Institute of Education Press, 76–98.
Coffield, F. (2020) *Devolution for the North East*. Newton Aycliffe: Newton Press.
Collet-Sabé, J. and Ball, S.J. (2023) Beyond school. The challenges of co-producing and commoning a different episteme for education. *Journal of Education Policy*, 38(6), 895–910.
Department for Education (2021) *Skills for Jobs: Lifelong Learning for Opportunity and Growth*. London: Department for Education, CP338.
Elliott, L. (2023) Levelling up. A century-old strategy that must not be put off any longer. *The Guardian*, 30 October, 29.
Fielding, M. (2016) Why and how schools might live democracy 'as an inclusive human order'. In Higgins, S. and Coffield, F. (eds) *John Dewey: Democracy and Education: A British Tribute*. London: UCL Institute of Education Press, 114–130.
Frankfurt, H.G. (1988) On bullshit. In Frankfurt, H.G. (ed) *The Importance of What We Care About*. Cambridge: Cambridge University Press, 117–133.
Hargreaves, D.H. (2019) *Beyond Schooling: An Anarchist Challenge*. London: Routledge.
HM Government (2022) *Levelling Up the United Kingdom*. White Paper, CP 604, HMSO.
Institute of Fiscal Studies (2023) *Social Mobility Continues to Fall – and Moving up Is Harder If You Grow up in the North or Midlands*. London: Institute for Fiscal Studies, 7 September.
Institute for Government (2022) *Levelling up and Skills Policy*. Insight Paper, July, London: Institute for Government.

Judge, Lord (2023) Obituary in *The Guardian*, 20 November, 6.

Labour Party (2022) *A New Britain: Renewing Our Democracy and Rebuilding Our Economy. The Commission on the UK's Future*. London: Labour Party.

Mawson, J. (2020) *Current Conservative Agenda in the Run Up to the Autumn White Paper on Devolution in England*. County Durham Fabian Society.

Monbiot, G. (2023) The Earth's systems are warning us: we must act now. *The Guardian*, Journal, 1 November, 3.

Murphy, R. and Hines, C. (2023) Our savings could be key to ending austerity. Letter to *The Guardian*, Journal, 28 December, 5.

Newsom, J. (1963) *Half Our Future*. A Report of the Central Advisory Council for Education (England) by the Ministry of Education. London: HMSO.

Ofsted (2023) *T-Level Thematic Review: Final Report*, July 2023. London: Ofsted.

Joseph Rowntree, Foundation (2023) *Destitution in the UK 2023*. York: Joseph Rowntree Foundation.

Runciman, D. (2013) *The Confidence Trap*. New Jersey: Princeton University Press.

Tomlinson, M. (2004) *14-19 Curriculum and Qualifications Reform*, Final Report of the Working Group. London: Department for Education and Skills.

Index

For Product Safety Concerns and Information please contact our EU
representative GPSR@taylorandfrancis.com Taylor & Francis Verlag GmbH,
Kaufingerstraße 24, 80331 München, Germany

Printed and bound by CPI Group (UK) Ltd, Croydon, CR0 4YY
08/06/2025
01897002-0014